Whiteness and Teacher Education

Routledge Research in Education

For a full list of titles in this series please visit www.routledge.com

Whiteness and Teacher Education

Edie White

Routledge
Taylor & Francis Group

LONDON AND NEW YORK

First published 2012
by Routledge

2 Park Square, Milton Park, Abingdon, Oxfordshire OX14 4RN
711 Third Avenue, New York, NY 10017

Routledge is an imprint of the Taylor & Francis Group, an informa business

First issued in paperback 2018

Typeset in Sabon by IBT Global.

Library of Congress Cataloging-in-Publication Data
White, Edie.
  Whiteness and teacher education / Edie White.
    p. cm. — (Routledge research in education)
  Includes bibliographical references and index.
    1. Multicultural education—United States. 2. Minorities—
Education—United States. 3. Race awareness—Study and
teaching—United States. 4. Teachers, White—United States.
5. Multiculturalism—United States. I. Title.
  LC1099.3.W49 2011
  370.1170973—dc23
  2011018105

ISBN: 978-0-415-89889-8 (hbk)
ISBN: 978-1-138-37806-3 (pbk)

Contents

1 Introduction

On the first day of sixth grade a new student came to my school. Her name was Nicole and she was African American. Her family was the first African American family to move into the neighborhood. She was the first African American I ever knew. The other kids in class called her "that Negro girl"; I just called her Nicole.

Although Nicole and I were in the same classes, we were not always treated in the same manner. Because we were chatty twelve-year-olds, Nicole and I were often separated and seated on opposite sides of the room. In our language arts class we had read the *Miracle Worker* and learned how to sign all of the letters of the alphabet. Nicole and I soon discovered that learning sign language afforded us the opportunity to continue to talk during class regardless of how far apart our teachers sat us. Because we only knew the letters and not the signs for whole words, we had to spell each word out; understanding each other required serious concentration. One day Mrs. Donahue, our language arts teacher, saw us signing across the room to each other. She stopped talking for several minutes while she and all of our classmates watched us. We were oblivious to the silence until she interrupted our secret communication and told us she wanted to see us in the hallway. She first spoke to Nicole and told her that that was not the way we behave in class and that if she wanted to be successful she had to pay attention like the other kids. She looked at me and told me she was disappointed because I should have known better.

When our parents went to parent–teacher conferences, Nicole's parents were told that she "could be a smart child," but she was not taking advantage of the education she was receiving at our suburban school. Her parents were told that she needed to learn how to act appropriately in a school setting. Mrs. Donahue assured her parents that Nicole was getting the same opportunities as everyone else but that she was making a choice to be a distraction to her peers by her constant chatter. My parents were told I was a good kid who was excelling.

In May of that year as Nicole and I were walking home together (like we always did), about twenty of the kids in our grade started running after us. We ran as fast as we could, but were quickly overtaken. We curled into balls on the grass as we were kicked and punched and told to "go back where we came from." I didn't realize at the time that they were not talking to me—that is until they added the "N" word. Eventually they stopped, and we gathered our things and continued to walk home. The only thing breaking the silence was the sound of an occasional sob. As we approached our street, I said, "Nicole, they'll leave us alone now and forget about us." She looked at me with fresh tears and said, "They'll never forget that I'm black." I told her that it didn't matter what color she was. She just shook her head and continued walking. The next day I got a new bike so that I wouldn't have to walk home from school; Nicole had a for sale sign in her yard.

On the day they sold their house, I was filled with sadness and cried to my mother because my best friend was really going to move. My mom reminded me that her father got transferred to Pennsylvania and that they had to move. She suggested to me that I should be happy for her. I disagreed. Remembering what Nicole had said, I told my mom that Nicole was moving because she was black. My mother said that I was being ridiculous and that our neighborhood was a good, safe place and the fact that her family was able to live there was evidence of their success. My mother assured me that times were different and that a person's race didn't matter anymore. She told me that success was determined by how hard people worked, not by the color of their skin. Although what she said greatly contradicted what I had experienced during my sixth-grade year, I believed her because I so desperately wanted it to be true.

I thought Nicole and I were best friends because she was the same as me in that we thought alike and had similar interests. But I was wrong. We were not the same; we experienced the world in very different ways. I didn't realize the disservice I was doing her by expecting that she should have the same experiences as me. I remember telling her I didn't see her dark skin, I only saw her as a person, not realizing that subtle implication I was making about our differences not being worth noticing. By pretending to not see her skin color, I was not acknowledging how her skin color made her experiences different from mine. Because I never thought about my race, I became frustrated with her when she thought about hers. When her family wasn't invited to the block party, I tried to convince her that the invitation must have gotten lost in the mail. But she was convinced that no one liked her parents because of their skin color. When her house got tpeed and her family cars got egged, I told her that it was just crazy teenagers who randomly picked her house, but didn't have an answer when she asked why they randomly selected her house so many times. In annoyance I asked her why she had to make a big deal out of everything. When we rode our bikes to Baskin Robbins to get an ice cream cone, I thought Nicole was being overly sensitive because she was afraid and thought that everyone was staring at her. I didn't understand; neighborhoods that weren't safe looked different than ours. I had been in those "unsafe" neighborhoods coming home from Chicago when my father told us to lock our car doors. It never occurred to me to question my own racist beliefs about an African American neighborhood not being safe. I never considered that Nicole's race physically defined her to others just as I felt mine did when I was in Chicago. Since she lived in my community, I thought she was different from the inner city people. I considered her one of us and in doing so expected her to act, understand and interact with the world like one of us—a white person.

While she was trying to communicate to me that race was still an issue in the world, I was trying to convince her that it wasn't. Because my race did not compromise me, I believed that sometimes things just happened and it wasn't ever about race—those days were gone. Yet in the back of my mind I was confused by what I had experienced and what I had been taught. I saw what had happened to Nicole and her family, but I had been taught at home and at school to believe that people created their own circumstances. If they were struggling, it was because they hadn't taken advantage of the opportunities that were available to everyone. I was taught that racism was about individuals who harassed and discriminated against people who were racially different than them. Nicole was trying to tell me that it wasn't just a few individuals, but that it was everywhere. In her own way, she was trying to tell me that it was embedded in the culture, even within me, but I wouldn't listen. I didn't understand how from a very early age, social structures influenced my ideas about equality and race. I didn't consider how the notion of equality and the American Dream were myths perpetuated by a force much greater than my parents or my teachers.

WHITENESS AND CULTURAL DIVERSITY

Despite current studies regarding privilege as it relates to whiteness (Lipsitz, 2006; Kendall, 2006; Dyer, 2005; Doane, 2003; Rodriguez, 2000; hooks, 1997; McIntyre, 1997) white privilege for the most part persists as an unmarked narrative. When white people are not seen or named, the implication is that they are the norm while all others are raced (Dyer, 2005). Yet, how one comes to understand the self and others is largely influenced by systems of normalization learned through school, religion, the media, national folklore and other means of education which in the United States privileges the socialization of white people.

In considering an ideology of race, whiteness must be understood as a racialized social system that is contingent upon historical, institutional and social influences (Kendall, 2006; Doane, 2003). These social relationships are created through dominant discourses that are used to racialize groups of people. Whereas people's individual notions of truth are influenced by the ideologies of the society from which they are a part, these ideologies are explained through discourses that are passed from institutional and political sites. These discourses work to normalize a notion of what is true through the education and indoctrination of the citizens in a society. Foucault (1994) argues that

> each society has its regimes of truth, its "general politics" of truth—that is, the types of discourse it accepts and makes function as true; the mechanisms and instances that enable one to distinguish true and false statements; the means by which each is sanctioned' the techniques and procedures afforded value in the acquisition of truth; the status of those who are charged with saying what counts as true. (p. 316)

Yet, discourses of truth cannot be separated from discourses of power. Whoever has the power makes the discourse. White people have historically had the power to produce and control the discourses that become the official regimes of truth of society. In the United States, a white version of knowledge has become the official version of knowledge (Apple, 2000).

Interrogating whiteness is crucial as the population in the United States continues to grow more diverse. While the 2005 "minority" population in the United States represented 33% of the total population, by the year 2020, the "minority" population is predicted to be 39% (National Center for Educational Statistics, 2006). The increasing racial and ethnic diversity in the United States can be witnessed in the schools as well. In 1993, 66% of the student population in all national schools was categorized as white whereas 34 % was classified as non-white. By the year 2003, 58.7% of the total student enrollment was white while 41.3% of the students were identified as nonwhite (National Center for Educational Statistics 2006).

While the nation's student population continues to grow in ethnic diversity, the racial diversity of teachers has stayed relatively the same with white teachers representing approximately 84% of all teachers working in elementary and secondary schools over the last decade (National Center for Educational Statistics 2003–2004). The fact that our nation's schools continue to become more diverse whereas the teacher population continues to be predominantly white has become a growing concern for educators who are concerned with all students being given the opportunity to experience success (Howard, 2006; Ladson-Billings, 1995; Rodriguez, 2000; Lipsitz, 2006). As the number of students from racially diverse backgrounds continues to increase, teacher educators urgently need to turn their focus toward preparing both practicing and pre-service teachers to work with culturally diverse students. The teacher population must become more knowledgeable about contextualizing teaching practices to meet the educational needs of diverse populations of students—the future of our country—who will provide the nation with the intellectual resources to participate and compete in a global society.

SITUATING THE STUDY

At State University students are grouped into cohorts. They proceed through a five-semester teacher certification program in which they take all of their education classes together. I met one of the cohorts of twenty-four in the autumn of 2006 during the second semester of their journey. I taught two literacy methods courses to the group. The cohort consisted of twenty-two white students and two students who self-identified as biracial.

In addition to incorporating course readings that addressed the theories and methods behind teaching literacy, I also included readings that discussed how literacy is understood in social and political contexts. I wanted to offer my students the opportunity to understand the importance of making the content and lessons of their classes relevant and accessible for all students. As an educator, I found this information invaluable. Yet, I was surprised at the apathy that bled through our class discussions. I did not understand the tacit resistance from my predominantly white students whenever we discussed strategies for teaching children who come from marginalized communities.

In order to better understand what I perceived as my students' apathy, I asked if the group expected to have an entire class of children who looked like them and who had similar schooling and life experiences as they had. I asked if they saw any importance in learning how to develop their practices in ways that would meet the diverse needs of all of their students. While my questions were for the most part met with blank stares, one student, Brittany, stopped my line of inquiry by answering, "Of course we care, but we already talked about diversity and culturally relevant pedagogy last semester. We don't need to talk about this anymore. Besides, no offense, but we're different from you and most of the teachers we had growing up. We have friends from all different ethnicities from all over the country and all over the world. We don't have the same hang ups about race that your generation has."

Brittany, like all of the students in the class, was born after 1980. Much has been written about this group—often referred to as the millennial generation. Recent research suggests that due to the rise of internet use and a move toward globalization, millennial students have more experiences with people from diverse populations and are more accepting of cultural diversity (Greenberg & Weber, 2008; Howe & Strauss, 2000; Rainer & Rainer 2011). Indeed, the common view of millennial youth appeared to be true with my cohort.

After Brittany shared the beliefs and attitudes her generation had about diversity, many of the students in the class offered stories recounting their daily interactions with people from ethnicities and cultures different from their own. The students in the class also shared that some of their friendships with culturally diverse people were started and continue to exist on facebook and other social networking sites. They were pleased to speak of the ways they were connected to others.

Intrigued, I asked the group to talk more about their various interactions with diverse groups of people. Several of the students in the class talked about the plethora of volunteer hours they needed to graduate high school and get into the university. They shared stories about service-learning projects in which they had to work with underserved communities in order to earn credit in their college courses. Without a doubt, my students had many more opportunities than I did (or did many of my contemporaries in their forties and fifties) when I was their age to interact with those who are ethnically and culturally different from themselves.

When I asked the students to share with me what their experiences with diversity taught them, they overwhelmingly agreed that "people are people, we're all the same" and that "it doesn't matter where you come from or who you are, we're all on an equal playing field now." I was somewhat taken aback by their answer. While I agreed that there is a degree of consistency in the human experience, I disagreed that there is an equal playing field. Upon further discussion, it became clear that they didn't see the complexity of cultural diversity in quite the same way that I did; they weren't conscious of the role that one's culture played in determining whether an individual might be socially, politically and economically privileged or marginalized. Despite what we had read in class or what the two people of color in the cohort had to say about their experiences, the twenty-two white students were particularly resistant to critically examining the ways their race afforded them privileges while at the same time marginalizing others. What was missing from the discussion of their experiences with cultural diversity was a critical reflection about how structural and institutional beliefs and practices have created, and continue to create, inequity.

I have shared this story to offer perspective on an all too common occurrence in teacher education classrooms. While many white youth from the millennial generation believe they are more accepting of cultural and racial diversity than previous generations, their life experiences of privilege too often bump against their notions of racial acceptance and equality. Studies discussing the experiences of pre-service teachers (Artiles, 1998; Villegas & Lucas, 2002; Cochran-Smith, 2004; Gonsalves, 2008) show that white teacher candidates often resist forms of socio-historical analysis of their own schooling. Because so many have benefited from the school system that privileges those from their own socio-cultural upbringing (white, middle class), they are unlikely to acknowledge the presence much less the effects of institutionalized racism within the educational system at large (Villegas & Lucas, 2002). Furthermore, Gonsalves (2008) suggests that questioning the norms of the dominant culture often leads to feelings of guilt and confusion which result in denial and other performed acts of resistance.

Because of the resistance I encountered from my white students when I asked them to reflect on the ways their personal experiences shaped their notions of teaching and learning, I began to focus my energies on helping teacher candidates move past this resistance. I felt it was important for them to acknowledge and understand difference and inequalities so that they would see the need to develop practices that serve culturally diverse populations. Yet, in order to prepare prospective teachers for working in a diverse world, it became apparent to me that teacher educators need to offer authentic opportunities for their students to interrogate their personal beliefs and experiences and reflect on how these shape their teacher identities with respect to notions of teaching and learning. Helping pre-service white teachers explore the ways they are situated in the world juxtaposed with the experiences marginalized groups encounter in various social systems can give these teacher candidates the needed insight to develop pedagogies and craft their practices in ways that prepare culturally diverse students for a changing world.

THE STUDY

This study examines the life histories of five, millennial, white pre-service teachers. It explores how they have come to see themselves and unpacks the spoken and unspoken biases that shape who they are and who they imagine themselves to be. The study looks to answer the following questions: How do white prospective teachers discuss and understand their life experiences and the ways these experiences shape their teacher identities? How do white prospective teachers discuss an equitable pedagogy and how do they imagine practicing this pedagogy? How can our understandings of the intersection of life experiences and pedagogies of equity be developed in teacher education programs so that teacher candidates are given the opportunity to consciously develop practices that meet the needs of all of their students?

The stories you will read are the individual stories of five participants as told in their own words. Yet, they can be viewed as a microcosm of white teacher candidates across the nation who struggle with understanding the ways their own socio-cultural heritages shape their professional identities. It was important for me to include the participants' stories, uninterrupted, as told in their own words. The purpose of this was so that the readers of this work have an opportunity to study the speaker as well as the experiences themselves.

The stories are then interpreted using Bakhtin's notion of the development of the self. What makes this analysis so revealing is that Bakhtin's theories allow us to study the language the speaker uses when looking back on the experienced life; that is to say we are not looking at the just the stories the participants tell to make meaning of their lives, but we are examining the language that the participants use to give the experience meaning. What this gives us as readers is a chance to study the speaker as well as the experience being described.

In a time where being white still carries privileges, teacher educators need to provide a space for pre-service teachers to reflect on how their life experiences, at least in part, shape who they are as teachers. It is also important for teacher educators to help white pre-service teachers understand the ways people of color may interpret and respond to whiteness. When a space is provided in teacher education programs for prospective teachers to reflect on the similarities and differences between their own life experiences and the experiences of people of color, to understand how their spoken and unspoken biases have shaped how they make sense of the world and the ways they interact with others, teacher candidates can more clearly see and respond to schooling discrepancies across cultures. Armed with this potential for developing cultural awareness, teacher educators can help pre-service teachers develop appropriate pedagogical approaches, frame curriculum content which is accessible for all students, and create a supportive social context of learning for all students, but especially ethnic minority populations.

2   The Making of a White Teacher

This chapter examines the role that teacher education programs play in facilitating the development of a teacher identity with their pre-service teachers. It explores how teacher educators have attempted to help prospective teachers, specifically white and middle-class prospective teachers, reflect on their individual and social identities as they develop their professional identities. Beginning with the Multicultural movement through current practices, I trace the ways that teacher education programs have incorporated strategies for teaching diverse learners.

EDUCATION AS A POLITICAL PROBLEM

The unacknowledged norms that are used to develop teaching practices and student evaluation are unquestionably linked to the broader society. The accepted Discourse (Gee, 2005) of the educational system honors a certain way of thinking, talking and behaving that promotes the ideologies of the dominant culture—that is to say the white, middle-class culture. The crisis we see regarding inequitable schooling conditions and educational experiences for socially marginalized students is not merely based on policy problems (although we can certainly look to policy as a contributing factor), but rather it is the political nature of schooling that leads to inequitable policies.

Most white people's first experiences with schooling have socialized them into believing that education is the great equalizer in society. Villegas and Lucas (2002) argue that this erroneous belief is based on two false assumptions. The first is that the notion of meritocracy is based in the idea that all individuals can be identified and measured using objective criteria. The second assumption is that all schools are fair and equitable in their practices. Cochran-Smith (2004) argues that "schools (and how 'knowledge,' curriculum,' 'assessment' and 'access' are constructed and understood in schools) are not neutral grounds but contested sites where power struggles are played out" (p. 18). Teachers who develop ideologies and practices of the dominant culture re-inscribe inequity in the schools. Teachers who resist the accepted norms and develop practices that are multicultural in their approach to both teaching and learning challenge the status quo. Either way it is impossible for a teacher to teach in a way that is not political. It is for this reason that teacher educators have turned their attention to considering how Teacher Education Programs can help prospective teachers experience success working with all children in the political arena of the school system.

MULTICULTURALISM AND TEACHER EDUCATION

In the late seventies and early eighties, teacher educators began responding to the need to develop theories and practices to include all children in the educational experience. There became an increasing awareness that the gap between the life experiences and the school experiences of white children and the life and school experiences of children of color needed to be closed. One way to close this gap and create a space for diverse voices was explored in the Multiculturalism movement that gained momentum in the early 1980s and still exists today. Early Multiculturalists emphasized the appreciation of differences and the celebration of a collective oneness. In schools this implementation of early notions of Multiculturalism often translated to celebrating the contributions that different cultures brought to the United States through mini school-wide festivals. These celebrations were considered special days where community members would come into the school to share their cultural food and dances with the student body. However, as Ladson-Billings (1995a) argues,

> these demonstrations were often reduced to trivial examples and ar-
> tifacts of culture such as eating ethnic food or cultural foods, sing-
> ing songs or dancing, reading folktales, and other less than scholarly
> pursuits of the fundamentally different conceptions of knowledge or
> quests for social justice. (p. 56)

While these mini festivals certainly exposed children to cultural practices that were unfamiliar to them, they did not allow or encourage children to examine epistemological differences between cultures.

Educators began to look at the way pre-service, as well as in-service teachers, were being educated in diversity to help schools bridge the chasm between the students' school and home lives. Teacher Education Programs began responding to an increasingly racially diverse student population and a consistently white teacher population by adding one or two classes on Multicultural Education, but typically left the rest of the curriculum in tact. The implication of this was that issues of diversity could be separated from the rest of the teacher education programs (Garibaldi, 1992; Zimpher & Asburn, 1992; Ladson-Billings 1995; Zeichner & Hoeft, 1996; Goodwin, 1997; Villegas & Lucas, 2002; Gonsalves, 2008). A study conducted by McIntyre (1997) concluded that this add-on approach left most white pre-service teachers with the idea that Multiculturalism was about studying "other people" rather than understanding the effects of oppression and inequality on non-whites as well as whites.

In an attempt to bring the issue of diversity closer to home, Teacher Education Programs began placing their white pre-service teachers in urban settings so that they might have first hand experience working with students who were racially different from themselves. The hope was that this practice would facilitate their understanding of educational inequity and would Multiculturalize the teacher candidates. Goodwin (1997) followed eighty-three students (fifty-six white and twenty-seven students of color) through the course of a semester seminar of student teaching in urban schools. She asked them to write vignettes about their Multicultural experiences in their schools. Many of the white students wrote about the shock they felt by the disparities they saw in the way students of different races were treated. They talked of being discouraged by the blatant racist attitudes and behaviors displayed toward the non-white students by many of their white peers and teachers in the school. Furthermore, they felt helpless about doing anything to alter what they witnessed. Goodwin concluded that it was naïve and irresponsible to place white teacher candidates in schools with diverse populations and expect them to experience success armed only with their course work in one or two Multicultural Education classes. Goodwin's findings support the argument that traditional pre-service teacher education has not prepared prospective white teachers to teach diverse populations (Zeichner & Hoeft, 1996; Ladson-Billings, 1999a; Gomez, Walker & Page, 2000, Gonsalves, 2008).

The main criticism with adding one or two courses in Multicultural Education and/or placing white teachers in racially diverse school settings is that the majority of prospective and practicing teachers are middle-class whites who have lived all or most of their lives in the suburbs (Villegas & Lucas, 2002; Cochran-Smith, 2004; Gonsalves, 2008). White teacher candidates did not often have or make opportunities to have contact with people who were different from themselves. Without contact with people from various socio-cultural groups, white pre-service teachers miss the opportunity to see and understand the daily realities including the struggles, interests and concerns of marginalized people and families with whom they will eventually encounter in their classrooms. This isolation affords them the comfort of accepting without question the status quo (Villegas & Lucas, 2002). The education system worked for them; therefore, they are often not likely to question school practices. This too often leads to the gaps in educational achievement being blamed on the students rather than critically examining the social and institutional practices that contribute to this gap.

NEW IMAGES OF TEACHER LEARNING

For the past two decades, teacher educators have developed a new image of teacher learning. Rather than looking at teacher training as one dimensional (learning methods and then practicing teaching) this new image was informed by looking at how teachers think about their work. The emphasis in teacher training has shifted from considering solely what teachers do to examining what they know, what sources of knowledge they have and how these sources influence what they do in the classroom (Shulman, 1987; Barnes, 1989; Cochran-Smith & Lytle, 1990; Lampert, 1990; Cochran-Smith, 2004). This new approach to teacher education recognizes that prospective teachers come to Teacher Education Programs with prior knowledge (that is both social and specific) which they bring to all new learning situations. Additionally, with this recognition comes the understanding that active learning—merging prior knowledge with new understandings—requires a prolonged span of time rather than a few isolated moments (Cochran-Smith, 2004). This awareness for teacher educators helped, at least in part, explain why the previous practice of including one or two Multicultural Education classes within an established education program was having little impact in producing teachers who were cognizant of why and how to develop practices that were culturally relevant for their students.

The new image of teacher learning is based on the premise that what a teacher knows and believes informs the way she acts, decides, interprets and develops her practice. Relationally, this means that the prospective teacher must negotiate what she learns in her teacher education classes with the knowledge and beliefs that she brings into the Teacher Education Program all the while thinking about what she will teach in her classroom (Borko & Putnam, 1996; Wideen, Mayer-Smith & Moon, 1998; Hollins & Guzman, 2005). New attention is being paid to what teacher candidates are learning and how they think about the content of their teacher preparation classes.

PROSPECTIVE TEACHERS' RESISTANCE
TO CRITICAL REFLECTION

Su (1997) concluded (from investigating the attitudes of African American, Asian American and Hispanic American prospective teachers) that non-white teacher candidates, because of their marginalized experiences within the dominant culture, come into Teacher Education Programs with a stronger commitment to issues of social justice within the educational arena. They are also more likely to see themselves as change agents than their white peers. Similarly studies (Artiles, 1998; Villegas & Lucas, 2002; Cochran-Smith, 2004; Gonsalves, 2008) show that white teacher candidates are more apt to resist a socio-historical analysis of schooling than their non-white colleagues. The resistance that many white prospective teachers feel is often performed as an act of denial of widespread educational inequalities. This denial can take the form needing to defend dominant social values from which they have personally benefited. Additionally, their denial may be a defensive reaction to challenges posed to their core beliefs and sense of self or individual identity. Gonsalves (2008) calls this denial a blindness that "operates as a defense against critical awareness of how educational inequality against others is intrinsic to maintaining individual privilege for some" (p. 5). Many of the white prospective teachers' lived experiences have reinforced the belief that society is unbiased and that education is the great equalizer in society. Because the school system has worked for them, they are unlikely to question the reasons for their academic success or look to see the effects of institutionalized discrimination (Villegas & Lucas, 2002).

Yet Gonsalves (2008) suggests that it may be the very act of questioning the established norms of the dominant culture that leads to feelings of confusion, guilt and shame which are performed as acts of resistance. Furthermore, Gonsalves contends that "resistance to new information and the interrogation of personal beliefs may spark an ethical and moral dilemma in which the pre-service teacher must reconcile competing values about education, equality and privilege" (p. 8). The moral dilemma requires further examination.

MORAL DILEMMAS AND SOCIAL CONSCIOUSNESS

Many educators and researchers alike contend that teacher education can contribute to the agency of prospective teachers by focusing on the moral and ethical dimensions of education (Tom, 1984, 1997; Goodlad, 1990; Fullan, 1993, 1999; Villegas & Lucas, 2002). This is not to suggest that educators should deliver a moral imperative in order to indoctrinate prospective teachers, but rather teacher educators should focus on the moral dimensions of education as they impact the teacher candidates' evolving identities.

The essence of the ethical or moral dilemma involves making a choice based on conflicting values, beliefs and then acting upon that choice. This choice can be distressing and at times emotionally challenging as the exposure to new information that contradicts deeply held beliefs initiates a sense of confusion in the individual. This confusion often leads to a self-induced blindness and consequent paralysis (Gonsalves, 2008). Yet, teacher educators have begun to foreground the moral purpose of teaching by highlighting the place of social justice in education. This entails teacher educators engaging future teachers in a critical inquiry and analysis into the political nature of education, the social and institutional practices that result in inequities, as well as the reflection of their own roles in social and institutional contexts (Villegas & Lucas, 2002). Once prospective teachers become cognizant of social injustice, they can no longer assume to be objective. Developing a socially conscious understanding of the way the educational system privileges some and marginalized others, forces the teacher candidate to make an ethical decision—to either perpetuate the inequities by doing nothing or to actively work against the prevailing injustices.

Cochran-Smith (2004), a strong proponent of incorporating principles of teaching for social justice into Teacher Education Programs, contends that learning to teach for social justice at least in part involves unlearning racism and problematic stances that are often hidden. In order to help prospective teachers unravel the complexities of racist ideologies, teacher educators have begun to see the need to help their students develop a social consciousness. In part this means helping teacher candidates develop an awareness that the way an individual views the world is not neutral, but rather is shaped by her life experiences and is mediated by how she is located and locates herself in society with respect to race, gender and class (Grant, 1991; Sleeter, 1992; Banks, 1993, 1994; 1996; Cochran-Smith, 1993; Bennett, 1995; Howard, 2006; Villegas & Lucas, 2002). Additionally, gaining social consciousness requires teacher candidates to see and understand that traditional schools, as political sites, play a significant role in reproducing social inequities even as they appear to be equitable and fair.

LEARNING COMMUNITIES

Rather than using traditional teaching methods to teach social consciousness, (teacher lectures where students are expected to hear about and then remember different theories in order to reproduce this information in the form of quizzes, tests and papers) educators are calling for teacher educators to incorporate learning communities as a way for prospective teachers to gain new knowledge and new understandings. Cochran-Smith (2004) argues that teacher education for social justice is not about providing scripted lessons and activities that work for all students and all teachers, nor is it about developing a specific knowledge about particular cultural group. Rather learning to teach for social justice involves all people in the Teacher Education Program, students, instructors and faculty alike, working together in as a community of learners, educators and activists.

Cochran-Smith (2004) envisions these new learning communities as places built on mutual respect in which members are committed to not only their own professional development, but to the growth and development of all members in the group. In the new learning community all members take an inquiry stance. This requires new and experienced teachers and teacher educators to work together to "generate local knowledge, envision and theorize their practice and interpret and interrogate the theory and research of others" (p. 14). It allows prospective teachers and experienced teachers to question one another. This process invites teacher candidates to bridge their particular students to larger educational ideas and frameworks. Within these communities, pre-service teachers have opportunities to see how experienced teachers construct problems, struggle with uncertainty, and how they question long established practices or assumptions (Cochran-Smith, 2004). This exposure to experienced teachers also allows pre-service teachers the chance to see how teacher mentors working to incorporate notions of social justice in their classrooms create knowledge and develop interpretive frameworks for crafting their daily practices.

MOVING FORWARD

Assisting prospective teachers to develop social awareness has become one of the aims of teacher educators today. Teacher educators are working to help prospective teachers create conditions for all children, regardless of their socio-cultural backgrounds, to have positive and successful experiences in the educational system. Teacher educators have begun encouraging teacher candidates to examine their own social positions and question the ways they have formed their beliefs. For white teacher candidates, this means becoming aware of the assumptions they make about those who are culturally different from them. Additionally, in order to induce prospective teachers' to think about assumptions promoted by institutions, teacher candidates are being asked to contemplate their beliefs and assumptions about the role of schools, the value of diversity, and their notions of knowledge, learning and teaching (Feiman-Nemser & Melnich, 1992; Cochran-Smith 1995; Farber, 1995; Feiman-Nemser & Remillardi, 1996; Villegas & Lucas, 2002).

Gonsalves (2008) argues that teacher educators must help prospective teachers re-evaluate their assumptions in order to recognize beliefs that are grounded in racist ideologies. He contends that changing inherent racist beliefs to more socially conscious attitudes requires careful introspection and a reassessment of one's social positioning. This transformation does not happen over night, but rather it is a process that evolves over time and very often involves oscillating between struggling with the deeper levels of resistance that often surface as new awareness opens up (pp. 16–20).

FACILITATING THE PROCESS

There are many avenues that teacher educators use to help prospective white teachers begin the process of developing a social consciousness. Within learning communities teacher educators have begun incorporating generative ways for prospective teachers to reconsider their personal knowledge and experiences.

Life History Work

Life history work asks students to consider their own histories as human beings and educators. Drawing on the work of Wijeyesinghe, Griffin and Love (1997) Villegas and Lucas (2002) suggest that students explore their earliest memories of their personal socialization process including their own cultural, racial and linguistic backgrounds as well as their schooling experiences that all work to shape their evolving teacher identities. Invariably, embedded in these life histories are the social ideologies and assumptions about the self and others that inform the prospective teachers' understandings about the role of teaching and learning in society.

Life history work can take the form of writing personal narratives or the oral sharing of life stories. The sharing of life histories is important because it allows the teacher candidates in the community of learners to explore their experiences for themselves, but also provides for the other community members a sense of who they are as human beings as well as learners and teachers (Cochran-Smith, 2004). Additionally, sharing one's life stories allows the teller to see the self reflected back from the group members. Through their interrogation, the group members can further question and share insights about potentially unexamined assumptions and the influence of the teller's beliefs and assumptions on her attitudes and practices. Furthermore, Cochran-Smith suggests first person accounts have "the capacity to contain many of the contradictions, nuances and complexities that are important for understanding the roots and twists of racism and the many ways that they interact with social life" (pp. 91–92).

A study done by Gomez, Walker and Page (2000), however, contradicts the findings of Cochran-Smith. These scholars found that personal narratives did not always support peer and self-critique and could potentially reinscribe life experiences as guidelines for a developing teacher identity. In particular, Gomez, Rodriguez and Agosto (2008) suggest that each story told is a "particular cultural performance—an attempt at an effective presentation of their identity for a specific audience at a particular time and place" (p. 1648). Their contention is that even as people reveal their life histories, what stories they choose to tell and how they tell these stories is influenced by how they are hoping to be perceived. There exists the inherent risk that a prospective white teacher may consciously withhold racist elements of their experiences in order to be perceived as socially conscious all the while harboring prejudice beliefs and attitudes.

As Gomez et al. (2000) contend, while an individual can choose to cling to her ideologies regardless of what is shared or challenged during a class discussion, the interrogation of one's life experiences is still a worthwhile tool to help deconstruct and transform racist ideologies when used in conjunction with other approaches. Establishing a learning community, as previously mentioned, may be one way to establish a space for teacher candidates in the class to do the work of transformation. This is significant as the other members in the group can challenge, provided they are in a safe and non-threatening environment, assumptions and contradictions in the speaker's shared experience that the teller might not have seen otherwise. In this sense, while there is no guarantee that all class members will learn from the shared life experiences of the self and others, the opportunity for all group members to learn from the teller's life experiences is heightened.

Personal Reflections

Educators have also begun using personal reflections and journaling as a way to help teacher candidates reflect on their ideas about culture and education. Studies by Garmon (1998), McFalls and Cobb-Rogers (2001) and Obidah (2000) conclude that students do, in fact, learn through written reflections. The students' writing suggested that understanding of bias and cultural assumptions about teaching and learning increased, and they were more able to critique their own assumptions as well as those of others.

Not all studies have been as hopeful, however. Through examining student reflections about multicultural attitudes and beliefs, both McIntyre (1997) and Katz (2000) found that while students did in fact grow in their knowledge of racial disparity, many did not change their attitudes or beliefs and still considered discussions about racial inequality as being about "other people."

Although teacher educators cannot force a student to change his or her beliefs (nor should they strive to), they can support prospective teachers' increasing awareness to other perspectives. Through their responses to student writing, teacher educators can challenge the teacher candidates' standing assumptions by encouraging critical reflection (Ladson-Billings, 1991; Zeichner, 1996; Villegas & Lucas, 2002). Other members of the learning community can also support the prospective teacher's growth by authentically responding to their peers' reflective writings. Like the sharing of life histories, the sharing of personal reflections provides the writer the opportunity to see the self through the eyes of another and can enhance opportunities for critical reflection.

WHAT IS STILL MISSING?

While teacher educators working to help their prospective teachers examine their own identity development is a vital part of teacher education, what is absent in most teacher preparation programs is the presence of diversity, specifically people of color. Whereas teacher educators can have their students read narrative accounts from people of color, white prospective teachers can stand to substantially benefit from learning directly from their peers of color as well as faculty of color who may have had life experiences that are radically different from their own. These alternative perspectives could serve as a powerful impetus for the white teacher candidates' critical reflection. Additionally, hearing first person accounts could also serve to heighten their "cultural sensitivity, interracial understanding, and sense of social responsibility that is needed to teach a changing student population" (Villegas & Lucas, 2002, p. xv).

Without authentic encounters with real people of color, white students often view class discussions about diversity as liberal indoctrination. They learn the right things to say, what they call the "politically correct" things to say, in order to appear to have the right disposition to survive in schools of education across the country. When they do not have to answer to real people of color, those who are sitting in front of them, for their attitudes, words or actions, they risk going through an academic exercise without any cause for real reflection or insight.

Furthermore, while there are certainly moral and personal reasons for white teacher candidates to explore their white privilege, teacher educators need to facilitate white pre-service teachers to move beyond the exploration of the personal perception of themselves and others to become advocates for their students. While it is not likely that teacher educators can erase in their pre-service teachers years of socialization regarding privilege and racial superiority, teacher educators can help pre-service teachers understand and negotiate their biases in order to become knowledgeable in ways to provide support to their ethnically diverse and underserved students. As the cultural diversity of the United States continues to grow, it is imperative that pre-service teachers understand the urgency to develop pedagogies and contextualize practices that provide the same support to their culturally diverse students that they received in their schooling. Preparing culturally diverse students to participate in a global society, benefits not only those individuals but society as a whole.

3 The Emerging Self
A White Identity

A discussion of what it means to be a teacher cannot occur simply in the realm of the role one plays in the school system. A person does not simply become a teacher after completing a teacher certification program and finding a job in a school. Rather a teacher identity is influenced by a multitude of factors that shape who that teacher is as a person. To understand how a teacher self evolves then, it is important to examine both the individual and social identity that one brings to the role of teacher.

A persons' identity is unfinished and fluid—always in the state of becoming rather than something that can be permanently constructed and singly situated. With respect to a person's active engagement with the world, one does not have a single identity, but rather individuals are always evolving with various aspects of their identity existing in different times and spaces in the social and material world. In actuality, we all have multiple identities wherein the performance of any single identity is actually a hybrid of the multiple contexts of the self. To further explore the notion of identity, I turn to the works of Mikhail Bakhtin.

BAKHTIN AND IDENTITY

Identity is always shaped in part by past experiences and past ways of understanding the world. The past shapes the individual in the present as well as impacts the future understanding of the self. For Bakhtin (1993), identity is shaped not from a single event, but from the ongoing lived experience of each event in an individual's life. Every individual experience that a person has, or *once-occurrent event* as Bakhtin calls them, carries with it all events leading up to the moment. This accumulation of experiences creates a standpoint from which the individual understands and acts in the world. In terms of identity, the development of the evolving self incorporates the history of the lived experiences of each unique individual.

Yet, there are many experiences that an individual cannot choose. People cannot choose the class they are born into, their gender or their race. However, individuals can choose many of the events that happen in their daily lives, as well as how they might respond to these events. The choices they make are drawn from the series of events or experiences that they have lived. More simply, the choices individuals make in the present are impacted by the how they have come to make sense of their past.

For example, neither my parents nor I had the money to pay for my college education when I graduated from high school. Despite the fact that my father had paid for the higher education of my four older siblings, my family's financial circumstances dramatically changed by the time I was ready to attend college. Yet, I saw how doors opened to my siblings once they had earned a degree, and I was determined to create that same opportunity for myself. I had always dreamed of being a teacher and had experienced academic success during my years in school. From my past schooling experiences, I believed I would find the same academic success at college if I could just find a way to get there. I also knew the ways to turn my dreams into a reality. In order to pursue my goal, I applied for school loans, found a full time job and attended a junior college for a year so that I could save money to go on to four year college where I could get a teaching degree. Although I could not choose the financial situation in which my family found itself, I could choose to see myself as academically competent and could develop a plan to achieve my goal. In other words, the choices I saw for myself were determined by my life experiences up until that point.

In addition to the series of one's lived experiences, identities develop relationally in response to structural features in a society including but not limited to race, ethnicity, gender and class. Furthermore, identities grow out of "historically contingent, socially enacted, culturally constructed 'worlds': recognized fields or frames of social life" (Holland et al., 1998: p.7). In other words, there are multiple influences that work simultaneously to shape the ways that individuals make meaning in the world. Whereas individuals do in fact have unique experiences, they do not become the self in isolation; rather they evolve through their interactions with individuals as well as social ideologies.

The intersection where the two meet, the place where individual discourses as well as social discourses converge, is what Bakhtin (1981) refers to as dialogism. Bakhtin (1984) contends that "two embedded meanings cannot lie side by side like two objects—they must come into inner contact; that is, they must enter a semantic bond" (pp. 188–189). It is in the dialogic place where the social ideologies as well as the personal experiences intersect that individuals form their unique identity and determine how they will act in the world.

In looking at the above story I shared about earning my college degree, my understanding of my possibilities was influenced by multiple discourses. My understanding of success was based on the societal notion that one must earn a degree from a university to be successful and have further opportunities later in life. I had seen my siblings experience success, so I assumed I would achieve my goal as well. I never seriously considered that there might be race or class barriers that could prevent me from achieving my goals. The unseen privileges I had been granted as a middle class white person allowed me to assume that I would be given money to pay my tuition; I never contemplated the possibility that I might be turned down for a loan on the basis of my race. Nor did I consider the possibility that if my parents did not belong to the middle class (and thus co-sign my loans), I could also be turned down for the loan. My understanding of my possibilities was determined by the social discourses that operated in my own world that I had come to know as truths.

AUTHORING OF THE SELF

At the age of eighteen, I had developed an orgulous attitude. I believed that my peers who did not go to college were destined for a life of despair. I had no understanding, much less empathy, for those who did not have the same options that I had—I assumed everyone had the same opportunities as I did. I saw the world as a reflection of myself and my circumstances. I did not understand the ways I used my privileges to other those different from myself.

It wasn't until I was in my sophomore year of college that I had an awakening. I met peers in my classes who shared their personal struggles based on their race and class and described the setbacks they had encountered while attending the university. I became outraged at the inequalities that existed in society as I started to see the world through the eyes of my classmates who had been marginalized. Hearing about the struggles of others juxtaposed with my experiences allowed me to explore the ways that unspoken ideologies worked to privilege some and not all. I could no longer view myself or my life in quite the same way. For the first time in my life I began to see the relationship between myself and others, between my privilege and the denial of these same privileges to others. I came to see how socially constructed hierarchies contributed to my own life circumstances as well as the life circumstances of those less fortunate than myself. I realized that there was no seeing myself without seeing myself in relation to others. In this sense, understanding who I was, or authoring myself as Bakhtin calls it, took a distinctly different form from how it had in the past.

This new understanding of the other in relation to myself was an act of empathy. Bakhtin (1993) argues that empathizing requires seeing an object of being "from inside its own essence;" and involves "a separation of it from oneself" (p. 14). For Bakhtin, empathy requires a shift in perspective—rather than looking out at the world from the eyes of the self, empathy requires viewing the world through the eyes of another. This shift of position offers individuals an opportunity to expand their understanding of the world and the multiple perspectives of experiences.

However, in order for the experience to have meaning for the individual, it is imperative that this concern for the other's perspective be followed by a return to self-consciousness. Bakhtin (1990) argues that only from the return to the self "can the material derived from my projecting myself into the other be rendered meaningful ethically, cognitively or aesthetically" (p. 26). If individuals do not take what they have learned from seeing the other's perspective and integrate this new knowledge within their own life experiences, they risk being infected with the other's understandings. The point of empathy is not to become the other, but to use what has been learned from the other's experiences to get a better understanding of the self.

The act of empathy not only allows an individual to see the other from the other's point of view, but it also allows an individual to see the self through the eyes of the other. Seeing the self through the other's lens has the potential to allow individuals to see how they are perceived by others. Holquist and Clark (1990), drawing on Bakhtin's work on identity, suggests that

> in order to see ourselves, we must appropriate the vision of others. Restated in its crudest version, the Bakhtinian just-so story of subjectivity is the tale of how I get myself from the other: it is only the other's categories that will let me be an object for my own perception. I see myself as others might see it. In order to forge a self, I must do so from outside. (p. 28)

Bakhtin (1990) calls this awareness of the way the self is perceived by the other a *surplus of vision*. This surplus of vision affords individuals the opportunity to develop a more expansive understanding of the self—one they could not have seen without empathizing with the other.

This dialogic notion of self embraces the mixing and exchanging, the intersecting of values between the self and the other. As Bakhtin (1993) suggests, "empathizing actualizes something that did not exist either in the object of empathizing or in myself prior to the act" and "through this actualized something Being-as event [the living self] is enriched" (p. 15). It is in the boundaries and tensions of the merging of the self and the other that new meaning is formed and the individual's identity evolves.

Yet authoring the self calls for more than contemplation by the individual; Bakhtin calls for an engagement with the other. This engagement involves the bringing together of the multitude of voices that speak to and through individuals in order for them to make unique sense of their world. Bakhtin (1981) asserts that "the living utterance having taken meaning and shape at a particular moment in a specific environment, cannot fail to brush up against thousands of living dialogue threads, woven by socio-ideological consciousness around the given object of utterance" (p. 276). Individuals cannot escape the influences of other individuals nor can they escape ideological conditions that exist in their social world.

What individuals say, think and do is shaped by their life experiences and reflect the particular position from which they make sense of the world. Individuals author themselves through negotiating the multitude of social discourses that make up the "living dialogue threads." Bakhtin (1981) refers to this tension as part of the process of ideological becoming which involves "selectively assimilating the words of others" (p. 341). Drawing on this, Halasek (1999) asserts that this place of choice is one in which individuals consciously select which utterances and ideologies, of the many voices that bombard them, they come to make our own.

My new awareness of the ways in which some people are marginalized while others seem to coast through life allowed me to see myself in a different light. In the past I had not considered the version of reality that many marginalized people lived. I only saw it through my understanding of the world. My initial response when hearing the plight of my collegiate peers was to be angry for the injustice they had to endure. This quickly turned to paralyzing feelings of guilt when I considered how easy things seemed for me. I went through waves of dismissing their struggles (because I felt there was nothing I could do) and moments of wanting to fight on their behalf. But neither reaction felt right to me. I could not ignore their plight; yet fighting their fight seemed to further marginalize them.

In my early attempts at empathy, I succumbed to the others' consciousness adopting my peers' understanding of the world. In contemplating injustice, I sought to understand it from the perspective of those who had experienced it. Yet, as Holquist and Clark (1984) warn, when individuals see the world through the other's eyes, they risk falling prey "to the limitations of the other's horizon" (p. 78). In my attempts to understand the other, I lost myself by taking on the other's point of view while ignoring what my own life experiences had taught me.

However, a shift happened within me when I began to alter my thinking by assimilating the experiences of my peers with my own experiences. Rather than singly viewing the world from the eyes of my peers who had been marginalized, I came to see the ways that each of our lives were impacted by the socially accepted norms that lead to inequality. I couldn't do anything about the early experiences of my peers, but I came to see that I could do something about my future experiences as well as the experiences of my future students. I turned my focus toward developing a teaching practice that would work against false notions of equality and began to look to ways that I, as a future teacher, could develop equitable practices in my classroom that could help my students have opportunities for success that were similar to my own experiences. In this sense I was moving from internalizing the worldview of those whom I saw as others back toward integrating my new understanding with my own life experiences. By contemplating the experiences of others side by side with my experiences, I was becoming something more than I was before my encounters.

IDENTITY AND ETHICAL CHOICES

The question of ethics asks how one *ought to act in a specific circumstance.* Rather than rely on a moral imperative, ethical moments are found in each utterance and act. That is to say that the ethical moment is found in the particular, not the universal. In looking at a dialogic encounter, individuals determine how to act by considering whom they are directing their words or actions toward. Thus part of how individuals determine how to act depends on whom they believe is being addressed. Additionally, the possibility that an addressee might respond back shapes how one determines how to act. Yet this consciousness does not always assure that individuals will make ethical choices.

Bakhtin offers a way to conceptualize a notion of ethics and provides a possible framework that can help the individual make ethical decisions. Bakhtin (1993) argues that although there are no absolute moral norms, there is what he calls a *superaddressee,* a divine unseen observer of dialogic encounters. Bernard-Donals (1994) suggests that Bakhtin, through the notion of the superaddressee, sought "an experience that one could liken to that of the divine in the everyday" (p. 21). Nolan (2004) claims that this third party witness acts as an "ideal consciousness," or maximum authority, to which individuals frame their utterances (p. xvii). Bakhtin proposes that individuals relate with this unseen other, this divine witness, through aesthetic reflection.

For Bakhtin aesthetic reflection allows individuals to imagine a superaddressee who is an empathizing witness to the encounter. When individuals orient the self toward a sublime witness, they are able to see the self as they imagine they are seen by the superaddressee. The orientation of speech (and actions) toward this third party witness gives individuals a basis for determining how they ought to act in a particular moment. What we ought to do becomes clearer for us when we consider an addressee who is an actual participant in the event. For Bakhtin, it is to this addressee, or superaddressee, that individuals must orient their choices if they are to act ethically. Yet, ethics also involves what Bakhtin calls answerability.

Answerability requires individuals to take responsibility for the choices that they make without making excuses or justifications. Bakhtin (1993) calls one aspect of answerability the *non-alibi in Being.* He argues that individuals cannot escape their accountability or answerability for an act by using an alibi, but instead must assume responsibility for the totality of their role in the act.

Additionally, answerability involves taking responsibility for the emotional connection, the relating of the experience to the self, what Bakhtin (1993) calls the emotional-volitional tone. He describes this as "the experiencing of an experience as mine relating a given lived experience to me as the one who is actively experiencing it" (p. 36). As each thought and action is answerable by the individual, so too is a person accountable or answerable for the emotional connection he or she attaches to the experience.

Our identities are shaped by the individual choices we make throughout our lives. Our day to day decision making regarding how we ought to act in a particular moment in time, our notion of ethics, is influenced by whom we believe we are addressing, how we believe that person might respond to us and how we imagine we might respond back. In the authoring of one's life, or the becoming of the self, individuals are answerable for the choices they make not only in the specific events in their lives, but in the culmination of their life choices ultimately shaping their identity.

THE SOCIALIZATION OF WHITE PRIVILEGE

As the works of Bakhtin suggest, individuals do not develop identities simply from the unique experiences which they have in their lives. Rather, they evolve through their interactions with individuals as well as social ideologies. Bahktin (1993) contends

> an act of our activity, of our actual experiencing, is like a two-faced Janus. It looks in two opposite directions: it looks at the objective unity of a domain of culture and at the never-repeatable uniqueness of actually lived and experienced life. (p. 2)

When considering the ways that social ideologies shape a person's becoming, it is important to look at how constructed worlds emerge. Specifically, looking at the role that whiteness plays in shaping one's identity, it is important to examine how discourses that normalize whiteness contribute to the dialogic process of becoming.

Considering the social construction of whiteness, understanding the ways one might author the self in a Bakhtinian framework requires an examination of how a notion of whiteness is both produced and enacted. The act of becoming with respect to whiteness influences how individuals come to understand the world and negotiate a space for themselves in relation to others. As individuals internalize what it means to be white, they also conceptualize what it means to not be white.

This is not to suggest that one's race is the only aspect that goes into the creation of an identity. Whiteness is, like other facets of identity, important in the creation of a hybrid self. What I am seeking to understand is the extent that whiteness inflects other aspects of identity and how it in part shapes the ways prospective teachers understand their roles in the school system.

The ways that white individuals talk about their life experiences provides insight into how their emerging identities are influenced by ideologies that normalize and privilege whiteness. Furthermore, how they justify their life choices offers a glimpse into the ways that their white legacy shapes the ethical decisions they make about how to act in the world.

CONTEMPORARY IDEOLOGY OF RACE AND DIFFERENCE

Historically speaking, white privilege in the United States was something that was produced and constructed by white European settlers. These settlers came to author themselves in relation to those who did not look like them establishing monological notions of inherent worth based on one's fair skin tone. Although the white settlers, and those who came after them, acknowledged the physical presence of non-whites, what they did not develop was what Bakhtin (1993) terms empathy for those who looked different from themselves. Rather than seeing and understanding non-whites from what Bakhtin says, "inside [their] own essence" (p. 14), they chose to contemplate non-whites solely from their white position.

This single and limited perspective also prevented whites from having the opportunity to see themselves refracted back to them in the eyes of non-whites. Instead they viewed whites and non-whites as coming from disconnected worlds providing them the justification to treat non-whites in a discriminatory manner. The construction of white privilege was shaped by a monologic position which considered non-white others as an inanimate objects rather than living beings with whom a dialogic relationship existed. Racial tensions mounted as non-whites, who held no significant power in the United States, were forced to see themselves through the eyes of whites while the whites continued to turn a blind eye toward understanding the ways that non-whites shaped the social becoming of whites.

Even today, ideologies that create and sustain privilege continue to be protected from political critique. One obstacle that often prevents contemporary whites from being able to clearly see the privilege that their whiteness affords them is the notion of meritocracy which can work in hidden ways. This invisibility helps maintain the illusion that success is something that an individual earns through hard work and determination rather than being tied to an unnamed privilege based on whiteness (Lipsitz, 2006; Rothenberg, 2005; Fine 2004). Many whites are too quick to deny responsibility for the way by which the privileges that work to *their* advantage marginalize non-whites. When non-whites demand to be given the same or equal opportunities as whites, whites often see this as unfair and feel as if opportunities are being denied them. This perceived inequity is named as reverse discrimination in which non-whites are blamed for "playing the race card." In this sense there is not an absence of consciousness about racism but a dysconscious (King, 1997) notion of racism that impairs their ability to see the historical contingency of discourses about race and equality.

Denying the ways whiteness is produced in contemporary society allows whites to continue to privilege particular discourses that normalize advantages that whites receive. Bakhtin (1993) argues that dialogism takes into consideration individual experiences as well as social ideologies. When whites call out reverse discrimination as people of color receive what whites perceive as advantages, ideologies that encourage justifications and alibis for whites to maintain their privileged position in society are being perpetuated. In this sense discourses that position non-whites as deserving of the same opportunities that whites have are discounted in order for whites to continue to see people of color as outside of themselves without whites having to be answerable to the privileges they receive. Whereas this allows whites to at least acknowledge non-whites, it does not create a space for whites to develop what Bakhtin (1993) calls empathy in which whites are able to see their social position from the position of non-whites. Instead, subscribing to social ideologies that ignore social inequities works to shape many whites' beliefs about being entitled to particular privileges.

Another obstacle that hinders whites from acknowledging the privilege that their race carries is the belief that there is an equal opportunity for all people, regardless of race, to have the same opportunities to experience success in the United States. Because many white people do not see their whiteness, they are unable to see that their image of the world is created from their self-image of white dominance, and they cannot see their whiteness reflected back to them (Dyer, 2005). Many white people often assume that people of all races think, feel and act like them. Yet, this is not the case. bell hooks (1997) suggests that people are

> socialized to believe the fantasy, that whiteness represents goodness and all that is benign and non-threatening [and that] many white people assume this is the way black people conceptualize whiteness; [however,] they do not imagine the way whiteness makes its presence felt in black life, most often as a terrorizing imposition, a power that wounds, hurts, tortures. (p.169)

Although there is much talk of equality and equal opportunity in the United States, what is not recognized is that success is often tied to an individual's willingness to assimilate to societal norms and values which represent white norms and values (King, 1997). Built within this assumption is the notion that individuals, by their own will, can assimilate—the social structures that are in place that keep people locked within a particular social status are not taken into account.

Because white privilege is an unspoken norm even today, many white people never have to look at their own whiteness or examine the implications of the advantages they receive. Their identity is shaped, in part, by the unspoken notion of what it means to be white in the United States. The life experiences of many white people support the idea that an egalitarian society exists. Because they have been granted access to privileges throughout their lives, they assume non-whites have as well. The accumulation of their life experiences allows them to understand the world from their own perspective never having to empathize with the position of the non-white. Bakhtin (1993) suggests that the act of empathy allows individuals to become something more than they were before the act was performed. When whites fail to develop empathy, seeing people of color from a position that has been historically and socially marginalized, they are missing an opportunity to develop the self in a more socially conscious manner.

Furthermore, when whites continue to see and interact with people of color based on a social construction of white privilege perpetuated through institutionalized racialization, they deny what Bakhtin (1993) calls answer-ability for their privileges. The assumptions many whites make about people of color deserving fewer opportunities than whites works to continue the production of whiteness as privilege. These assumptions and cries of injus-tice by whites are often oriented toward other whites who feel the same way they do. Whites are often unprepared to respond to people of color and white advocates of social justice who might challenge these assumptions in the name of equality.

Examining the ways that one facet of identity, whiteness, influences teachers' understanding of their role in the schools and informs their decision making can help teacher educators develop meaningful Teacher Education Programs. Pre-service teachers need to be prepared to develop practices that are grounded in promoting equality in which all students are prepared to compete in disciplines that require high levels of cognition. Teacher educators need to find ways to assure that pre-service teachers have these opportunities.

4　The Examined Life

The participants of this study shared their life histories over the course of eighteen months. At the time of the first meeting, all of the participants were twenty-one years old and in the third semester of a five semester teacher certification program. During our meetings they had the opportunity to reflect on their life experiences and share stories of their social becoming. In contemplating their construction of the self, they addressed, among other things, their conceptualization of their whiteness as well as well as how they had come to understand the racialization of non-whites.

Understanding how individuals negotiate their sense of self—how they negotiate their identities to themselves and with others—must begin with an attempt to understand the world in the way they see it. The stories that the participants chose to tell reflect the particular ways they came to author themselves in relation to the world. Mischler (1999) contends that *"narratives are identity performances"* in which narrators express and explain who they are and who they imagine themselves to be (p. 19; italics in original). Subjects of life histories choose the stories they wish to tell, the stories that they deem important and the stories they value as mattering in describing their reality. Becker (1966) claims that

> to understand why someone behaves as he does, you must understand how it looked to him, what he thought he had to contend with, what alternatives he saw open to him; you can only understand the effects of opportunity structures, . . . social norms, and other commonly invoked explanations of behavior by seeing them from the actor's point of view. (pp. vi–vii)

Yet a life lived is not lived in isolation. The participants in this study, like all of us, are social beings influenced by individuals and society.

Embedded within the participants' stories about their lives are their understandings of the way the world operates. McAdams (1993) argues that subjects do not suddenly invent notions of how they should be in the world. Instead, our knowledge of how to be in the world is based on what McAdams calls societal myths—widely accepted stories that contain a truth about life for a given culture. Myths capture a society's given "psychological, sociological, cosmological and metaphysical truths" and "reflect the most important concerns of a people" (p. 34). In order to project a particular image, narrators have to have some understanding of the myths that are valued in a given society. This understanding is not developed instantly. Instead, this knowledge of societal myths evolves over time.

Social discourses as well as institutional discourses (both which create and perpetuate social myths) work within and through the participants as they share and make sense of their life experiences from their particular situated place in the world. Indeed, authoring of the self is a dialogic process that encompasses the multitude of discourses that shape life experiences. Bakhtin (1981) argues that the "word in language is half someone else's. It becomes 'one's own' only when the speaker populates it with his own intention, his own accent, when he appropriates the word, adapting it to his or her own semantic and expressive intention" (p. 293). How a subject decides to narrate and interpret a life experience, the stories participants choose to tell and the language they use to convey their meaning, can be just as revealing as the experience itself. In other words, what makes a Bakhtinian analysis intriguing is not the events themselves, but the language that the participant uses when looking back upon the events, that is to say, how the participant uses language to give the experience meaning.

As you read the life stories of the participants, it is important to consider that they were orienting their stories to me as the researcher as well as toward future readers of the study. Inherent in this orientation is the tellers' anticipated expectation of all who would come to hear their stories. In other words a narrator's stories are always oriented toward a listener. Linde (1993) contends that "a narrative is not a soliloquy; it is told to someone, and it must elicit some response from its addressee" (p. 102). Speakers look for how they think their words are being perceived and interpreted "from the alien conceptual system of the understanding receiver" (Bakhtin, 1981, p. 282). While the participants speak their stories, they are simultaneously internalizing the context with which they believe I am hearing their words. My reactions, responses and questions as the listener/researcher influenced how they thought I might be making meaning out of their words. This, I have no doubt, helped them to determine what stories they would tell—and within those stories what they would include and what they would leave out.

Narrators may say some things in order to project a particular image to the listener. In terms of discussing race, this has become quite apparent in the over emphasis of the phrase *politically correct* or the overuse of air quotes to signify correctness by those who come from a dominant social position in order to project an image of cultural sensitivity. Each of the participants employed an understanding of political and social correctness at some point during our meetings.

The examination of the life histories of a small group of white pre-service teachers reveals particular social ideologies about race, privilege and power that shape the way the participants make meaning of their lives. But we can move beyond the stories of the participants in this study to develop more expansive categories of understanding. Goodson and Sikes (2001) contend that

> analyzing the experiences and attitudes of an individual, we always reach data and elementary facts which are exclusively limited to this individual's personality, but can be treated as mere incidences of more or less general classes of data or facts, and can be used for determining laws of social becoming. (p. 6)

A broader interpretation of this study reveals a deeper understanding of how white teacher candidates in general might come to interpret the intersection of their lived lives and their teacher identities. Considering the ways that white pre-service teacher interpret and perform their racialized identities provides an opportunity for teacher educators to help white pre-service teachers interrogate how they understand those who are racially different from themselves and how this impacts their notions about teaching and learning. Furthermore, interrogating their own social becoming provides an important foundation to help white teacher candidates understand the need to develop more meaningful and equitable practices for their culturally diverse students.

PARTICIPANTS' NARRATED LIVES

Each of the life stories in the following chapters is composed of the actual words of the participants during the interviews. I have chosen to present their stories in a first person narrative so that the participants might speak their story to you, the reader. This was done so that the reader would become an addressee, or a participant, in the subject's life history rather than simply relying on my analysis as the researcher. As readers of the participants' stories, we are viewing the speaker as the speaker views the past self from the position of the present self. What this gives us as readers is a chance to study the speaker as well as the experience being described.

In transcribing the narrated life, I have eliminated only interruptions, questions asking for clarification, pauses, interjections, and opening and closing chit chat about unrelated issues so that the participants' stories are for the most part uninterrupted. Within the story, I used italics to inform the reader of moments when I prompted the participants to share more details, when I redirected the conversation after it became sidetracked, or when I asked the participants to further reflect on any experiences which they shared. The names of the actual participants have been changed.

5   Desiree

For the most part, everyone was white in my childhood neighborhood. I think there were maybe two black families in my community. I say maybe because I really don't remember anyone who wasn't white. But there had to be some non-whites. There were probably some Hispanic people, too. But I didn't notice. I mean, well, of course you would notice if someone had different skin color than you did, but to be honest, I didn't ever think about it. Everyone was the same to me when I was a kid.

When I was in elementary school, both of my parents went back to college after working blue collar jobs. My dad became an engineer and my mom went into real estate. When I was younger, I remember that our house wasn't as nice as most of my friends. But after my dad became an engineer, we moved into a nicer house in the same community and were able to have more of the things that our friends and neighbors had. I guess you could say that we lived in a really good neighborhood. But it was a conservative neighborhood. People had kind of an uppity attitude. For instance if you didn't have a nice yard or nice cars they kind of looked down on you. I hated that attitude.

When my mom was a child, she lived in a major US city. Whenever we went to visit her parents, I sensed it was a really big deal. I remember my mom being more protective of us. When we were driving she always locked the car doors, something she never did when we were driving around our community. I could obviously tell that the people in the city looked different. Like if we were driving through an area of the city and there were darker skinned people, she would tell us to duck down. She never told us why, but when I looked around and saw people who looked different than me, I couldn't help but make assumptions. As a kid, I think I thought that if one of those people saw us, they would kidnap us and do horrible things to us. I had heard enough stories about crime in the city and I remember always looking for bullet holes in the houses and cars that we passed.

When I got a little older, maybe junior high age, an African American family moved into our community. They didn't live in my neighborhood; they lived in a poorer section of town. There was a girl my age. She was a pathological liar. She would constantly tell us that she was moving to our part of town and that her family was going to have a pool. I remember asking her why that mattered. It was like "We know where you live. We know you're not moving." I don't know if she was ashamed of where she lived or if it was a culmination of other things. I never asked her.

[*In a previous discussion Desiree had mentioned that her parents were divorced. She had said the divorce was amicable and she was fine with it. I asked her to talk about how she felt that might have shaped her experiences growing up.*]

When my parents got divorced, my mom did her best to make our lives seem unchanged. She was a big shopper and always took us with her. I always dressed in clothes from stores like J Crew or the Gap. I didn't have Chanel, but I had the kid version of expensive clothes. When we turned sixteen, my twin sister and I each got cars. Looking back, I don't know why each of us got a car. I mean we probably could have shared one.

My mom also kept the big house. When I asked her why, she said, "Well, it was important that you kids maintained the lifestyle you had before we got divorced." It's funny. That house was so important to my mom. But when people would say to me, "You have a really nice house," I would say, "Oh, it's so boring." I was kind of embarrassed. Because after a while, you just sort of feel like it's not fair or something. You kind of feel bad. But on the other hand, you're used to having a certain lifestyle and somewhere along the way it's like you should feel bad for living a certain way.

I started wondering what other people were thinking about me and what I was thinking about them because they didn't live in a neighborhood like mine. I just became really conscious of how people think about each other. It's like people want to put a certain attitude on you because you have a nice house and I think, I don't want to be associated with that snobby attitude. I don't want people to know where I come from because to be honest, there is a stereotypical white, middle class uppity attitude there. And I'm not like that.

My mom used to tell us when we were little not to have a racist attitude. It was like she was sticking up for the people of color who lived on the other side of town. But, the neighborhood that I grew up in has changed since I was a child. Now that there are more black and Hispanic people living on our street, my mom seems to have a different attitude. She refers to them as "those people." She'll say things like, "Those people are throwing trash out their windows. Those people don't say hi to you when they pass you on the street. Those people don't have any respect for the neighborhood."

My mom spends a lot of her time buying and fixing up houses. She has one particular house that she rents to an extended black family. She says things like "Those people ripped out my carpet. They have too many kids. The kids smell. Those black people are smelling my house up."

It's hard for me to listen to and I'll say, "Mom, you need to think about why people are the way they are. Maybe they have a different idea of how to keep up a house." But she says, "I need to make those people change or make them leave." And I get so mad because she is being so racist.

But when I go home to visit, I know that I have been influenced by her changing attitude. It's like I only feel safe when I am walking my gigantic dog. The thing is there are a lot of black men in the neighborhood. They walk in the streets. They don't walk on the sidewalk. I don't know why that is. I've seen them checking out the cars in the driveways. If I come home late at night and I see a black man sitting in his car, I won't get out of my car. He's probably just waiting for someone, but I feel afraid all the same. And I hate myself for it.

I wonder if maybe I have always felt that way. Maybe I have always been a little afraid of black men even if those feelings are unfounded. It's like I see Mr. Smith walking down the street and I'm afraid. But Mr. Smith has never committed any crimes. So why am I suddenly afraid? Why do I want to run up to anyone's house and yell, "Let me in! I'm in danger!"? And I catch myself thinking these things and I'm like, "Oh crap. I'm one of those people. I have these racist feelings, too." It's frustrating because I don't know how to get rid of these feelings. And then I think, thank God I am at least aware that I have these feelings. At least I know what I need to change. But as wrong as it is to feel that way, I don't know how to make myself stop feeling afraid. Talking about it is helpful, but if I talk, does that mean I won't be afraid anymore? I don't think so.

K–12 SCHOOLING

I feel like my schooling before college was, intellectually speaking, pretty uneventful. My schools were pretty typical white suburban schools. There were some minority students in my schools. I know there were some Jewish people in my community, but to be honest, everyone acted the same way and pretty much looked at the world in the same way. It just seemed that everyone's lifestyles and morals were the same.

I wouldn't say that my school was diverse. We did have some students who were not white, but they were few and far in between. Being in the AP track, I never saw them in my classes. I have a few memories of being in the hallways without a hall pass and not being stopped, but then seeing a black kid get stopped by the same hall monitor that just said hi to me when I passed. If you were a person of color in my school, you would get stopped and challenged on everything. I would walk out of the building because it was a nice day and I wanted to go home and no one would stop me. But a black kid who had a bloody nose would be stopped on his way to the bathroom. A white kid who dressed the same as a black kid, you know baggy pants and a too big sports jersey, was not treated the same way as a black person. So you can't say it has anything to do with dressing like a gangster. It definitely had to do with race and people's perception of it. If you were a person of color in my school, you stood out. You were an easy target and everything bad that happened was blamed on you first.

[Desiree said she was having a hard time thinking of what to talk about in regards to her schooling. I prompted her to talk about her curriculum by mentioning some of my experiences teaching high school English.]

The way I was taught for twelve years was the same—no diversity of thought. The teachers always had us look at situations in the same way. For example, I never was required to read anything that was written by anyone who wasn't white. We read Dickens, Chaucer, Milton, Fitzgerald and Salinger. I read Toni Morrison's book *Cry of the Beloved* on my own. We read a lot of poetry by the typical dead white men. I probably read Emily Dickenson, but I don't remember. It was like everything I was required to read was safe. I'm sure they were all things that were on the AP test. When I got to college and people started talking about the books they read in high school written by minorities, I felt like I was so illiterate.

There was an opportunity for me to read works from diverse authors. It was when I was in a World Literature class. But we just read Shakespeare's plays and some of the works of Dante. I always thought the world was a little bigger than England and Italy. But as far as world literature goes, that was as far as we traveled in a literary sense. I can tell you anything you want to know about the Elizabethan Era. Sadly, we read all of the tragedies except Othello. So what does that tell you about what they were and were not willing to expose us to?

History was traditional white history. Of course, I learned about slavery and how bad that was. But it was just more in passing. We never had any in depth discussions about why things were the way they were. I mean we had discussions about what was fair and what wasn't and about how to treat people. So you have the discussion, but you don't really have the discussion. Without a doubt we never talked about white privilege. I didn't even know what that was until I came to college.

Some of my friends said that they had classes that made them think about things in a different way, but I guess that I wasn't lucky enough to have the right teachers. We just learned about history as if there was one way to see things. And that one way had everything to do with passing the AP test. I didn't know any different until I came to college. I mean, of course, the Native Americans and African Americans would have a different version of history, but I never even thought about that possibility. When I think about it, it's kind of scary that I was taught one way to look at things and never even considered that there might be another way. But even if I did think about that, I'm not sure I would have said anything. I was the good little white girl in my K–12 schooling.

I graduated high school with a 4.0 grade point average. I was in all honors classes. I'll say it over and over again. I got a 4.0 because I did the work. I figured out what the teachers wanted from me and then gave them exactly that. I was a good student. I would never have been someone to make waves and challenge the way things were taught. I think most of my education was about having the right answer. You either had it or you didn't. To be honest, I would say that most of my teachers never promoted anything but the answers they had in their heads. It was more like every question I was ever asked in school already had an answer. And I was a perfectionist. If I didn't know what they were looking for, I didn't raise my hand. Don't get me wrong. I was social with my friends during lunch and outside of school. But once I was in a class, I became mute.

That makes me sad because I have been working in the schools for a while now and when I see students who never talk, I try to reach out to them. I think my teachers always had a tendency to reach out to the students who weren't doing well and spent all of their energy trying to motivate them. But for me, it was expected that because I was doing well on all of my assigned work, I was fine. No one, and I mean no one, in all of my schooling ever once asked me how I thought or felt about something we were learning.

I only have one memorable teacher. He was intimidating which is probably why I remember him. At any point he would just call on you and if you weren't paying attention he would embarrass you. And he would ask questions, and students would come up with sugary responses that weren't very deep, but they were trying to sound deep. They would basically just repeat something he said earlier in the class or the day before. And he would tell them they were brilliant. It was pretty disgusting.

COLLEGE CAMPUS LIFE

When I first came to the university, someone was making a film and approached me and asked me what I thought about diversity on the campus. I said, "I hear it's diverse, but I don't really see many people of color." I don't really see what the campus likes to pretend that it is. My classes have been diverse as far as gender goes, but they are mostly white. You know, you walk into class on the first day and notice that there are one or two students of color and the rest are white.

I don't really feel like I fit in with the typical university student. I don't like going to sporting events and I don't want to get drunk every weekend. I like to seek out experiences that are new. There is this one place called The Lion's Den that plays Latin music all night and people do Salsa dancing. But a lot of times when I go there, I feel like an outsider. I really want to hang with the Latino people who are there, but I think it's hard to approach them. People don't come up to you and include you like they do at other places. That's so hard for me to grasp. When I'm with my friends, I would want people to feel like they could come up to us because I think that's cool to be with lots of people who have different backgrounds. But I don't feel like the Latinos at that particular place are as welcoming.

Every month, I also go to the Soul Sessions they have on campus. There is a lot of hip hop music playing and everyone dances. I love watching the people there dance. And people read their poetry. I am totally jealous of the people who can go up to the microphone and read their poetry. The things that come out of the minorities' mouths are just amazing. It's like they understand things that everyone should understand. They feel things I have never felt in my life. And they are so positive and full of hope. It's one of the coolest things.

But when I'm there, I go every month, I feel like maybe I shouldn't be there. I see some of the same people every month. You think they would acknowledge me a little bit by now, but they don't. I say hi if I see them on campus, but for some reason, I don't feel comfortable approaching them at these events. I feel like it's out of my element to approach them there because I am the outsider.

Up until I started seeking experiences where I could be around a diverse group of people, I never thought about being an outsider. In one of my education classes, I read a piece by an African American man. He talked about walking into a store and having to think about being dressed to impress the people working at the store. If he wasn't dressed a certain way, he felt they would think he was a shoplifter. I remember thinking that that would never cross my mind. He wrote with a very angry tone in that piece. And I totally understand that. I feel a lot of anger when I read it too, but it's not the same.

I feel it is unfair and I get embarrassed about the way things are for black people when they are around white people. People who are not privileged need to figure out how to make it in a white society. White people never have to think about that. They just go about their business because the world is set up in a way that works for and advantages them. But that isn't true if you are not white. But it's not just black people who are looked at suspiciously by white people.

[*Desiree talked a lot about her feelings about the injustice that people of color experience on a regular basis. I asked her to talk about any firsthand experiences she may have had witnessing racial injustice.*]

Two summers ago I was in Los Angeles at Venice Beach and I bought some food. The guy totally shorted me by five dollars. I went back up to him and said, "Hey, I gave you a twenty and this is what you gave me back." I showed him that I still needed five dollars in change. He said, "Ok," and gave me the rest of my money. That was the end of it and I walked out. Two Latinas who walked out right after me said, "That would have never happened to us." I asked what they meant and they told me, "If we would have gone up to him, he would have said, 'Get out of here'. And we wouldn't have gotten our money back."

I said, "Wow. That's really weird. I never thought about that."

And they said, "Of course, you didn't." Then they walked away. That has stayed with me. It just never crossed my mind. I never even hesitated about going back to the man and getting my money back. It was no big deal. But not everyone can do that, I guess.

I had a TA from Africa for my very first education class. He would argue with us that there was nowhere on campus where he felt welcome. He said there was nothing that spoke to or welcomed people from different cultures and different ethnicities. He would tell us that it was all very white. He was honest and people did not like to hear that. They would say that there is a very German looking place at the Union where students of all colors meet. He would laugh and say, "Look at me. What is welcoming about a German restaurant for me?" And then he would ask us to look around the class. He would say, "You're all white. What does that say about education in the United States?" And people would take it personally and get really mad.

My classmates would accuse him of being racist. They would tell him that he was in the United States and he shouldn't expect to find anything ethnically African. I never spoke that semester. I was doing the classic Desiree thing. I knew what he was saying was right, but I didn't know the right way to talk to my peers about it. So, I didn't say anything.

The people in our cohort who are not white don't speak up much. I have asked them how they feel about these kinds of conversations. I'm not asking them to speak for their race. I want to know how they personally feel about what they are hearing. Early on in our education classes, they would say, "People see me as one way because of my race, but I am really just like them." But sometimes, it feels to me that they want to use the color of their skin when it works to their advantage. I feel like they identify with a lot of the experiences that the white people in our cohort have, but when they go into the schools or we talk about race, they try to make their problems and struggles about their race. And I want to say, "Well, which one is it? Do you identify with whites only when it works for you? Are you a person of color when things aren't going your way?"

It doesn't bother me, but there are times when I think it's not fair. I remember one of the students of color in the class crying because she said that people treated her differently when she was growing up because of the color of her skin. I do believe that she felt those things, but part of me wonders why those stories only come out when it is convenient or when they want something. It just feels like these two girls can change how they feel depending on the situation. When one of the girls with color has a break down, some people will comfort her, and other people will say under their breath—loud enough so people around them can hear—"Here we go again—time to feel sorry for her." It's hard to say anything because I don't want to draw everyone's attention to the rude comment that was said quietly.

I'm getting better at challenging people when they say insensitive things. But there are still times when, because I don't know what to say, I don't say anything. I was in the car with two guy friends and one of them was white and the other was Jewish. That's what they call him—his nickname is Jewish. He is totally cool with it. He doesn't practice his religion and he makes racial jokes about Jewish people. Everyone laughs including him.

Another one of their friends is part Mexican and they call him "Taco" and he laughs about it. One time I wasn't feeling very good, I may have had the flu. I felt really nauseous. One of the guys told me to "Just do what Taco does. Drink some hot sauce. It will make you throw up. That's what Mexicans do because they don't have insurance." It makes me really uncomfortable, but it's hard to interrupt that when they are just having fun and the person it is aimed at is playing along with it. I know it's not appropriate, but I understand the reference. It's just that if you say something you feel like you're being a killjoy, but if you don't you feel guilty.

TEACHER EDUCATION TRAINING

My student teaching experience has been somewhat frustrating. I chose to go to a major city to do it. The school was originally set up to have 40% African Americans, 40% whites and 10% other. That's pretty loaded—to put kids into three racial categories. It's pretty close to that. About 55% are black and 35% are white. Most of the teachers in the school are white.

I think there is an expectation that because we have a diverse school, the kids would all hang with each other. But it didn't work that way. The kids all hung around with kids of their own race. One time I saw two Mexican boys walking down the hall and one of them was calling the other a racial name. Both boys were laughing. I didn't know what to do. Do you challenge everything that comes out of their mouths? What do I say to the biracial African American/ Korean boy who calls himself Blackie Chan? Do I make him stop? Do I have a right to impose my perceptions about the N word when I hear African American boys call each other that? How does that work when you are a white woman?

I didn't get to the school until January, so the environment was pretty much already established. My cooperating teacher was an African American woman nearing her retirement. Her age might have had something to do with her attitude. It was like she gave up on a lot of her students. She just had them do worksheet after worksheet. I was bored. I can only imagine how bored the kids were.

I was the third student teacher the kids had that year and it was only January! There were definite discipline problems in the class. The kids were unruly. I just felt like I walked into a situation where there were a lot of unsaid things going on and they had been going on for a long time. I went on a field trip with them to the symphony. It was just down the street from the school so we walked there. Thirty kids. You'd think they would be able to walk in two straight lines. But they couldn't. The kids were running, chasing each other and pushing each other down. My cooperating teacher was in the front of the line and I was in the back. Despite what was going on behind her, she just kept walking. And I was like, "You've got to be kidding me!"

Then I looked across the street and I would see all the other kids from the other classes walking there. They weren't running or pushing. I just kept thinking how is this still possible in January? Why hasn't she stopped this behavior? Doesn't she care what the other teachers and kids think about her and her students? Why hasn't she taught them self-discipline?

[*I asked Desiree to talk more about her student teaching experience by trying to recall any situations where she was directly involved.*]

There was one African American girl in the class who was just blatantly disrespectful to me. I would ask her to put something away and she would say, "No." I would ask her to take a piece of paper out to work on a piece of writing and she would say, "No." She was not like that with my cooperating teacher. It was like she was trying to tear my head off from the first day I walked into the classroom. Eventually a meeting was set up with her parents. They called it an intervention. But I was not invited to it. I just wanted to be part of it, but when I asked, my cooperating teacher told me it was only for the principal, the parents and her. So, I felt like I never really connected with my cooperating teacher. It was like she never saw me as a colleague.

Mr. Jones, an African American teacher, was more open with me. I learned a lot from him. He was very honest with me about my perceived presence in the classroom. He said, "You're going to walk into a classroom—white female teacher. Good luck. Kids will say things about you. Parents will say things about you. I've had parents say to me, I'm so glad that you're black. My kid doesn't respond to a white teacher."

He was right. One day a little African American girl's grandmother was at school helping out. This was not the same girl I was having problems with. When she introduced me to her grandmother she said, "This is Miss Desiree. She doesn't like black kids." I was floored and angry. I had never done anything to her to make her feel like that, but here she was pulling the race card. I said, "Becky, that's not true. Why do you think that?"

In front of her grandmother, she said, "You say things like—all you black kids, you need to pay attention. She never says it to the white kids." That was an absolute lie. I never said anything like that. I was devastated. Afterward, I talked to Mr. Jones about it. He kind of smiled as if to say, "I told you so." He told me I have to be maybe more conscious about what I am saying and doing and what I'm not saying and not doing than the African American teachers. He told me that I always have to be thinking about who is listening to what I am saying and how might they be hearing it.

And I started thinking more about that. I mentioned earlier that I had had an awareness about the hidden fear I have toward the black men in my neighborhood. Was that coming through in my day to day interactions with my students? But I don't look at my students that way. I don't look at my students—like my little black boy is my black student. I think it's so cool that they are all so different. I'll meet the parents and when I do, there's no problem. The dads don't frighten me. Maybe part of that is that they are coming to my school, to my comfort zone. I don't know.

But if I saw those same parents walking down the street when I was leaving the school, I think I might unconsciously be afraid that they might pull me away or something like that. And I am really, really ashamed when these feeling creep up. I feel like such a fraud. I mean here I am volunteering to work in an inner city school because I want to help disadvantaged kids, and I am just as bad as the bigot in the suburbs. I think I never wanted to admit that, but if I'm going to be honest, that is who I am.

[*Desiree became silent and had shared feelings of disappointment in herself. Yet, I knew from our conversations that she was committed to her self-growth and was intent on developing a socially just practice. I asked her to talk about her commitment to social justice.*]

Maybe that is why I feel such a pull to develop socially just teaching practices. I think I'm a pretty introspective person, and I am just realizing some of these things about myself now. I'd like kids to be able to work through these things at a much younger age than I am. For me social justice education is about becoming aware of yourself and others. I think it's about really digging down into who you are—your identity. After you do that, you learn the perspective of others. We are always learning about the perspective of others. But we don't spend much time thinking about our own way of understanding the world. It's like people assume that we have all thought about our own thinking. Look at me. I'm twenty-two and I am just doing that now.

We talk a lot about social justice, but when it comes down to it, it is really about how we treat others. It's nothing magical. We need to think about how we understand them, how we handle situations, rethinking why things are the way they are. Those things influence how we react and what we do. I think teachers have to be listening to what their kids are saying because that gives insights into what they are thinking. Teachers shouldn't tell their kids what to think, but we have to get them thinking about different things. It's really about showing them different perspectives. I don't think you can possibly ensure that kids will leave your room thinking about equity and justice. But teachers have to bring up these things within the curriculum and create environments where it is ok to talk about these things.

I think as students of teacher education we have to be taught how to do this. To be honest, most of us have gone into education because we've wanted to be a teacher since we were kids. I've wanted to be a teacher since I was five or six. I used to play school all of the time. We go into our first education classes excited about learning how to teach and instead we get bogged down with all of this stuff about race and class. It was over my head. And then you think—oh yeah. That's why I'm in education. But no one wants to admit that they've never thought about these things before. It's just assumed that we have and that we are going into education to promote equity and justice. It's not like we don't want to do that. We just never thought that deeply about it before coming into the program.

Something happened in my first semester education class. The teacher was amazing. He completely altered my thinking on education. And yet, everyone chose to argue with him. He was just in our face with a different perspective and for some people that was too much. So maybe his approach was too aggressive. But we need that. People really don't want to rethink who they are. It's really tough to do. It's much easier to talk idealistically and to read assignments for class. But it needs to start with understanding your own perspectives in order to begin to see value in other perspectives.

Even more than this though, the school of education itself needs to become more diverse. I mean I am going to feel more comfortable talking about these issues with people who are more like me. But that can only go so far. Where does it get you when everyone agrees with everything you say? You have the opportunity to gain a lot more if you get people in the room who are different. It's not that we're all not different, but we all come from a similar perspective. But you need other perspectives to have a meaningful conversation.

The trick is how you choose people to go into the program. I'm sure the people who admit us have the hope that those who they pick want to come and talk about social justice. But a lot of people aren't thinking about these things before they get into the program. They're just not. They don't even realize that they are going to deal with it. I know it's tough though. You can't control who applies to the program. So what do you do? Go out and recruit minorities? That doesn't make sense either. It has to start in elementary education.

6 Emma

I was raised in a large city in the Midwest. Actually, I lived in the same city that the university is in. The community that I live in is very liberal in its thinking and behaviors. The people accept differences, so I don't recall any community tension at all. People just kind of did their own thing and minded their own business. My neighborhood has changed somewhat from when I was a child. I grew up on Lake Comet. The houses used to be affordable for the average middle-class family. But now, the home values have skyrocketed in value, and it is virtually impossible to buy a house there unless you are well-off. The houses aren't even that big, but it has become a very desirable place to live. The new families moving into the area, I guess, are richer than the families who originally bought the houses.

There is no way my family would be able to buy a house there today. My father is a vice principal at a school in a suburb about twenty-five minutes away from the city. And my mother is working with ESL students as a teacher's aide making about $8.00 an hour even though she has a Master's Degree. My mom stayed home with us when we were little. I don't know exactly how much money she inherited when her father died, but I know he owned a very successful furniture factory. That inheritance, I think, helped them pay the bills.

The neighborhood I grew up in is known for being extremely liberal. The schools that I went to were economically and racially diverse. But my neighborhood, including the few blocks surrounding my house, was all white. Rather *almost* completely white. The kids who weren't white often had to walk through our neighborhood to get to their part of town, so it wasn't like we never saw people of color.

I'd like to say that my family was active in giving to the community but we really weren't. Every once in a while we would do some volunteer work, but nothing substantial. I never knew how much money we had, but I did know that we weren't lacking for anything. I played on travel sports teams and I know that you couldn't do that if you were poor.

My dad had a rule that we couldn't do anything that he didn't want to watch. So, my sister and I were not allowed to take dance lessons or do gymnastics. I played basketball, soccer and softball. It takes a lot of money to play club sports. And your parents have to be able to drive you all around town in the middle of the day and on weekends. Because of the economic division in our community, the club teams were made up almost exclusively of white people. My basketball team had only two African American girls. The rest were white. Soccer and softball? All white.

It was odd traveling to the suburbs for competitions. We would hear parents tell their kids to be sure to walk with a friend because the kids from the city were tough. When they came to our city to play, they held their things close to their bodies. It was like they were afraid we were going to jump them or attack them or something. I had some friends who lived in a nearby suburb and they told me that when they came to the city to play our team, they would always lock their doors. After the game, they would grab a bite to eat on the way home after they left the city. It was like we were stigmatized as being aggressive and dangerous city kids.

As kids, our social groups were mostly formed by our interests. It's not like it was forbidden to mix races. But it was rare that kids from different races would really mix. Your interests and hobbies are just different and that, no doubt, has to do with how much money your family had. I was really into soccer, and I was friends with people who shared that passion. I mean we went to practices every night and spent the weekends traveling to and playing our games. So that makes sense, but we were all white. So it wasn't like we didn't want to be friends with people outside of our race; it was just we didn't have time to.

[*Emma was talking about the reasons why she did not have many experiences with people who had different experiences than she had. I asked her to try to think about any direct experiences she may have had with people who were socio-culturally different than herself.*]

I remember being in first grade and being invited to go to a boy's house to sleep. I didn't really want to go, but my mom made me. He was a Mexican boy who had two mothers. But that wasn't why I didn't want to go. I was more of a homebody and was afraid I would miss my mom. But she told me, "You have to go this once. You were invited. Just once you have to go and see what it's like. If you don't like it, that's ok. Just be polite and next time we'll just say you have plans." I thought it was weird. They had rice and sausage for breakfast. I tried it, but I was raised as a vegetarian, so I was completely grossed out.

I don't know if there is any relation to that experience and my parents' decision to take us to Mexico, but shortly after my sleepover we took our first of many trips there. My parents are both fluent in Spanish and wanted my sister and me to be also. They had an educational expense account—that's what they called it—that they would use for extensive travels. I know they took money out of my education fund to pay for some of our trips. We drove all over the United States when I was growing up. We went canoeing, camping, and we roughed it in the wild out West. My parents also sent my sister and me to camps every summer, so we got to see a lot of the United States.

When we went to Mexico, we didn't stay at resorts. We would fly to Mexico City and take a second-class bus and stay at the hotels that the locals stay at. That was their way for us to get to know the real Mexican culture. My parents thought that if we stayed at the resorts we would grow up thinking that the world was just like America. I'm really thankful that they did that. I totally value other cultures now and want to travel and learn as much as I can about people who are different from me.

But my sister isn't like that. I love pushing the boundaries and traveling to countries where I don't speak the language. I like trying to get by and figuring things out. My sister thinks I'm crazy for that. She likes to travel through Mexico because we've been there and we all speak Spanish. She's afraid to travel to some place that she's never been because she fears that she might say or do something disrespectful. Me? I have no problem finding a local and saying, "Hey, I don't understand. Can you help me?" I know that natives know more about their culture than I do. If I make a faux pas, I'll say, "I'm sorry," and move on. Those things happen, but you shouldn't let that stop you from experiencing different cultures.

K–12 SCHOOLING

I would have to say that my schooling experience is completely different from most of the people I am friends with today. The biggest difference between where I grew up and where other people grew up is that my schooling emphasized the backgrounds of different cultures and how important that was. I was brought up with the perception that you should care about what other people have been through and what they think about and how they perceive you.

I remember when I was in fourth grade asking my mom if white people had ever done anything important. My school curriculum was heavily focused on how white people had been terrible to the Native Americans and how their culture had been destroyed by whites. We learned a lot about African American history and women's history. I guess our curriculum emphasized non-whites to compensate for, I guess, not having done so in the past. I mean when I glance through textbooks now, I do see a white version of history. So I guess it was good to do that.

But I remember feeling like being white was kind of shameful. It was like, "Look what our culture has done to people. We've ruined the Native Americans. We ruined African Americans. We've ruined Latino Americans." I felt like my experiences were about learning other cultures, which is good. But it was also partly about, "Well, look what you've done. You've been in power and you really messed up everyone's lives." I have to admit, though, when I got to college, I was clueless about the traditional history curriculum.

But I would say that my K–12 teachers were dedicated to socially just causes in education. And I think I am too. I think part of the reason my education was the way it was is because I live in the city that the university is in and so many of the teachers had been trained there. So I would say that the socially just thoughts and values of the School of Education infiltrated within the public K–12 schools that surround it. I guess I could say that I'm a product of what the university stands for.

So, I think it's good to learn about many different cultures. And that's what we did in our curriculum. But something that I think was bad was that we didn't really celebrate cultures. Oh, sure we had a medieval festival when we were learning about that in history. But as far as a celebration goes, we were not allowed to celebrate anything. No Santa. No Halloween. No Valentine's Day. No Hanukah. No St. Patrick's Day.

I think it gets too sensitive. Everyone is afraid they are going to offend someone else. And when it gets like that, it's like we are pretending that people do not have their own customs. I think that public schooling has moved away from celebrating individual's identities to pretending like we don't have cultural customs. It's like the whole color blind thing. You know. If I pretend I don't see that someone's color is different from mine, then it won't be. If I pretend no one has any differences in their cultural traditions, then they won't have any.

And they wonder why people of different races don't mix. It's like they are forcing us to deny our differences even though we all know there are some. I say celebrate *everyone's* diversity instead of *no one's*. I just get really defensive when I feel like, in the name of social justice, I'm being asked to get rid of my identity so that I can blend in with everyone around me. I think—I can't help what I was born with. Why can't we celebrate everyone's uniqueness?

[*Emma was talking a lot of the ideologies of difference in her education. I asked her to share some of the specific ways students interacted with one another and the ways the performance of difference were witnessed.*]

Even though the curriculum represented diverse perspectives, there were still the same old stereotypes among the students. At school there was a very distinct economic status. I'm sorry to say that it was defined mostly by race—whether it was true of not. Most of the white kids were middle class, and most of the black kids were not. So there was some definite tension there.

My high school also had a tracking system. I was in the Honors Program, so I had most of my classes with white students. I'm not saying that non-whites couldn't be in those classes, but for the most part, they weren't. I was smart and I was expected to be the good white student. I was expected to be high achieving and to not act out in class. I really worked to maintain that, too. I was the one who always followed directions and turned everything in on time and was nice to everyone. I never spoke unless I raised my hand, and I never raised my hand unless I thought I had the right answer.

But then I would go home and just be so exhausted. I would just scream at my parents or my sister for the littlest things. I couldn't be that nice to everyone all of the time. But at school, I worked very hard to be the person they expected me to be. I don't know if my desire to be perfect at school was self-imposed or if it was a result of the expectations on me.

There were some non-whites that were in the Honors Program. But they were constantly harassed by their peers because they were told they were acting white if they were performing well academically or if they were following the rules. And the white kids who were not performing well were called "black" or "whigger" by their peers. The tension was only among same colored peers though.

I felt a little picked on because I was the smart, white girl. I remember standing in the lunch line in the cafeteria, and a group of students just came up and cut in front of me. They were African American students and one of them said, "Oh, we can budge her. She won't do anything about it. She's white." They were right. I didn't do anything. I think there was a lot of that behavior going on toward a lot of the white kids.

I had one seriously disturbing situation with a black girl. Out of nowhere one day, I got called to the counselor's office. This African American girl told her counselor that I wouldn't hang out with her because she was black. I was like, "What?! I have no idea what you are talking about." The assumption was that if I didn't want to be friends with her, there couldn't be any other reason for it besides the color of her skin. I was called a racist. This happened every week for a couple of months.

Every time I was in the counselor's office, I tried to explain that it had nothing to do with race. It was about not having any classes with her. No common interests with her. I hung out with my soccer friends and she didn't play soccer. But I couldn't get through to her. She would cry and scream and then the counselor would say the meeting was no longer productive and he would send me back to class. I will admit that like after the third time, I became defensive and put up walls and stopped listening to her.

So, when it came time to schedule our classes for the following year, the counselor suggested that I sign up for a class called Multicultural Perspectives or something like that. I resented the implication that I was a racist, but being the good girl, I signed up for it.

The class was taught by a woman and the focus of the class was basically racism and how it affects all different things. I don't think she had a syllabus for the class. It was like she would see something in the paper that caught her attention and we'd talk about it or write about it. Like one time we read a one-page article about the high suicide rate of Native Americans. We would talk about why that was happening and what we thought about it. The class was pretty interesting.

I remember reading this article about whiteness and feeling frustrated. I was like, "This sucks." I sometimes still have that reaction when I read about whiteness. I feel like things aren't presented in the right way. Who knows. Maybe the goal is to get people to have a reaction. I just feel like they dump all this information on you about how bad the white race is. But it's just depressing if they don't go any further. I mean I get it, but I need to know something I can do to change it or it is just depressing.

I will say that one of the good things about the class was that it was racially diverse. We had Native Americans, African Americans, Asian students, Latino students. There were only a few white students in the class. So I felt like I couldn't wallow in guilt or pity because I was constantly hearing the perspectives of my classmates to bring me out of it. I felt like hearing their perspectives gave me some hope.

COLLEGE CAMPUS LIFE

Coming to college was actually a bit of a shock for me. I met my first Republicans there. Honest to God, I'd never met one before. In my family, in my social circles, in my schooling, I was just taught that there was a certain way to think and be. So I came to college and all of my friends were suddenly from small towns with much more conservative viewpoints than my own. It was a real adjustment for me. So many times I had to bite my tongue or I would get into a fight with my friends.

I went out with a guy I thought was pretty cool. Somehow the conversation got to abortion one night. I said it was a woman's choice and he said I was going to go to hell. There was just no way getting around the whole God thing. I stopped talking and he told me I was acting like a faggot. I couldn't believe it! I had lived my life in a city with a very high gay and lesbian population, and I completely respect that lifestyle. But I told him he was being totally disrespectful. You know, he was actually a friend of mine and I learned that you have to put aside your views a little bit to be around someone like that. I can't stop him every time he says something like that.

It's not quite the same when you're talking about race. People don't really say the N word anymore. But, whenever some of my friends see a black guy on campus they will say, "Oh, he must play football" or "he's here to fill the quota." I hear the athlete thing a lot. People assume that if they see an African American guy on campus that the only reason he goes to the university is because he is an athlete. When I hear people say that, I think, "Yeah, well, I'm here on an athletic scholarship, too." I would have gotten in anyway, but my soccer skills assured my acceptance.

There is kind of an attitude among many of the white, conservative students. It's like if you don't agree with them, you need to just be quiet. No one ever says that, but I feel like it is there. If you do try to disagree with something someone says, you are silenced. People will look at you funny or change the subject. So, I would say that in my circle of friends, there is an accepted way of seeing the world. It's like they will be my friends as long as I keep my political views to myself.

So, coming to college has really opened my eyes a little bit. I came from a place that accepted diversity. When I came here it was like, "Wow. There really are people who aren't open to differences and don't believe in what I believe in." I also didn't hear a racial joke until I came to college. I didn't even know they existed. So I guess I was kind of sheltered growing up. I didn't realize that this stuff was still going on. I learned about blatant prejudice in elementary and high school, but I didn't think so much of it was still alive. I had no idea there were still people who thought like that and talked like that. My mom has told me that living a sheltered life might not have been all good because I was not prepared to understand what a lot of people hear and deal with on a daily basis.

[Emma had shared a great deal about her direct experiences with her peer group. I asked her to talk more about the racial divide on campus.]

People are also pretty racially divided on campus. The Union does have live music and dancing, so I would say that is the one place where there is a racial mix of people socializing. But I believe it is mostly white people. People still tend to stay in their racial comfort zones even if they are all in the same place.

The bars, for example, are pretty homogenous. The white students go to most of the bars on campus. There are very specific locations you would go to if you wanted a diverse crowd. Most of the non-whites go to the bars off campus. They are located further in the city and farther from campus. I actually go to them sometimes. There is one particular bar where a lot of Latinos go. I like to go there to practice my Spanish and just get away from the same people. I love the Latino culture.

Actually, I like learning about any culture that is different from mine. I worked at the Treehouse. It's a place where minority students can go to get tutoring. I'm pretty sure that white students are not allowed to go there. They have to use other resources on campus. The tutors are definitely racially mixed which seems odd—letting white people work there. I mean there is obviously a reason that it is only for minority students, but it seems like kind of a weird message having white people tutor.

I like working there because I love having the experience of being exposed to students who I might not normally see in my classes. I love the chance to meet people who aren't like me. Once you get into your major, you're kind of stuck with the same people in all of your classes. At the Treehouse, I get to meet people who are younger than me, have different majors and just different life experiences.

I meet with a Korean woman once a week. We are conversational partners. She's trying to learn English, so we just talk about everyday things. She practices her English and I get to learn some Korean. So, I'm really enjoying that. But you have to seek these kinds of experiences out. If you don't, you could leave this university without really ever having to dialogue or share the same space with someone who is radically different from yourself. That would be a real shame.

TEACHER EDUCATION TRAINING

I can't believe I got a job even before I'm done student teaching! I will be working in Mexico next year. I interviewed for jobs in El Salvador, Colombia, Ecuador, Puerto Rico, Nicaragua, Venezuela and Mexico. It came down to that I wanted to go to a Spanish speaking country because I would like to come back totally fluent and get a bilingual certification. Seventy-five percent of the staff is native Mexican, so it should be a great opportunity for me to learn more about the Mexican culture.

It is a private school for the children of wealthy Mexicans. Apparently it is one of the top schools in the country. There are some Americans, Canadians, and Asians whose children will be going to the school as well. I will be teaching language arts. The students are not meeting grade-level standards, and my job is to get them there. The standards are based on the standards in the United States, not Mexico.

I'm actually pretty excited about this. Before I started in my education program, I lived in Santiago, Chile for six months. I took classes there. Everything was in Spanish because the people do not speak English. I had to negotiate everything for myself from my housing to getting my credits transferred to the university here. I was definitely an outsider and had to find my way around.

Anyway, teaching in Mexico will be an interesting experience for many reasons. There is some racial tension in the area. Mexico is a lot like the United States in the sense that the lighter skinned people are more privileged than the darker skinned Mexicans. I had a great experience when I was student teaching to model one way to handle tension when it arises.

[*Emma and I talked briefly about her student teaching placement. She mentioned that she had a great role model in her cooperating teacher. I asked her to talk more about that.*]

I was in a sixth grade class in a school in the East part of town. I would say it was about 50% white and 50% non-white. Two African American girls were fighting and one said to the other one, "You should just go back to Africa." I heard they were comparing skin tones to see who was blacker. Being blacker was a bad thing to them. My cooperating teacher heard the whole thing and called the girls aside.

He told them, "Stop that right now! Ok, now I'm going to give you a history lesson. Do you know who started saying things like that? Do you know who first said that black skin was ugly?" He took it back to slavery and explained to the girls that it was the slave owners and masters who said that to make the slaves feel inferior. He made the girls understand that repeating the things that the slave owners had said was something they didn't want to be a part of.

By the time he was finished with them, the girls were saying, "Okay. I get it. I guess I probably shouldn't do that anymore." It was really good for me to see a white teacher have the guts to step into that. I think a lot of times white teachers do not know how to respond when African American kids make racially insensitive comments to one another. I've also witnessed a racial incident that was not as easily handled.

In the same class, we have an African American girl who has real issues with a sub whenever she comes to fill in for my cooperating teacher. Every time the sub is there, the girl says, "She is being a racist toward me." The first time she said it, I was horrified. I pulled her aside and asked, "What happened? What did she say or do?" She didn't give me any specifics. She just said, "She's picking on me."

I said, "Well, if that's how you really feel, maybe you should talk to her about it. Would you like me to come with you?" I was trying to help her out, but she just kept saying the same vague thing over and over again. I started paying more attention to the sub that day, but I couldn't see anything.

When my cooperating teacher came back, he had a talk with her. He said, "Listen. This is a really serious accusation. We are taking it very seriously, so don't say it if you don't mean it. If you really think that's what's going on, then we're going to step right behind you and make sure this is resolved. If you are saying it because you don't want to do the work she gives you, then don't call her a racist." And then that was the end of it.

But it is sticky, because you want to support the student, but if she can't substantiate her claim, then what can you do? You don't want to accuse someone of being a racist if they haven't done anything wrong. You don't want to give her the opportunity to accuse someone of being a racist every time they ask her to do something. But you also want her to know it is safe to call out racist behavior.

When I first came to the class she didn't like me either. I quickly made it a personal project of mine to get her to like me. She's a great kid, but she just doesn't like to do anything you tell her to do. She tests people. For example, one time I told her to sit down, and she said, "I'm not sitting down just because you tell me to." So you have to find ways to ask her so that she wants to do it. If you tell her what to do, things can escalate in front of the whole class and then her walls quickly go up. She just feels like that whenever you tell her what to do you are picking on her. You could say the same thing to everyone in the class, but she is the only one who will hear it like that.

So this is where educating for social justice comes in. To me, educating in a socially just way means you have to treat all children fairly. It may not be equal, but it has to be fair. You have to give each child what they need and not everyone needs the same thing at the same time. This girl maybe needed to be spoken to in a different way. For some reason she resisted being told what to do, so maybe she needed to be handled more gently.

I also think it means making all kids feel valued. Their cultures should be accepted and respected. You do this by making things relevant and interesting and by bringing their home cultures into the school culture. You get kids talking about racial issues, and economic issues—those kinds of things. You get them to do more reflecting on experiences in their own lives.

[*Emma had some definite ideas about how to incorporate socially just practices in her classroom. I asked her to talk about the influence that the Teacher Education Program may have had on her developing pedagogy.*]

I think the school of education really prepared me to teach this way. I mean the ideas were always in the right place. We were exposed to readings to let us know what's out there and how we could develop our practice in ways that were socially just. I didn't always agree with the way the ideas were presented to us though.

The first class we take in the School of Ed is an Intro to Education class. It's really like an introduction to Multicultural Education. Our discussions centered on what our education was like. For me Multicultural Education was nothing new. But a lot of my classmates talked about how they were never exposed to viewpoints other than the traditional ones.

We spent a lot of time reading about white privilege. I think this was good. But I also think everyone was very uncomfortable. It's difficult to talk about white privilege when the majority of the people in the class are white. Most people had the same perspective. You know small town, middle class, white. But we also had two or three students who were not white, and I think everyone was on their tiptoes not wanting to say anything offensive even though some of the things in their backgrounds are not that positive toward non-whites.

The people in the class turned to the minority students as if to say, "Oh here. A representative from the other side. What can you tell us? Speak on behalf of your race." They would talk, but they said many times that they did not want to be responsible for sharing the opinion of millions of people.

And then it got to be a competition about who was the most commit-ted to social justice. It was like if you stated an opinion that wasn't what they believed, you were attacked. No one said, "It's okay that you believe differently. We're just getting opinions out here. We're going to talk about it. You may change your mind." It was more like, "You're wrong. You're a horrible person. You come from somewhere that's horrible and everything you stand for is horrible." The conversations usually ended up with some-one crying

I don't think that's the way you win someone over. You can't attack things like family values or community ideals–things that are central to who people are—and expect them to just give up those things so easily. You can't just come out of the box saying all white people are terrible. All white people don't care about black people. All white people are racists. All white people don't think about other races. Put it out there. Show the evidence—really discuss it. Ask for opinions. Then ask for counter opinions. But don't try to make people feel bad about where they come from. And don't just tell them what to think. Show them a better, bigger way to think.

It's like with white privilege. I still have issues with the guilt associated with it. At times, I want to say, "Yeah, I know it is all out there. But does that really shape every aspect of everything that happens in the world?" I guess maybe it does, but it would be nice to get a reprieve from it once in a while and think we can all get along and be happy. What we need to do with teachers is to make them believe in social justice instead of doing something out of guilt. There's just no hope when you come from guilt. It's like where do I go from here? It's like, yes, I know I'm privileged, but unless I'm given the tools and strategies, the practical things that I can use to make the situation better, I tend to put my fingers in my ears and say, "I can't take it anymore! It's just too upsetting! Enough! I can't have this same discussion again." I want to know how I can fix it in the school I am working in right now.

The approach of "This is who you need to be" doesn't work if no one ever asks me who I am first. There were times in my education classes that I felt like I was being grouped with every white person in my class. I had one instructor who made comments like, "I'm assuming none of you have ever been in a situation where you were the minority. I'm assuming you've never had any black friends. I'm assuming anything I want about you." He made a lot of assumptions about me and he didn't even know me.

I think it would be good if attempts were made for our professors to get to know us as individuals. And I think we should be given the opportunities to know our classmates as individuals. We should be asked to write more about our experiences and our reflections about those experiences. We should reflect on what we read. And we should share those with everyone in the class. Not just the instructor, but everyone. Typically, it was like "Here's the assignment. No one is ever going to read it except me. So make sure you say exactly what you think I want to hear."

And that's what a lot of people do. A lot of people faked their reflections to make themselves look socially conscious, and then would rip on the School of Education as if they didn't believe anything they wrote. What good is that? What has been learned except how to play the game?

I would have liked to write more about my own life experiences and I would have liked to have heard from my classmates. I think that is a really crucial part of learning to teach for social justice. Without doing reflection about your own life, what's the point about learning about other cultures? If you don't think about where you are initially coming from, how do you know how to move forward?

7 Alex

I grew up in a mid-sized city in a Midwestern state. The city was pretty much white people and then a solid amount of Hmongs. We always thought it was about one-third Hmong and two-thirds white. But I think it is actually maybe one-fifth, at most, Hmong. We just always thought there were so many Hmongs. I think my city had the most Hmongs per capita in the United States. So we always joked that our city was the designated city that all of the Hmongs had to immigrate to.

People referred to the area where they lived as the Hmong ghetto. It's not like it really was a ghetto or anything. But it was really run down, probably the worst housing in town you could say. They were very poor. I didn't know one Hmong person who wasn't poor.

I knew a guy who lived in the Hmong apartments. The three buildings were right on top of each other. The apartment complex was right next to a cheese factory and then there were train tracks leading into the woods where the Hmong village was. It was literally a Hmong village. There were tons of huts and chickens running around. And when we walked past it to get to a bridge we used to jump off of to go swimming, we would tell each other, "Oh, you don't want to go down there."

[Alex stopped his story there. He continued when prompted to talk about why people were afraid to go near the Hmong village.]

I got to know this guy Khong really well when we were in middle school. One day he asked me to be in his gang. I said, "No, no, Khong. That's not cool." I was afraid of the initiation. They would beat the crap out of you with bats and things. I think the gang's name was MOB. But there was another gang. I forget their name, but there were a couple of serious gangs. I don't know what kind of violence they did. I mean you'd see the spray painted buildings and you kind of knew they were there and that they were bad, and they were dangerous. And then when I was in high school, the city did something and then gangs weren't as prevalent. I don't know what they did, but things changed. The gangs that I'm talking about were all Hmong. There weren't any other gangs in the city.

I guess people were afraid of the Hmongs because they were so different and real mysterious in a way. There were a lot of people in my city who didn't like that they tried to keep their culture and traditions. Eating dog was always such a huge joke to everyone in town. If you wanted to rip on a Hmong, you would just say, "Go eat a dog." People would yell that all the time to Hmongs at school and passing by in the street. There was a lot of crap talked about the Hmong people. People would just come right out and call them "gook" or something. And the Hmongs always just ignored it. I guess people just didn't like that the Hmong people were not assimilating into the city. The Hmongs weren't ready to learn a new way.

But the city tried to assimilate them. When I was in elementary school, there was a movement to integrate the schools. The schools were basically segregated because of the division in housing and boundary lines. So schools were either all Hmong or all white. The city council tried to change that by making a K–2 school and a 3–5 school. But that required bussing the kids to different parts of town. It didn't affect me because I went to a Catholic school, but it affected my school. All of a sudden, the parochial school enrollment skyrocketed. And people were furious. For whatever reason, people didn't like it. They said it was inconvenient to have their kids travel across town to go to school when there was a school just a few blocks from their homes. I don't' know if the argument was racially intended or not. But it went back to how it originally was. The bussing thing only lasted a year or two. I think both sides were happy about that.

People thought the Hmongs didn't like white people. There would be times when I would hear people say, "I tried going up to them and talking to them and they just shooed me away." That was true actually. The Hmong crowd just didn't want a lot to do with the white people. It was because they were holding strong to themselves and within their communities and they didn't want outsiders coming in. They just wanted to be in the city, close to the north woods and have a nice house and maybe get up the hill.

[*"Up the hill" was a term that had a definite meaning in Alex's town and he provides further explanation when asked. He had assumed that the phrase meant the same thing in all social circles, and was shocked at my confusion.*]

Living on top of the hill was the goal for the people in the city. On top of the hill was very white–probably all white. And they were very wealthy. The people that live there are nice, but there is a definite separation between racial backgrounds of the people who lived at the top of the hill and people who lived lower down the hill. And there is definitely a separation between where the rich and the poor lived. The more money you had, the higher up you lived. Several blocks away from the hill is where the Hmong village was. I lived at the bottom of the hill.

I always thought I was poor when I was growing up. I had a paper route and had to ride my bike up the hill everyday and deliver papers to these amazing houses. Don't get me wrong. I was super fortunate in the way I was raised. I had a nice house. But I remember hearing my parents talking in their bedrooms—our house was nice, but small, and you could hear everything—about how they couldn't pay their bills. We had an 89 Chevy that basically had the whole front half ripped off. I remember being so embarrassed when my dad would drop me off at middle school. I just remember getting out and walking as fast as I could so people didn't know I came out of that car. You just didn't want people to know that you were one of the non-wealthy ones. Someone growing up poor doesn't want to admit it. And they'll try to hide it with anything that they can, be it nice sneakers or clothes or anything. And I was the same, and I hated that feeling.

To put our financial position in perspective, I'll give you a specific example. I'm almost finished with college and this past Christmas I just got an iPod from my parents, and it's the cheapest kind you can get. It only holds a couple of hundred songs. But it is easily the most expensive gift I have ever gotten from my parents. And I know they were so excited to give it to me. And I was really grateful for it. I knew that they had to sacrifice getting something for the house or the car or getting each other a Christmas gift so that they cold give me the iPod. And that part sucks. So I think in a way I related to the Hmongs because they were poor, too. I wasn't as poor as them, but I didn't grow up with a lot of extras.

K–12 SCHOOLING

Going into eighth grade, I thought it was really cool to be dumb. You go through that stage—it's cool to be stupid. So I was really hitting that hard. I had just gotten contacts and was starting to get into the "in" crowd, and I was trying to be cool. But I had a teacher named Mrs. Morris who really pushed me with academics. She wasn't the type who said, "You need to do your homework." That wouldn't have worked. I probably would have said, "Screw you" or something. The first assignment we had that year was to write ten similes and metaphors. We had to go up in front of the class and read them. I thought mine were hilarious. I wrote things like, "My biceps are lethal weapons." Stuff like that. I went up and read mine thinking I was going to shock her, but she said she thought they were great.

Then it was like she started testing me. We had to write a research paper. I went up to her desk because I couldn't get started. She said, "Well, first you have to write a thesis statement." And I was like, "What the heck is that?" She was appalled that I didn't know what a thesis was by eighth grade. She said, "Okay. Well, you're going to have to work hard, but I'm going to teach you how to write."

So, during every study hall and a lot of lunches and recesses, I would go into her classroom and she would teach me about literacy. That might not make sense because what cool kid would meet with a teacher on his free time? I think I went because I thought she was cool. She let me be me and she let me joke around. I could sit in the back of the room and joke with my buddies and not pay attention. And she never stopped me. And when I did work, she let me write about things that I wanted to write about. She was really genuine. You knew she was serious if she said something. You just knew she cared and that she was authentic. When she told me that she thought I was a good writer, I believed her.

The night before a paper was due, I watched *Shawshank Redemption*. I thought it was the coolest movie ever. And I wrote a story about a jailbreak. It was almost exactly like the movie. She could have given it back to me and said, "You copied this." She had to know the movie. But she didn't. She said, "This is really good. Now you need to make it better." She could have reamed me out, but she saw that I was really excited about it and she focused on that. I don't remember her being like that with anyone else. But for some reason she took a liking to me.

I had multiple teachers who were just really good. I realize now that Mr. Zands, who was my high school math teacher, who hated my guts, was a good teacher. So many times he told me that he wanted to throw me out of the window because I was a goof off. But I still managed to learn a lot. I would go to him for extra help during my study hall, and he was cool and would work with me. This happened a lot to me. I was a real trouble maker. But I was still a good student and my teachers knew that and believed in me.

I will say that overall, my history classes sucked. I didn't know it at the time, but looking back, I would say they were definitely bad. We didn't learn much about Viet Nam. We felt gypped. We watched one movie. *The Killing Fields*. It was violent. It portrayed the US as invaders. But that was all we learned about. A whole era of history and one movie to sum it up. It was a missed opportunity. Because our high school had a large Hmong population, I think we could have had some really serious, meaningful conversations [about race relations during the Vietnam War]. But we didn't have any. And that is a real shame because there was some very real racial tension in our school.

The tension was unspoken. Very blanketed. There was never a discussion that I could remember. You know, no teacher ever said, "There are a lot of Hmong people in our community. And a lot of them are poor. A lot of them are not getting financial aid that was promised to them from the government. What do you think about that?" That could have been a really important conversation to have to get us thinking in a bigger way.

We were separate entities in our school. There would be some Hmong people that would talk to white people and some white people that would talk to Hmong people. But it was rare. You might have your token Hmong in your AP class or your token white in the remedial class, but that was basically it. Outside of school we just never saw each other.

There was one place where I was able to interact with Hmong students. In high school we had homeroom every day. I was kicked out of my first class and placed into the ESL room. The room was in this random corner in the back of the school. It was more of a makeshift room. It was me, a few other white students who had been kicked out of their homerooms, and then the rest of the students were ESL—mostly Hmong. Everyone was cool with each other in there. It was like you came to homeroom and it was your clan. The Hmong people, in general, were very, very shy and timid. They didn't talk much. Maybe it is a cultural thing.

But my white buddies and I—we were like, "Hey, let's do something. Let's hang." So that's when we started making our homeroom more fun. We had a great homeroom teacher who basically let us run the class. He wouldn't always show up, so I would take attendance and do whatever. So we watched movies, had rock-paper-scissor tournaments, and we had contests to see who could eat the most hot sauce and stuff. It was a great experience.

In our society, I see that—I think racism is a double-edged sword. I just think a lot of racial assumptions are made. I don't think we are going to get nearly as far as we could, or very far at all, if it's only one-sided. If only white people would stop having racial premonitions about others, we can only get so far. So if we can have opportunities like my homeroom, where people can really get to know each other, that is a really good start. Once you get to know people you realize that you're not so different. Sure, you're different, but when you can really talk to each other you start to think, "Yeah. We're different. So what's the big deal?"

[*Initially, Alex could not think of any ways that he had interacted with the Hmong population outside of the school setting. When I suggested he think about after school activities where different groups of people interacted, he was able to recall the following examples.*]

Outside of school, people played soccer with the Hmongs. They were really into that. And they were really good. Better than any of the white kids. Maybe that is why soccer was kind of the sport for non-whites at my school. I played football, basketball and baseball. There was maybe one Hmong that played basketball, but that was about it. Most Hmong people played soccer or wrestled. I met some Hmongs in the high school weight room when I would go lifting. But you just kind of surface talked. You didn't go out with them afterward. You might say hi to each other if you saw each other a lot there. But it never really went any further than that. But there were also a lot of Laotian kids that were in the weight room, too.

There is a fairly large Laotian population in my city as well which is odd because up until I came to high school, I thought they were all Hmong. I guess the Laotians and Hmong do not get along. One of my Laotian friends told me that it had something to do with them coming from border countries in Southeast Asia. So I guess there is a history there. But I don't know much about it. I just know at times it was awkward in the weight room when there were Hmongs and Laotians in there together.

I also interacted with some Hmongs at the YMCA when I was in high school. I always went there to play basketball. There weren't ever any Hmongs that played, but afterward, I would see them in the game room.

That was one place where they always could go to hang out. There is a Boys and Girls Club there and it is a place where Hmong and white kids go to hang out. So, I guess that's pretty cool. But I didn't go there after school when I was in elementary school. I didn't really talk to a Hmong person until I got to middle school. But I wasn't afraid to talk to them. I was the new kid from the Catholic school. I was an outsider just like them on that first day of sixth grade.

COLLEGE CAMPUS LIFE

I lived in one of the big dorms at the university, so there were approximately 2,000 people who lived there. It was one of the older and dirtier dorms, not to mention, the cheapest dorm on campus. It was one of the most diverse environments that I have ever lived in. One of my roommates was Egyptian and the other three were Caucasian. But I was exposed to more ethnicities than I had ever been before. That was cool. I got to know three or four African American girls on the floor. We became really close. I didn't notice any racial tension in the dorms. It might be completely different for someone who was a minority. I wouldn't know about that.

You commonly saw people of similar ethnicities and backgrounds sitting together in the cafeteria and hanging out. There was maybe some racial divide, but I would say in general it was not very strong. There certainly wasn't any visible tension. Everyone was pretty tight.

I would say that there is more of a class distinction on campus and in the dorms than a racial distinction. The rest of the dorms were nicer than ours. The people were dressed nicer. There was a lot more Greek activity in those dorms. And the people went to different bars than the people from my dorm. They were more high class. A lot of the people in the nicer dorms went to Eddie G's. It's the bar where all of the African American athletes go to. So in that sense, it is for more privileged people. We went to the bars with more townies. No dress codes—you can just be whoever you want.

I got to learn about different cultures, I think, because of the dorm I lived in. There was more diversity. My Egyptian buddy used to go to Ramadan meals and I would go with him. One of my friends is African American, so I would go to his house if he was having a party with his African American friends. It was me and a couple of white dudes with all African Americans. It was pretty cool.

I've also gotten into these hip hop sessions. I think it's just a cool form of expression. There are just way more minorities there than anywhere on campus. I've been going for a few years, so that has helped me meet more people of color. I just like hanging out with people who have had different experiences than me. But when they go to the microphone and speak their words, I feel their pain like I never have before. It's tough when you're not white.

I have gotten some flack for having African American friends. One time I was with an African American girl who was a friend of mine. We were going to a play for class. We were just walking down County Road and an African American dude, I think he might have been homeless, was riding his bike next to us and just taunting me the whole time. He was bitching out my friend for hanging with a white guy. It was just really awkward. I still wasn't comfortable with the whole race thing, so I didn't really know how to respond to him.

This other incident happened three weeks ago. I work at a parking garage and I work in this booth that goes up into this helix where the parking lot is. You're not supposed to walk down the helix; you're supposed to take the elevator because it's dangerous. So, I'm sitting in this booth and this African American dude comes walking down the helix. He's a young guy, about my age. As he walked by, I said, "Hey man, next time, can you take the stairs or the elevator? It's safer."

He just looked at me and was like, "What the–." I was like whatever. I really debated about saying anything to him at all in the first place because he was African American and I think a lot of white people that I know don't want to be judged as racist for saying something to an African American. So he passed me.

Then about five minutes later, he just walked into my booth. We have these packets of money that you take with you when you start working. They have about $150 in them. So he walks in and just reaches up on the counter and grabs one of the packets and walks out quickly.

As he was walking out, I was like, "Whoa. Dude. What are you doing?" I've never seen this guy in my life and I've worked there for over a year, so I know most of the people who work there. And he was like, "I'm working, man." And I said, "Where's your shirt?" We have to wear these yellow shirts and he didn't have one on. We argued for a little bit and I said, "What's your name?" He kept saying Jackson. I went over to the schedule and said, "There's no Jackson here, man. Where are you working? What location?" He wasn't answering my questions, so I'm like this guy is robbing me. He gave me no intention that he actually worked at the garage.

Finally he walked over to the schedule and pointed. "Right here, Walker. My last name's Walker." And he walked away. And I was like oh, crap. This does not look good. This looks really bad. So at the end of his shift, he came back down and I apologized more than I have ever apologized about anything in my life. I told him that I knew it looked like I was profiling, but I wasn't. It just didn't seem like he knew what he was supposed to do at work.

And he just said, "Whatever, dude. F—- you." And he just kept calling me a racist when I wasn't. And all the way out I kept yelling to him, "I'm sorry, I'm sorry." But he complained to my boss anyway, and I was going to be charged with racial profiling and all of this crap. He just would not let it go. I told my boss I felt terrible, but I wasn't profiling him. I ended up quitting over the whole thing.

It was just really weird and awkward. I felt bad for a little while, and then I realized that this changed my point of view on race. I didn't feel bad anymore because I realized that he was profiling me because I was white. I wasn't rude to him. But he thought that because I was white I was stereotyping him. Just because a person is white does not mean that they cannot be discriminated against. That's crap. It really changed my thinking about multiculturalism and the idea of embracing minorities.

I had thought about my whiteness before, but I hadn't experienced it in such a powerful way. Before this experience, my whiteness was a burden for others, but this time it was a burden for me. But I think it's a discredit to whites to assume that we do not have a culture. Multiculturalism should be about embracing all cultures. Not just anyone who isn't white because in a sense that is profiling as well.

I know someone else who was accused of profiling when he wasn't. He works at the Union, and there was an African American event that was shut down because of a lack of security. Normally, I'm like that is crap. That is racial profiling to shut an event down because there isn't enough security. It doesn't happen at events that whites throw. But a few weeks ago, there was a hip hop event with a DJ and it was sweet. So there were some teenagers there goofing around and throwing sugar packets and water bottles and just making a mess of the whole place. So my friend, who's white, is the building manager and went up to the kids and asked them to stop. He walked away and gave them a few minutes. As he walked away, they jacked him and they beat him up. Three or four dudes just kicked his ass pretty badly. And another guy came up to help my buddy, and they beat him up, too. Then the kids ran away.

There was an article about it and my friend was asked to describe what the kids looked like. He said, "Well, they're African American teenage males, and so—so tall and what not." There's been a sound board where you can voice your opinion about what happened. He told me that on one sound board there are like twenty claims that he was racially profiling the kids. He's gotten a lot of things sent to his personal email calling him a racist and that kids are just kids.

It's tough. He got his ass kicked. He's not going to like the people that did it regardless of their skin color. But it's like taboo to mention someone's race because if you do, people can use it however they want. It's just weird. He's being profiled because he mentioned a race. It's just frustrating when people who are trying to do things about all the crap that has been done to minorities are being called out as racists. Whatever bridges are being made are crumbling because of this. The effort to change cannot just come from the white people. If he would have said the kids were white, would he have been called out as a racist, too? I don't think so. What if it was an African American worker who got beat up? Would he have been able to say the kids were white without being accused of profiling? I'm pretty sure he would.

I mean, I get that there is a history there. But people use history to make their assumptions. It's too bad though, because you want to move on. I'm trying to be careful here because I don't want to sound like black people need to be the ones stepping forward. But there needs to be a unified leap. Obviously I speak so much of African Americans because these examples are specifically about them, but this applies to all races and ethnicities. It's just like, yes. I was born a Caucasian. I can't control that. But I can control what I do and that is what I am working on.

TEACHER EDUCATION TRAINING

There have been a lot of things that I have done along my route to becoming a teacher that helped me really understand people from backgrounds different than my own. I went and lived and worked in a homeless shelter in Boston for a week over spring break. I worked with immigrants on the border in Texas for three weeks. And I taught summer school in Englewood in Chicago for a summer. All of these opportunities were offered through the university, so I took advantage of them to help me become a better teacher.

My experience in Chicago was life altering. I taught seventh grade literacy in a summer school. My class was made up entirely of African Americans except for one Mexican boy. He spoke limited English and there was no support for him. The class met Monday through Friday from 8:30 until 12:30. They weren't supposed to get a break in that time period. In defense of my students, with that structure, they were not going to be angels. I started with twenty-two students, but two were kicked out, so I had twenty for the summer. Most of them were in summer school because they were suspended too many times throughout the year. They clearly had behavioral problems. They were seventh graders, but most of them were already sexually active. One of the girls was pregnant.

Most of them walked to school. They would meet at an agreed spot and then walk together in groups. Maybe it was a safety issue, but it wasn't a violent area during the day. You could look down the street and see people walking to the bus stop or what not. And this is a testament to those kids. They kept coming. I mean it was summer. There had to be other things to do. But each day they showed up. They were incredible people—extremely strong.

My students had very negative premonitions about me, where I came from and what my intentions were. At one point during the six weeks I was there, my students legitimately thought I was trying to fail them. It was very hard. Every day there were issues.

The first time I spoke in the class, I said, "Hey, my name is Mr. Johnson. I'm a white dude from a northern state." I was very forward. I was not going to put our racial differences under the blanket and act like it wasn't an issue. I don't know. Maybe that gave my students the right to be very forward with me.

The first week I was an anomaly. They were fairly okay because they were kind of in awe at having someone new in their class. I wouldn't doubt that I was the first white person they interacted with on a daily basis who wasn't a lawyer or a cop. The teacher I worked with was on the exterior a very large African American woman. She had a lot of African features, but she was actually bi-racial. She sat in the back of the room on her cell phone for four hours on the first day. So, I thought, Ok. I guess I am teaching the class this summer. Each day she would come in the room in the morning and say, "I want you to teach about this or that today." And that was the only direction I received.

The first day I had ten minutes to prepare a cause and effect lesson, so I quickly Googled the history of the Englewood neighborhood to find out something about their community. I found out that the neighborhood started out affluent and then the trains pulled out, and Sears pulled out, and the shopping mall went down, and it became poor. Then it became more violent. So my first question was why is Englewood so violent? I read to them that in one year 600 people were killed from the neighborhood. In one summer over 200 were shot. I was very conscious that I was talking about their neighborhood and that they would have some pride connected to it. So every time I read a fact, I told them I was reading it online.

So we analyzed why things were the way they were. So from day one that I was teaching, we talked about violence and poverty and the correlation. The next day we talked about education. There were no books in the classroom. No materials to use. And I had to fight to get a little green chalkboard wheeled in. The kids weren't stupid. They understand that the lack of resources showed a lack of respect for them as learners.

I was careful to tell them, "I don't know what it's like to live here. I have no idea what it means to grow up in Englewood. And I have no idea what it is like to go to this school." And I didn't. I may have taught there, but I lived downtown. I got to leave there everyday at 12:30. When they asked where I lived I told them. Most of the students had never been downtown. I'd tell them that I lived by Grant Park and they'd be like, "Huh?" They lived a very sheltered life. They hadn't been to the downtown of their own city. I guess they haven't had many chances to go there. They were only fourteen, maybe too young to go by themselves.

Within a few days they were calling me "cracker," "white boy" and "whitey." One girl refused to call me anything but "boy." "What do you want, boy? You're bothering me, boy." It was hard. It didn't really bother me. I mean I never felt down. I just felt annoyed that we couldn't get beyond that. I just got really sick of their blatant racism toward me.

One of the assignments I gave them was to research the biography of their favorite hip hop artist. I was teaching them to read for information, so I wanted to give them an assignment they might enjoy. I wanted to take them to the computer lab to do their research. I was told that we couldn't go. The administration was worried that my students would wreck the computers because of their past behaviors.

I went to the principal and told him, "I guarantee that if you let us go in there, nothing will happen." I think that made my kids start to respect me more. They worked on the computers and nothing was damaged. It was a great moment. But these kinds of days were few and far between.

My kids were nuts, absolutely nuts. If you can imagine a couple of tigers with some gazelles, and a couple of giraffes and then maybe a gorilla or two all trapped in a ten by ten cage. That would be my class. Just with their behavior alone, I was completely exhausted when I left at 12:30.

Every night I stayed up until about 1:00am preparing the lesson for the next day or grading papers. Every lesson I prepared I thought would be one that I would want one of my university supervisors to observe. I would think, "Today they're going to get it. This is the song I'm going to play, and they are going to love it. They're going to write and they're going to be pumped." And most days, they would take the lesson and throw it in my face. Sometimes literally. Other times just figuratively everything fell apart. We maybe got through a tenth of what I wanted to do each day.

Somewhere between the third and fourth week, I got totally burned out. I was really questioning if I could finish the program. I always had a lot of success in my practicum classrooms, and I worked really hard. But at this point I was working really hard to convince myself not to quit. So anyway, one night I said, "Screw it. I'm tired. We don't do anything in that class-room anyway. I'm going to play my guitar and go to bed."

So then the next day we didn't do squat. It was a circus as usual and I was like, "Whatever. Who cares?" But the thing is I felt really bad that afternoon. It was a wasted day. I mean my kids came to school that day. They picked up their friends and walked there, and I didn't bring it. The next day I came in and apologized. I told them, "What I did wasn't fair to you guys. You woke up at 8:00 to get here and I didn't come. That'll never happen again." It was about one of only a small handful of times that they were quiet.

I could tell from that point on that they knew I was there to help them. I don't want you to get the wrong idea. It wasn't like some made for televi-sion movie. Most of my days were still really challenging. But they knew that I was genuine because they saw me when I wasn't. And I was glad I didn't quit because I really did understand why so many people had quit on them before. It is really hard and draining. You wonder if you can actually be a teacher because you suck so bad. But when you get through to them and you see a level of excitement in them or you watch a light bulb turn on inside them, then it makes the bad times seem not as bad.

[*At this point Alex had talked uninterrupted for over a half an hour. He mentioned in our greeting as soon as I saw him that he had already been offered a teaching position. I asked him to talk about his teaching plans on the record and asked if he could connect his experience two summers ago with his future plans*]

I've already been hired by the New York City Public School System. I'd like to teach in Harlem. That is where I am going to apply. Once you get hired in the system, you have the choice to either be placed anywhere or interview at specific schools. In relation to my summer school experience over a year ago, I think I will be much more prepared. I didn't have as thick of skin as I have now. I forgot that those kids were just young minds. And so at times it just became too much for me. I took things too personally even though I thought I wasn't. After that summer I told myself, "You need to get stronger before you do that again." But I think I am totally stronger now.

I'm also a more confident teacher. I have a different agenda. I made the summer in Chicago about me. It was all about if I was reaching the kids. If I was experiencing success. Don't get me wrong. I was concerned about them, too. But I think a lot of my ego was attached to them being successful and them liking me. Those things are important still, but I am also concerned about their futures.

When I look at the specific school I would like to teach at and I see their test scores, I see that somewhere around 80% of the minorities are failing. That is just unacceptable. As teachers, we have to look at the community we are serving. We have to reach the kids in ways that are meaningful to them. I'm looking to teach in a poor community inhabited by mostly people of color. There is a high crime rate. I have to get them reading and writing and thinking about the things that are important to them in their worlds. I have to help them understand the whys of discrimination and poverty and how to break those cycles. We really have to have the conversations.

I think in Chicago, I directed those conversations. But since that experience I have learned to be more of a facilitator rather than a leader in class discussions. I understand that the kids I am going to teach are young minds. And that sometimes they will say things that might be offensive because they haven't thought deeply enough about the issues I would like to bring up. And I can't be afraid to have those conversations. It's better to make a mistake and back up and say, "Wait a minute. This is what I heard you say. Is that what you mean? Could you talk more about that? Wait, did you really mean to say, 'Ugh' there? Just because you do not agree with Susie's perspective does not mean you can disrespect her." It's better to use your authority to interrupt behaviors than to use your authority to silence any discussion.

For me that is what teaching for social justice is. It's about bringing the world into the classroom. It's about getting kids thinking about their own place in the world and how to change that place for their own betterment. It's about teachers making the space for that to happen by listening to all perspectives. It's about teaching kids to make that space for others, too. It's about open dialogue as a first step to creating change.

I really feel like the school of education prepared me to do that. I've had some really good TA's and professors who modeled that for us. We had some really important discussions. But we also had a divide in our cohort. We had people like myself who were really committed to teaching for social justice and people who felt very belittled and demonized because they came from the suburbs and are white. I think the idea of the evil white man in the suburbs was really played up. It was like we had to put the blame for inequity on someone and so it was put on the rich, white folks.

And I think a lot of the kids in the cohort thought, "Hey wait a second. You're talking about me here. I worked my butt off to get here. I want to help kids. Don't make me the bad guy." So I would say if you came from the suburbs and had a lot of money, you felt personally attacked.

But I will say I loved the program because it made me think about so many things I never thought about before. I felt like over the last couple of years I did a lot of soul searching. I just found the program to be such a great outlet. All of the teachers I have had have taken the time to talk with me individually about the things I am struggling with or having success with.

I would say, though, that the one thing the program is missing is more meaningful community experiences. We should be required to do more volunteering in the community that our schools are in while we are in the schools. There are some of us who did this on our own, but most people didn't. So when they talked about their experiences to the larger group there seemed to be little connection between what they were teaching and who they were teaching. This university puts such a strong emphasis on teaching for social justice, but doesn't have us truly experience its core. We can't just read about it or talk about it. We have to live it.

There are some things that you just cannot learn from your practicum or from course readings. I look at my experience in Chicago and think, sure, I could have read about someone who had that experience. Maybe I did read something similar to that. But it was so much more powerful when I had to live through it instead of reading about it.

8 Lauren

No one wants to say they're upper class, but I guess my family is. When you move away to college, you realize that everyone isn't like you. You get out of your own little bubble where you're surrounded by people like you.

I grew up outside of a large city on the East coast. We used to joke about living in a bubble. My suburb was very white. Everyone was the same. Well, of course everyone wasn't the same. Obviously there were people who looked different, people from different classes. So, there was some diversity, but it was really about where you fell in the upper-class spectrum.

My elementary school was all white—at least my class was. Then in fourth grade, we had a black girl move into the neighborhood. There was a lot of excitement about that because it was someone who was different than us. I mean we did have some kids who were of Asian descent, but I guess in our minds they didn't really count as different. Anyway, we all became friends with the African American girl. She became popular very quickly. She didn't live in one of the big houses. She lived in one of the duplexes. They were still very nice and very expensive. But still. I felt like people made some kind of correlation between how she looked and where she lived. You know, she was black and living in a duplex. Not a nice house.

Like I said, she had become pretty popular. There were times when it was awkward, though. For instance if we were talking about our hair color. Everyone wanted to be a blond, but she never said anything. Or if we were comparing who was getting the most tan in the summer, she was just kind of left out. I remember thinking, "Oh, do you talk about different skin colors? Is that something you can do?" But I never brought it up.

I remember, I didn't find this out until high school, but there was one girl in our elementary school who was not upper class. But it was never an issue. Kids don't really notice those things. But I remember going to the mall a few times with her in high school. When my dad would drive, he would always ask me if I needed money before I got out of the car. Her parents never asked her. So, I think it was then that I realized that maybe she didn't have as much money as the rest of us.

My parents were very careful not to spoil us. They would say, "Yes, we have a big house, but you're not getting everything you ask for." We had tons of conversations about how blessed we were to have so much. And every Thanksgiving we would go downtown to work in a food shelter. I remember going and just feeling really sad. We usually went about two or three weeks before Thanksgiving to hand out food. I remember seeing an African American family with a lot of kids, and I remember feeling really sad for them because they were not going to have a warm, cozy holiday like we were. I knew that in a few weeks we would go to my grandparents' house and we would have this huge meal with lots of family around us. You know—the whole traditional Thanksgiving thing.

My dad grew up in a different large city on the East coast. His parents owned a hotel and an apartment building. It was one of those old-fashioned ones with maid quarters and everything. They lived on the entire first floor of the apartment building. I mean the *entire* first floor. He went to a private boarding school and had to wear a tie to school every day. My dad's parents had three children. My dad and two daughters. I guess you could say that he's their pride and joy. But then, he married my mom who was this little Jewish girl who raised her children as Jewish. That didn't go over very well with my Catholic grandparents. I guess there were a lot of problems and tensions. One of the big problems was that we didn't talk about Jesus. We also didn't celebrate Christmas in our house which was sacrilegious, I guess. They just didn't like their grandchildren being raised as Jews.

My mom? She says she was poor when she was growing up, but she really wasn't. When she was small, she lived in a suburb outside of the city where I live now. When she was little, she had to share a crib with a sibling, but then my grandfather's business took off and they moved to a nicer house.

Both of my parents are attorneys. When I was born, my parents decided that one of them should stay home with me rather than putting me in daycare. My dad chose to be the stay at home parent. My mom is a huge feminist, and my dad is the same way. They both believe in equal rights. I have been told that my dad said to my mother, "Well, we want you to break through the glass ceiling. So, you know what? I'll stay home." It worked out because my mom's brother is also an attorney who does a lot of mortgage foreclosure work and he needed someone to do it near our city. So, he hired my dad who could mostly do the work from home. So, my dad found his little niche.

And my dad really got into it. He knew all of the stay at home moms and they would watch each other's kids if one of them needed to run out. For a couple of years my dad was featured in Mr. Mom type articles. One time we were featured on a special local news show. They were doing a piece on different types of fathers. I just remember a television crew following us around for a couple of days with video cameras. They did Oprah type interviews with our family.

My mom is one of the top voices in the major city I live near. Newspapers call her whenever there is an issue. Like the county board. Last time they appointed people who were old white men over fifty. And my mom was very vocal. She was like, "That is not what our county looks like. We have a lot of women who live here, too." She is constantly looking at things and saying, "We need more representation of women. Not everyone is a man. Not everyone is white. Not everyone is heterosexual. Let's spread out the power a little bit."

[*Lauren was speaking a lot about feminist activities, so I tried to bring her back to talking about race.*]

My mom is on a lot of boards. She works for a major law firm. Several years ago, she got them to build a major sports stadium. But then there were a lot of law suits because people didn't want their tax dollars going toward a new stadium. She eventually negotiated a deal where the owners of the stadium would have to donate some of their profits to organizations that provided services to the needy in the city. And the stadium was built. She is on the Women's and Girls' Foundation Board of Directors for the Southwest region of my state. She is also is on the board for a women's shelter. She's my role model.

[*Once again, I tried to steer Lauren to talk about race. She struggled to think of examples where race was fore-grounded in her experiences. After a few minutes, she came up with the following story.*]

I think maybe because there was a lack of non-whites in my life, I don't have many personal experiences to talk about. I was mostly exposed to non-whites through the media. I guess in middle school, we listened to rap music. This is somewhat vague, but I remember there being an issue when I was in sixth grade. There was a house for sale and an African American family was interested. I remember hearing people say that the sellers did not want to sell their home to them because they were getting pressure from their neighbors. I don't really know exactly what happened, but a few months later, a white family moved in. My parents were pretty fired up about it, so I didn't want to ask them any questions.

We also had a Venezuelan family move into our school district. But they didn't have any problems. I think both parents were doctors or something. They would be the only Hispanic family I can recall. I just didn't have much exposure to people from different races.

[*I then prompted Lauren to try and recall if she had been exposed to people of color through community activities. I knew she had danced and played sports, so I thought perhaps she might have had some experiences that she might be forgetting.*]

I played softball from kindergarten through eleventh grade and soccer through sixth grade. I played only on rec teams, so that meant I only played against teams in my community. This meant that everyone was white and upper class. My sister played high school softball, so we did travel to other communities to see her play. Some of the communities were racially diverse. But they were comparable in class to my community. So any tensions that came up were not racial; they were all economic. The rivalries were referred to as the "Caviar Kids versus the Cake Eaters."

We were the cake eaters. It's ridiculous. Even the local sports writers talked about us that way. It seems bizarre that you would write about economic differences in a sports column. But there was never any mention of race. Race was a taboo thing to talk about. I guess if we were basically the same economically, then we were pretty similar.

K–12 SCHOOLING

I was in mostly AP classes in high school. I will say that the hardest class I have ever taken was my eleventh grade AP US History class. It has been the only class I have ever pulled an all-nighter for. He really encouraged us to think. He was really into Civil Rights, and he was always bringing in other perspectives for us think about. For example, when we read out of our text book for homework, we would come into class the next day and he would ask us, "Do you think it could have happened a different way?" He'd go out of his way to find things written by minority groups who were there at the time. It was really interesting. I think up until that point in my schooling, I had never really had to do that. I mean I was from a predominantly white suburb, so I think it was really important for someone to do that. He would shake his head and say, "Remember, you are privileged. Not everyone is."

But he also showed us that he cared about us. He treated us like adults. In high school, the hall pass is key. He would tell us, "The hall pass is sitting up here. If you need it, take it so that you don't get yelled at by a teacher. Don't interrupt class to ask for it. You're sixteen. You know if you need to go to the bathroom. And you know if you're just bored and want to take a walk." Things like that.

I remember the night before a big project was due we ended up pulling an all nighter. One person in our group had mono and had been out of school for nearly a month. Another person in our group just broke up with her boyfriend. Something ridiculous. She had been crying all day at school. So we were all at one person's house just feverishly working trying to get it done. And he called the house to make sure we were all doing ok and getting the project done. He knew our group was especially stressed out. He just did things like that. You know, just really going out of his way.

I think that is the way it was for students in the AP track. I mean it depends on the teacher, I guess, but they had really high expectations for us. I knew how to meet their expectations. I was the good kid in class. I fell very much into the stereotype of the good kid who's going to sit there quietly and is going to get A's on her papers and is going to raise her hand if she wants to speak, but she probably won't participate a lot. I was the straight A student who blended into the background. There were a lot of classes where I wouldn't say a word the whole time. When the bell would ring, I would, of course, talk to my friends, but if we were working in groups I would mostly stay silent.

I would talk a little more in my English or Social Studies classes. But mostly in math or science, I wouldn't speak. I remember in those classes, you would be called on even if you didn't raise your hand. And I remember being terrified to give the wrong answer. I think part of that was being a teenager and having boys in the class. But part of it was that I never remember those teachers smiling.

As a good student, you want to please people. You want to give the right answer, and you want the teacher to smile at you. You want—I don't know. You want to make people happy by giving them the right answer. And if you can't give them the right answer, it's like, "I'm really sorry. I'll try harder."

[*Lauren was starting to talk much more about gender expectations. Although I did let her talk about that, I encouraged her to bring her discussion back to how she was taught about racial issues.*]

When I look back at pictures from high school and middle school, I see people from the same race. I just feel like the people, the whole educational system was very homogenous.

It's funny. But the only icons I ever remember learning about were Martin Luther King Jr. and Rosa Parks. I never even heard of Cesar Chavez until I got to college.

I remember, of course, reading the *I Have a Dream* piece. I thought, "Oh, this is cool." But then we just moved on. My sister became obsessed with the piece when she read it. She was just infuriated about the whole racial injustice aspect of it. Looking back, I don't know if she totally grasped it all and that we were living in a community where she didn't really have—not because of anyone's fault or anything like that—but I don't think she knew any African Americans. But she definitely took up the cause. I just went on to the next thing we were learning because that is what my teacher wanted us to do.

In elementary school, I never read anything from diverse authors or from a perspective different from my own. I remember a lot of Basal Readers. That type of mush. But I do remember going to the library to pick out books. The librarians always directed us toward the *Boxcar Children Series* or Nancy Drew nooks or *The Babysitter's Club Series*. I remember always reading a book and being able to see myself. I was like, "This could be me. This little girl in the book." Because I was white, I just assumed everyone in the books were white. I don't remember a single instance of reading a book where it was stated that the author or any of the characters were a different color than me.

In high school, we read *To Kill a Mockingbird*. I remember loving that book. Everyone loved it. In my honor's track we all loved it and talked about it a lot. In my high school, everyone was liberal, so we were all outraged about what happened in the book. We were like, "How could this happen? How could a black man be accused of a crime that he didn't commit?" But then when we finished it, we closed the book and thought, "Oh, thank God this happened back then." It was very much the "back then" mentality. We had some discussion about the race factor in the book, but it was more about the fairness of it. I just remember it being taught as a book about justice more than race.

The honor's track is ridiculous. It's all about building us up for the AP test. I remember having a teacher who was constantly complaining about teaching the required books when there were so many books that were written by minorities. I don't know if she taught the class after I had her. But I remember taking up her cause. I remember being angry that whole year because I was reading a lot of things about men. I wondered why anyone couldn't write a book with a female protagonist. It was like we were constantly reading about the world through male's eyes. But I don't remember race. Teachers were comfortable talking about race, but I don't remember many doing that. But if it came up, they would have definitely been comfortable.

I know we talked about the American Dream when we read *The Great Gatsby*. But our discussions were mostly about class. We never talked about how the American Dream might be different for different people. We never talked about things like how the immigrant might understand today's American Dream. If we focused on anything specific, it was about gender. You know–if I'm a woman, I can't necessarily achieve the American Dream.

We did have some activities where we talked about justice. For example, the student council did food drives and things like that. It was strange. It was like, "Let's do a food drive!" And everyone would be like, "Okay!" Then we'd pat ourselves on the back and be so proud of ourselves. Once a year, there was also a concert and all of the profits would go to some cause that was chosen. So again, whoopee! But we didn't do anything that required time or thought. Just our money to buy food to donate.

Our community was so proud of our schools. We had really strong academics and a really solid fine arts program. People just used to love to brag about our school. My mom just sent me an article about how my high school was rated by CNN as one of the top 500 high schools in the United States. Our test scores are amazingly high. So now people talk about how bright our children are and what wonderful teachers we have. But no one ever talks about why we have such high test scores or why we have the best teachers. They just talk about the fact that we do.

I remember going to other schools for football games. When we'd show up at the school and see that they didn't have artificial turf, we'd be like, "Oh, gross. The field is muddy. We're going to ruin our dance uniforms." I mean come on. We were in high school. There are colleges that do not have artificial turf. It was like that was all we had to complain about.

COLLEGE CAMPUS LIFE

I think I have an interesting way to look at the campus because I work for the university. I've actually had talks with the dean because I work with prospective students. I kind of have the spiel that the university wants us to say when people ask about diversity. I suppose it's not what they want us to say, but they want us to talk of diversity in terms beyond black and white. There's more diversity than just racial differences. There are people who are right wing or left wing. There's sexual diversity and there's gender and all things like that. I know you are wondering about race, but let's face it. The university reflects the state that it is in. It's a state school, so I guess that's what it's supposed to do, but I don't really see a whole lot of diversity.

Not to make myself seem all noble and colored blind, but I don't notice much diversity in the social life here. Going to football games is a big part of life at this university. A lot of people go to the games. But if you look in the stands, you see mostly white people. I do notice that the African American students tend to sit together. So, there is somewhat of a division. But we're all there for the same reason, so it's all good.

As far as night life goes, I don't see much diversity. I mean people who are really proud of their ethnicity want to identify with people like them be it African American, Asian American or whatever. So, they go to places where they feel comfortable. So maybe they go to specific bars, but because I don't identify that way, I don't go to those places. I wouldn't feel comfortable going there.

My freshman year I lived in the dorms where all of the athletes live because it opens earlier than the rest of the dorms. So if you were a football player or something, you'd be at this dorm because you had to be at campus earlier than everyone else for practice. I remember the people on my floor who were not athletes would always joke about how the only African Americans you would ever see on campus would be living in our dorm. They would say, "Why else would they be on campus?"

The African American athletes would say the same things. They would say, "I don't know what I'm doing here. I'm from Texas" or "I'm from California. I'm a black kid living in this state in the Midwest. I'm here because I'm an athlete." But in terms of injustices, they didn't really complain. Actually, they talked more about the perks, you know—the privileges that they received. They'd say, "Yeah, I'm here. I don't know if I would have picked this state to go to college, but they're giving me this, this and this. So, I'm here." And they would all laugh and high five each other or something.

But there were people who got upset when the athletes talked like that. I remember one particular time when one of my male friends started talking about the injustice of Affirmative Action. He said, "Can't people just get over it by now? I had to try really hard to get into this college. Everyone has to try hard to get in here unless they can run a nine second hundred. I don't think they should just pick someone off of the street and say, 'You have a different skin color. Why don't you come to our university? We don't really care if you can read or not'."

I remember being blown away. I had never experienced someone being so blatantly against something before. I've always been pro-Affirmative

Action and things like that. But when he said that I was like, "What are you talking about? What world do you come from? Are you insane?" Well, I didn't actually say that. I just made a confused face and I said, "What do you mean?"

He said, "Well, I tried really hard to get into this school and I got deferred."

I said, "I got deferred, too."

And he said, "Yeah, but you're out of state. It's harder for you to get in. But I live here. It's not fair that I got deferred when some guy got in before me just because he can play football."

I said, "Yeah, but we both got admitted in the long run, so what does it matter?" And that was pretty much the end of it. But people are sensitive when they see other people being given privileges or what they think are unfair advantages.

[*Because Lauren was talking about the advantages that athletes had, I asked her to share any academic advantages that she saw being given to any group of people on campus.*]

The athletes have specific people looking over them making sure they perform both on and off of the field. They have specific academic advising. They have to go to mandatory tutoring for three hours a week. But no one is finding me to say, "You're a fifth year senior. We're going to sit down with you and force you to study for three hours on Monday nights." They just assume I'm going to do it because if I fail out of class, I only hurt myself. If an athlete fails out of class, they hurt the university. I think the whole thing gets a little hazy. The fact that so many of our athletes are people of color sends a message about who needs academic help and who doesn't.

But it's not just athletes of color. There are special tutoring services specifically for people of color. There is one place on campus where if I am a person of color or an Asian American or a first generation minority, I can go there for help. But if I am white Lauren whose parents went to college, they won't help me. I'm not allowed to get their services. There is not a specific tutoring place for people like me on campus. It just seems a little weird. The assumption is that because I am white and educated, I will not need any extra help, and if I do need help, there are some places that I cannot go because of the color of my skin.

[*I asked Lauren to talk about a time where she was refused services, but she said she was talking hypothetically, not from personal experience. This prompted me to ask her if she had ever personally felt marginalized during her college years.*]

I've come to realize that I am very fortunate in that I do not have to pay to go to school. My parents pay for it. I realize every day that not everyone has that luxury and I am fortunate that I do, but to be honest, I don't like people to know that I come from money. In one of my education classes we were doing something where we shared parts of our background. After I went, one of my classmates said, "You're one of those really great people from the coast. You're from out East and your parents pay for everything, but I would never know that they do. I would have never guessed that you belong to a country club." When people find that out, I always tell them how much I hate it.

I thanked her. I heard that as a great compliment. And she said, "Well, you don't flaunt it around a lot. You're not wearing the obnoxious clothes and you're not talking about checks that your parents are sending you and you don't talk about calling them for money all of the time."

And the thing is I know if it came down to it and I really needed money, my parents would send it to me. They'd be like, "We'll send it to you. How much do you need?" But I don't want to be one of those people, but I know that we're fortunate enough that if I got into a bind, they'd help me. But I don't want people to think of me as one of those people. But there are still people that do, and it's really annoying. There are some people in our cohort that jokingly refer to me as "Country Club" or make fun of me for belonging to one. I always go along with the joke, but I would never call someone, "Hey, 'Subsidized Housing,' what's up?"

When we are having a class discussion about economic class, I notice myself, stepping back in the conversation and just opting not to say anything. I mean I realize that there are haves and have-nots in most classrooms. I realize it is the same in my cohort. I realize that the haves have a much greater advantage in schools. I know that and I know what end of the scale I come from. It's just hard to come in on a conversation and feel like I can talk about class on an even playing field as everyone else. I think I can talk about class, but I think other people would feel like I couldn't.

It's like as long as they don't know what my background is, I can talk freely and they will listen to me. Once they know where I come from, they'll be like, "Oh, you don't really know what it's like." It's just like when people find out the wealth of my family, all of a sudden, every opinion I have about what we can do to help students of a lower economic class is invalid or something. It's like people make assumptions about who I am because of the money I have, or at least the money that my parents have, without even getting to know me. It's very prejudice. Maybe not in a racial sense, but it is still prejudice.

TEACHER EDUCATION TRAINING

I'm nearing the end of my student teaching. I am teaching in a fifth-grade classroom in a relatively wealthy suburb near the university. My class has twenty-two children: ten girls and twelve boys. Four are special needs students, four of them are African American kids, one is an Indian child, one a Mexican child, one is from the Middle East and two of them are

ELL. Some of them overlap. So as you can see, I have a lot of diversity in my classroom.

Each year my cooperating teacher has her class organize a food and clothing drive for the community. When I first heard about it, I was like how much do they really need in this community? I wondered this because it is a, relatively speaking, wealthy community. I mean everyone appears to make and have a lot of money. There are some kids that get a free or reduced lunch, but nothing compared to the city where I did my practicum experiences. Actually the town that the school is in is a mix between wealthy suburbanites and farmers. But even the farmers in this community are wealthy.

But after exploring the school boundaries further, I discovered that there is one bus that comes from a specific neighborhood—Steeple Chase. I don't know for sure if the housing there is publicly funded or not, but it is economically poorer than the rest of the school district. And when the kids get off of the bus, you're like, "Yeah. That kid's in the principal's office a lot. That one is always in detention. That one is Special Ed." And nine out of the ten kids on the bus are kids of color. They weren't supposed to come to our school. They live outside of the district boundaries. Actually, they are not officially in any boundaries, so to be honest, no one wants them. But then my principal said he would take them.

One of the little boys in my class is from the Steeple Chase community. He is an African American who gets pulled out of class quite a bit to receive special help in math and literacy. So one day he stayed in for recess to work on some of the work he was missing. I said, "It looks like you're in here because you didn't do your math homework. So let's work on that."

And he goes, "You know what? I have a problem with math."

And I said, "Okay, well let's look at it."

And he said, "No, it's not that. My math teacher is a racist." I asked how he knew and he said, "Never mind." But I asked him again and he said that one day she made a face at him and he made one back at her and she got really mad at him. She gave him a little pat on the head. I wasn't there, so I can't say whether or not it happened. But I question a lot of the things that teacher does. No one will ever know what happened for sure in that classroom except the people who were in it.

I told him pretty much that. But I did tell him that if it happened again, he needed to find me. I didn't want him to feel like he couldn't confide in me next time. I promised him I would follow up on it if it happens again because I care about the things that happen to him. But I wasn't there, so there wasn't a lot I could do about that incident.

We talked more about it and he said, "The people in this school, they really—they really just don't like black people. I want to go to a school where there's less white kids because I don't like all of these white people." I asked him why he hates white people and he said, "Every time I try to say something, people correct how I'm saying it. It's like people are more interested in how I am saying something than what I'm saying.

And he's right. It seems like everyone writes this kid off. All day long you hear, "LeBron go over to Special Ed now. LeBron, keep working. LeBron, why are you out of your seat again? LeBron, you were late coming in for recess." He notices everything. He told me, "No one gets me. No one gets how I talk, how I dress, no one likes my music." So, then I asked him about the music he liked. He liked rap. So did I. When I told him, he didn't believe me. "Okay. Who do you like? Name one rapper." He was obviously calling my bluff, but I wasn't bluffing. I started naming rappers that I liked and we talked about music for the next twenty minutes. Now, he calls me by name instead of calling me, "Hey you." I feel like we really connected. I feel like a lot of the teachers in the school don't like him because they're so quick to- instead of saying, "Hey, how's it going?" When they see him in the hallway, the first question they ask is, 'Where are you supposed to be?'"

I guess that's kind of what social justice is all about. It's touching on the culture of each child in the classroom. It's about having these kinds of personal moments with kids. It's about breaking down stereotypes. It's about being conscious of how we talk about differences. It's teaching kids to critically look at things, and then critically analyze those things in the world around them. This has to be done in the curriculum as well. First kids need to see themselves reflected in the curriculum. And then they need to connect the curriculum to the larger world.

I feel like for the most part, I have learned how to do that while in the Teacher Education Program. I don't feel like I would struggle with teaching social justice through literacy or art or through movement. But there are some content areas where I would have no idea how to connect social justice with curriculum. I guess it is just hit or miss.

[*Lauren seemed reluctant to talk critically about the Teacher Education Program. This was evidenced by her covering her mouth after her last statement. I assured her that I did not know any of the TAs outside of literacy studies and reminded her that our conversations were confidential. I invited her to share more about the ways that the Teacher Education Program was hit or miss in preparing her to teach in a socially just manner.*]

I felt like our first education course was taught by someone who stood on a pulpit and told us what to believe and what to teach. For me, I was like, "Great, this is what I want to do." But I think for other people it was a little much. I mean we hear over and over again, "You should teach for social justice. I'm never going to tell you exactly what that is, but you should do it." And it was the same thing over and over again. And a lot of us felt like, "This is good stuff. I get it. But I don't know how I'm going to teach all of this and the curriculum."

I remember getting really annoyed in our Intro to Ed class because it seemed like all we ever talked about was race. And a lot of assumptions were made about us. He assumed that we were all white—all of us did not identify that way. He assumed that all of us wanted to teach in the sub-urbs. It was like he never asked us anything about ourselves. He just made assumptions about what he knew about white people, but not the white people in front of him. And we never talked about other forms of discrimination. And it was like, "I get it. I am a child of white privilege." But I also think I'm a woman and we didn't touch on that at all.

We had some heated discussions in our classes. I remember someone saying, "I'm not sure if we can talk about the holidays." And I said, "You can talk about the holidays, but you don't have to have a Christmas tree in the school. If you're going to do that you also have to have a menorah. You have to celebrate Kwanza. You have to celebrate Winter Solstice. You have to celebrate a lot of other things. You can't just focus on what the majority of the students celebrate."

And another girl in the class said, "Yeah, but there are so many holidays. How do you touch on every holiday? How do you do that?" I just remember it was one of those discussions where everyone in class had an opinion. And I just came out and said, "You can't teach Christmas." And she said, "But I want to have a fun classroom. I want to have a classroom where you acknowledge holidays and other stuff. How can I do that without spending the entire year on holidays?

And our teacher interrupted and said, "You will find a way because that is what you have to do. That is what a good teacher would do." It was like a light bulb went off in my head. A good teacher will teach for social justice and will find a way to do that with everything else she has to do in the curriculum. A good teacher will find a way no matter how hard it is.

But the thing is, we spend all of our time focusing on our students, which is good. But I don't feel like I ever had the opportunity to examine myself and my own background—like I was able to do in these interviews. I feel like it would have been important for the TA to say, "Okay. Let's look—we, all of us and realize there are twenty-five people in the room and all twenty-five of us are different with different social identities." I don't know. I just feel like there was a lot about the other, on our students, but it was never on us or our teacher.

We found out on the second to the last day that our TA had a whole family with kids, and we'd never known that. I remember feeling really betrayed. We had been forced to tell about our parents paying for college, and for me, I didn't want to do that. But at no point in the semester did he share that he had a small son. So it's a shame that we had a lot of teachers that didn't practice really good pedagogy with their Teacher Ed. students. I just feel that when teachers share it's good. That's what they're telling us to do. It's just when teachers keep their personal lives in, it changes the power dynamic, It's like, "I'm here, you all have to share with me, but I don't have to tell you anything. And if I do, it's going to be little pieces doled out. It's just about being authentic. Your practice should mirror your theories.

We talk so much about social justice in the Teacher Education program. About building community. And that means creating a safe environment where we can say things. Where we call each other out and maybe even the teacher if we see something that isn't genuine. And when I think about this it makes me think that teachers need to be authentic—share themselves and interrupt inappropriate behaviors. It's about empowering kids to be activists by being activists themselves. That's my practical version of social justice.

9　Sarah

I grew up in a small city in the Midwest. There are probably about 30,000–40,000 people who live there. The city itself had many businesses, fast food restaurants, grocery stores and even a few malls. I mean there were different classes for sure. There were the lower middle class who lived on farms and in apartments. And then you had the wealthy middle class where there would be rich neighborhoods, but they weren't really rich. They had big houses; they had nice jobs, but they weren't really rich. When I think of rich now, I think of CEO rich. We were more middle, middle class.

But outside of the city we were surrounded by miles and miles of farms. My elementary school was a country school that had about twenty kids per grade, but my middle school had a couple hundred kids. Racially speaking, my community was probably 90% white.

It wasn't until I came back for the holidays during my freshman year at college that I asked my parents why they chose to raise us in the middle of nowhere surrounded by people who for the most part looked like us. I wanted to know if it bothered them that there were almost no people of color in our community. My father said that both he and my mom grew up in New York City and they wanted to live in a place that was safe. So, they chose small town white America to do that.

I asked him if it bothered him that we were not exposed to diverse groups of people growing up. My parents did buy me white and black and brown dolls, but everyone I knew, everything I saw, even on TV, was mostly white. He told me that it was a compromise he was willing to make to assure that we grew up in a safe environment. He never said that not having people of color in the community is what made it safe, but I always figured that was what he meant. I mean I could have different colored dolls, but I couldn't live with people who came in different shades?

The other 10% of our population was Hmong. But they didn't move into our local neighborhoods. They lived more in the country and the outskirts of the city which makes sense for their culture. They farmed a lot, but, I mean, there were always problems because they had too many kids. They were immigrants and had a different culture. They ate different foods, talked different languages. And they were the only people who looked different in the community. My step mom is a social worker and she would say that the social workers would always be like, "Oh, we have so many of these Hmong kids and they aren't able to take care of all of their children. They run all over the town and are undisciplined, and their parents are nowhere to be seen." There were a lot of racial slurs said at places of work or school. But they were always said under the person's breath.

I never really noticed. I mean my town was all white. I never thought about it. I fit in. It never occurred to me that—I always said I was open-minded. I accept people, but I—it was never in my face at all. When I was in elementary school, a Hmong family moved in, and it was a smaller school, and I was young, so it was totally fine.

I had a couple of Hmong friends when I was young. My best friend was a Hmong girl. I loved that she had a ton of siblings. And all of their names, they had rhyming names, and I just loved it! I always asked her questions about her family. She would mostly come to my house, but one time, only one time, I slept at hers. For breakfast we had eggs and rice and I thought it was awesome. I was like, "Oh, I love this. I'll have to tell my mom to make this." But I think she was embarrassed or something because she never asked me to sleep over again. Her parents didn't speak English, and she spoke to her parents and grandparents in a different language, but I don't know if that was the reason or not. I always assumed it was.

When she moved away and I went to junior high; that's when I first realized how racially divided our town really was. I remember going from a class of twenty in sixth grade to a class of about 500 people in junior high. In my elementary school everyone was friends and there were no cliques. But in junior high everyone suddenly became separated. It was like in elementary school we didn't even, like, notice the differences. There were racial differences, but we didn't notice. All of a sudden it was like there were Hmongs and there were whites.

When I got to high school, the line of separation was definitely drawn. I thought it was odd that the Hmong students all sat together at lunch. I can't even think of a time that a Hmong would sit at a non-Hmong table. Maybe they were intimidated by us. You know, scared to approach us or ask us a question. They just had their table and we had ours. I think because you're in the same building everyday and because of the lack of communication between the two races and the two cultures you separate. I wish it didn't occur, but it did. To be honest, I didn't make any effort and try to be friends with them. I didn't want a Hmong friend just to have a Hmong friend. I mean I was always nice, but I mean my non-actions can definitely be perceived differently.

People never really talked publicly about how they felt about the Hmongs in our community until a few years ago. There was a hunting accident and a Hmong man shot and killed some white people. People were saying things like "those primitive Hmongs just don't understand the notion of private property. They think they can go wherever they want and hunt on someone's land. Those people are out of control." It was an accident, but it gave the right for people to start talking about their problems with the Hmongs. And because of this one incident, people felt like it was OK to say "OK, this is how I feel. This was my negative experience with a Hmong person or a group of Hmong people"

[*At this point I asked Sarah to talk about any memories that she had growing up where her parents may have interacted with the Hmong population.*]

When I was in high school, my step mom started volunteering at a community center called The Local. It was located near the Hmongs part of town. Mothers could go there to get food or drop their children off for daycare. It was completely free and mostly sponsored by churches, but they needed to fundraise. They had a lot of difficulty raising money. My step mom thought that was because it mostly served the Hmong population and there was a lot of tension between the whites and the Hmongs.

My mom was a teacher near the Hmong reservation. She was always filing grievances. She always complained about her school board not being supportive and that the teachers weren't respected by the administrators. They didn't really understand the difficult job that the teachers had everyday working with children who had to learn the school culture. She felt the teachers and support staff were not respected because the school board didn't respect the community it served. She was on the bargaining team and was always negotiating for higher salaries and better health insurance. The school board hated her. She's very vocal. My mom is very intelligent and would bring up things that they didn't have answers for.

My dad is a labor representative. That's his full time job. He has like fifteen or seventeen locals that he's responsible for and they would go to him with questions or issues. He determined what fires to put out and which ones were important to pursue. He helped them with writing and renewing contracts. I always felt like he was kind of a really low class lawyer even though he isn't one. A lot of times he would protect workers from losing their jobs. Everyone knew him because he really improved their benefits and, well, I guess their lives.

I think my parents' life choices and how they raised us impacted all of our career paths. I didn't always know that I wanted to be a teacher. I knew I wanted to work with kids, but I always thought I'd go into medicine. Then I started thinking, hmmm. I'm not going to get the relationships that I want with these kids. And I was like, I can't be a doctor or a nurse if I'm only helping people with insurance. That's not fair. I knew I wouldn't be able to handle that, so that was my deciding factor to go into teaching.

I have three brothers. One works with mentally disabled adults. One is a stay at home dad. My father was pretty much a stay at home dad. At least he had an office in the house so he was home most of the time. And my third brother is an artist. So for the most part, most of us have community-based and people-oriented jobs dealing with a segment of the population that is disadvantaged. I can attribute that to both of my parents and my step mom for always bringing to us awareness about issues in our community.

K–12 SCHOOLING

I'd have to say that my favorite teacher in elementary school was Mrs. Swanson. She was my teacher from third through sixth grade. She taught us all of the subjects except the specials like gym and music. I felt as if she cared about me and she really pushed all of us. I remember the first time that I had homework. I got it back and she wrote the word *sloppy* across the top in big red letters. After that she helped me with my penmanship and my spelling. I worked hard for her because I knew that she expected a lot from me. She also had a reward system. If you worked hard you got a special prize at the end of the day. I don't know if I would do that in my classroom because it punishes those who do not work hard. But it definitely worked for me.

She was one of those people who was really alive. She was very animated and she spoke very loudly. My family is really loud so maybe that is why I always felt like I had a connection with her. I had another connection with her, too. Because my parents were divorced, when I stayed with my dad, I had a fifteen-minute drive to school. She lived nearby and was friends with my father, so on the days I was at my dad's, she would pick my sister and I up and drive us to school. She did that for about three years. She never drove any of the other kids in the class, so I guess I always felt kind of special and valued.

My favorite teacher in high school was my Advanced Biology teacher. He honestly believed in everyone in the classroom and he believed all of us could learn. He taught me how to learn and think. Like if I didn't understand something, he taught me where I could go to find other resources, like on the internet, to get a clearer explanation. I remember being really frustrated about something about the breathing system. I went to his office and said, "Look, I just don't understand what this whole chapter is about. I read it and I just don't understand a thing about it." He grabbed my book and took a pencil and started underlining, circling and writing the words *why is this true* next to the sections I was having trouble with.

I was like, "No, you can't do that. This is a book,"

He said, "I can too write in this book if I want to."

And I said, "No, you can't. I'll have to pay a fine if you do that. That's what happened to my friend when she wrote in her math book."

He just smiled and kept writing in my book and said, "Well, my students are special."

That made me a little uncomfortable, but I will say that writing questions and underlining in my book made me understand things a lot better. And to be honest, in some warped way, doing something I knew I really shouldn't be doing made me want to read the chapter more closely.

AP Bio and Math were the only honors classes I took all through high school. I didn't realize it at first, but I was told when I got into high school that I had high math and science scores, so I was placed into an accelerated track for those classes. My sister didn't have the high scores and all throughout high school she was compared to me by our teachers. She always thought she was bad at math and science and most of her classes for that matter. She didn't try as hard and as a result got lower grades.

Even though we were both in the same track for English, she always felt like she was a bad writer. And I think teachers had lower expectations for her. I think they did for all of us who were not in the advanced track. We got full credit for writing any words down—even if we copied them right out of a book. I have to admit, I took advantage of that. Rather than writing a research paper, I asked my teacher if I could just write a bunch of journal entries instead. She told me as long as I turned in ten typed pages, that would be fine.

To be honest, I didn't really learn how to write until I got to college. I was intelligent and confident enough to fake it through high school. My sister wasn't as sure of herself. It got to the point that my mom wrote all of her essays for high school. She even wrote all of her essays for her college applications. It was ridiculous. We figured out the system and played it to our advantage.

History was the worst. All we did was read straight from the book. You know—this is what happened and this is how it happened. Very rarely did we ever talk about why something happened. You know—what structural features were in place to allow something to happen. Everything was very surface. Even when we talked about slavery, we were taught "oh, that's not right" or "that's not fair" but we never discussed why slavery wasn't right or fair. We talked about the atrocity of African Americans being enslaved, but we never talked about why the white slave owners thought they had the right to own slaves. We never talked about how social ideologies allowed something to happen. The teachers made it seem like it was the fault of the culture and that individual people had no responsibility.

Even when we learned about Viet Nam, it was in very cut-and-dry terms. This is where we were. This is what we were doing. It wasn't successful. I mean that would have been a perfect tie in with Hmong people in the class. We had a lot of Hmong in our school. It was very racially divided. Very racially divided. But not once did a teacher ever address the issue. Even if it would have made perfect sense with the content of the class, we never talked about it.

Learning about the Great Depression was no different. It was matter of fact. We were told that the people were poor and that they couldn't afford shoes or food. No one ever asked what people were poor? What did those people look like? Or why certain groups of people were poor before the stock market crash. It would have been a great way to bring in the economic disparity in our community. We could have talked about why one section of the city has three cars in every driveway while the other side of town doesn't even have paved roads. We could have brought the idea of the depression into our own community. But everything was always taught as if it happened "back then" and that everything is so different now. All any of us had to do was look out the window on their way to school to see the economic discrepancy in our own community.

But, the teachers didn't ask and the students didn't ask. I think it would have been OK to ask. I mean my school was a safe place to ask questions. But I didn't know how to ask questions like that when I was younger. I wasn't taught how to ask those questions. I was pretty much the quiet kid in the back of the room who almost never spoke in class. But I got good grades, so I think my teachers thought I was smart and knew the right answers even if I didn't raise my hand. Don't get me wrong. I went to academically good schools. Our test scores were really high. But I will say that I felt that there was a lot of hostility toward different opinions if you ever brought them up. It wouldn't have mattered much if I did know how to ask the questions.

[Sarah had talked a lot about the curricular component of schooling. I prompted her to also consider ways in which the Hmong students were socially constructed within the student community.]

At home, my parents would always read the news and follow politics and we would talk about the issues. But if I would go to my friends' houses, their parents weren't talking about these things. Even at lunch when we were with our friends my sister would bring up things about our community's lack of diversity or the racial disparity in our country. But people would say, "Yeah OK. I don't think that's true. You're just thinking irrationally."

I remember my friends telling me that I was cooler than my sister because they could rip on the Hmong around me, but my sister would tear their heads off. She's more outspoken than I am. Really she is. She will say what's on her mind. If someone says something that is politically incorrect, she is on top of them in a second. Me? Well, I think that wasn't right and I know why it wasn't. But I wouldn't say something unless I knew the person. But she would. And a lot of times that gets her in trouble. She would say things like, "How can you say a thing like that? And what makes you think that you're so much better than them?" I would think those things and sometimes I would even say them. But I always backed down when I felt like it was a losing battle.

I remember one time during lunch, my sister telling one our friends, who was racially insensitive, things about the Hmong—that the Hmong were people too. Just because they had a different culture and spoke a different language didn't mean they were not people with families. She said to the girl, "You should learn about their culture instead of ripping it apart."

And the girl said, "No, they're here now. They should learn about ours." And then she was in my ear about my sister getting on her about what she said. And that's just the way it was at my school. Most of the time what people said went unchecked. Especially if my sister wasn't around.

But classroom wise, I don't remember having that many great discussions. We almost never talked about cultural diversity in the classroom setting. I think the reason for that is probably that it's uncomfortable to talk about. Especially being white and having white privilege. If you're not used to talking about it, people don't know how to talk about it. It's a touchy subject and in an area like ours where the parents have so much say, it just might not be a safe or smart thing for a teacher to bring up.

COLLEGE CAMPUS

When I came to school, I started working with the EXCEL Organization. It's an after school program that's designed for homeless or at risk students. I worked there for three years, but I had to quit once I began my practicum work through the Elementary Education Program. There just wasn't enough time to do both. Soon after I started working there, I asked my boss what the phrase *at risk* meant. She never really answered me. I mean, because there were so many homeless children there, I knew it had something to do with the parents' financial situation. But there was something more going on. The homeless children were always black. But they couldn't accept everyone. The questions on the application only asked about income. But they were all black. I knew that there were people that were homeless that weren't black. Something didn't seem right to me.

I started being persistent with my questions. When my boss couldn't tell me what *at risk* meant, I asked my boss' supervisor. And then I asked her supervisor. I kept asking, "What's *at risk*? What makes them at risk? Are they at risk for becoming homeless or academically or for dropping out of school?" Whenever I asked, people just kind of looked at me. And they always said the same thing. "I don't know."

I understood it was an economic distinction. But I couldn't understand why they were all black. But, I mean, a fourth grader isn't at risk for dropping out. I just couldn't escape this nagging feeling that while a person's financial situation could label them at risk, there was something else going on that no one wanted to talk about. It was like the label *at risk* suggested that the color of someone's skin made them at risk for something too.

[*Sarah had strong feelings about the way that the children were constructed at her place of work. I asked her to think about the ways she may have experienced people of color being talked about in her university experiences.*]

When I came to the college campus, I started seeing more people of color that were my own age. I started paying more attention to the diversity in my own life at the university. I thought the campus was diverse because I came from a pretty much—besides the Hmong population, it was all white and everyone was in the middle class spectrum. I lived on the East side and because that neighborhood is diverse, I saw people of many different colors. On the campus, I would look around and see people who looked different from me, and I thought, "Yeah, this is diverse." But now I look around and think, "There's a lot of white people here." If we were really a diverse campus, I wouldn't notice the people of color as much. But they stand out.

Socially, I think the university does try to do a lot to bring diversity to the campus. They try to target students who consider themselves diverse. There is an event or program called "Achieve More" that the diverse freshman and new transfer students are invited to attend. But I feel like they trick the students. They get all of these diverse students, really anyone who isn't white, into one group. So they go, and they get to meet students in a social situation and they think there are a lot of diverse people on campus. And then they go to their classes on the first day and look at their classmates who are almost all white and they think, "What's this? This was not my impression at all."

They are not being prepared for the way it really is. It's kind of a double edged sword. On one hand it seems like someone is trying to provide a group for people that might have a racial comfort zone with each other, but on the other hand it singles them out, too. I don't really support the program. I think it gives the impression that the university is something that it is not.

But I do completely support the dorms that have multicultural floors. At first I didn't. I was like, "Well, I think that's weird. I wouldn't go live on a floor and just hang out with people because they looked like me." But I've come to realize that it does make sense. I think it would be a lot more comfortable and make the college transition easier. It would be a lot easier than living on the floor I lived on when I was a freshman. There were maybe three or four people of color. I'm sure those students felt singled out before they even opened their mouths.

I have some girlfriends who are black and I've heard them vent to each other. They will say, "Oh, this happened because I'm black. Or I was the only black person there." And everyone else will nod and say, "I know. The same thing happened to me." I think if they had to talk with white people about their racial experiences, most of the white people would say, "Oh, that didn't really happen because of the color of your skin. You're just imagining that." But when they can confide in their peers of color, they are probably listened to differently.

During junior year, I was a floor fellow [RH]. I heard a lot of negative language especially about people of different races. One time I was doing rounds and I heard someone talking about *coons*. The door was opened wide and I knocked and walked in. I asked why they just used that word. Someone pointed to the TV, and said, "Because of what that N—- just did." I told him I was offended by his language use and he got all defensive. He told me that maybe I shouldn't be listening in on other people's conversations.

I know this is an extreme example, but in this situation, the door was wide open and he was talking very loudly. Anyone on the floor could have heard him. We ended up bringing him to a mediator who talked to him about language and community. They talked about how language can disrupt a safe community. But you hear things like that all of the time.

I also worked at the Union at that time. I would hear things like, "Oh, a black fraternity is having an event. Someone should make a sign that says they are serving fried chicken and watermelon." And everyone in the group would laugh. It makes me mad, but I really didn't know how to approach them. I mean, it's things like that that cause racial incidents on campus.

Just recently, a Latina sorority was supposed to have a dance at the Union. It was cancelled because they were told they didn't arrange for proper security. I know the building managers and I would have done the same thing. I've seen what happens when the security is slim. Things blow up pretty quickly. But the sorority said it was a racial thing. I kind of see their point. I know they were supposed to bring their own extra security so that the policemen felt comfortable at the dance. But I wonder why the policemen felt uncomfortable at this particular dance. There are a lot of times when people don't bring additional security and the police feel comfortable. What was it about this event that made them nervous?

From my experiences working at the Union when there are dances organized by Black and Hispanic groups, there is often a security concern. I feel like the policemen are more on guard when there are going to be large numbers of people of color. When a predominantly white group has an event, the policemen and the managers at the Union seem much more willing to let it go on. It's weird.

I've also overheard conversations at the Union and have had conversations with my own friends, about Affirmative Action. They might say, "I need a job." And if a person of color got the job instead of them, they'll say, "This whole Affirmative Action thing sucks. It's not fair that they get a job just because they're not white. They should hire the best person for the job, not the person who will fill their quotas." So they make the assumption that the person who was hired wasn't a hard worker or wasn't qualified. At least not as qualified as them.

They'll also talk about who gets accepted into the University and who doesn't. It seems like everyone knows a white person who they think was "more qualified" to get in than a minority person who was accepted. It's like they don't look around and see 40,000 white people that did get in. It's ridiculous.

What's really scary to me is to hear the people in my cohort, who are going to be teachers, talking this way. One particular day in my Social Studies methods course, we were having a conversation about how race labels shape a person's experience. We had a list on the board of different terms that people use for race. We were talking about how if you are white you are assumed to be an American, but if you aren't white you hyphenate your race as in African-American or Asian-American as part of your American identity.

But then someone in the class said, "No, I don't think that's true. I don't think anyone has to prove they're Americans. People just like to call themselves a something hyphenated American. They create the separations by having the hyphens. If they just called themselves Americans, we wouldn't have so many racial problems in this country." She was really angry.

And then all of a sudden people started taking things personally. Someone asked that girl if she thought she didn't have opportunities that other people had because she was white. And then someone else said, "Well, I'm not responsible for what happened 200 years ago. Don't blame me for that. People create their own opportunities."

And then people started shutting down. It was a weird conversation. I didn't say a whole lot during that discussion. I'm still trying to find my voice. I think that the first semester of the education program, I was where some of the people are at now. For a while I felt guilty that I was white. Then I started wondering if I should even be working with non-whites. I mean, who am I and can I even make a difference in their lives? Then I just got to the point that there was nothing I could do about my skin color and I have to do what I can while being white. You try to understand something. Who you are and how it plays into society. And I think in a way, you should kind of feel guilty for a while. But some people never feel guilty. Some people feel guilty and never move away from that. And then some people feel guilty and then, because they don't want to feel guilty, they jump back and profess their innocence.

[*Sarah was relating experiences she had with her peers in her cohort. I asked her to talk about her reactions and potential interactions with the people whom she saw resisting ideas about privilege.*]

When people get defensive about race, I just try to put ideas in their heads without telling them they are wrong. I might ask them to explain something they said and then question their position. I might suggest a book for them to read that really changed the way I looked at things. I think for me, I just keep thinking about these issues and having conversations about them. I think because I was raised to see injustices, I realize that not everyone is as lucky as me and that there are a lot of social problems that need to be solved. Maybe I was more prepared to have the kind of discussions that we had in class that day.

TEACHER EDUCATION TRAINING

I see myself working with poorer families that don't have as many—specifically, families that don't have as many resources as other families. And they definitely have different experiences than what I have had. And with that, it just seems I'll be working with students who are racial minorities.

During one summer of my college years, I went to North Carolina and shadowed Teach for America teachers. I was in an all black school. The kids referred to me as "white girl." And it was all very apparent that I was the only white person in the room. I definitely realized what it felt like to be an outsider. I was like, "Yeah I have white skin." But as soon as I left that area, I didn't think about my skin color at all. As soon as I got back on campus, and I looked in the mirror, I saw Sarah. Just Sarah, not white Sarah.

That experience solidified my desire to work in the New York City school system. I've already been hired. During my interview I was asked how I would be able to relate to kids whose life experiences have been so different from mine. I explained that I knew I was an outsider and would be for a while. But I plan on moving into the area.

This is something we talked about in one of my education classes. We talked about school and community diversity and teaching for social justice. Our professor told us that we needed to live in the community that we worked in. Some of the people in my cohort said, "I don't want to live in the community. I want my life separate."

Our professor said, "Then you won't reach your kids."

And they said, "Well, I don't want to lock my doors when I go into the neighborhood that I teach in. I'll teach in a place where no one has to lock the doors." But I do want to teach in a community that is diverse. I want to work with kids who are minorities and who are disadvantaged. In that sense I'll be working for social justice.

I think teaching should be about being able to teach kids indirectly through a lesson. Like for example if you bring in a book and it has a lot of different topics you should choose topics that your students can identify with. My cooperating teacher just kind of slides away from anything that she thinks is too controversial. Like if anything about race comes up, she skids away from it. I would bring it up. I would say, "Let's talk about it. What do you see in the community? Where do you see this in the media?" I would ask questions and have students discuss things and bring in their own experiences.

When she was teaching the Declaration of Independence, she just stayed with the document. In the Declaration it says, "All men are created equal." And she just kept going after she read that. And I interrupted her and asked the class, "What were they talking about when they said 'All men are created equal?' Who were they talking about? Who were they not talking about?"

Then the kids started giving answers. Black men. Women. Men who didn't own land. And then it came out that they were talking about white men who owned land. I wanted to talk more about that but my cooperating teacher said, "Okay, let's keep going." And that was the end of it. I was so frustrated that we were focusing on the document alone when there was so much more we could have gone into.

[*Sarah was very passionate about the direction she felt the history lesson should have gone. I asked her to talk about how she might develop her practice in a way that would resonate with her notion of good teaching.*]

Obviously we don't live in a world that is fair or a nation that is fair. And if you look within small communities, there are definitely huge discrepancies. I think what I want to do is bring in more of the local. I mean you want to look at the big picture, but it would be good to look at the way things are on a local level, too. You know, ask kids how they see things and then build off of that. So, I guess I think teaching for social justice means teaching to educate students to look at the world around them. Even if a community seems the same, you don't have to look that far outside of the community to see all kinds of diversity. I don't know. I just see the world changing, and people really need to accept these differences and understand them.

I think we need to honor the students' perspectives and then try to bring in other perspectives. You could do that by bringing in many perspectives on a topic. You could bring outside speakers in. You could bring in movie clips or something from YouTube. Or an excerpt from a novel. It's all about having them experience ways of looking at things that they are not familiar with.

My cooperating teacher does try to incorporate student interests. Like for example, I work with the low group for math. She is having me teach the students math problems incorporating statistics from Jackie Robinson's baseball career. And the kids are really interested in it. Bu the thing that is weird is that the low group that I work with is made up of the six black kids in the class. The white kids don't do anything with Jackie Robinson. So, yes, she's trying to give them a cultural icon to relate to, but it's the same thing. You know. The black athlete. And why don't the white kids learn about the black athlete too?

On Fridays we go around the room and we share our weekend plans. They could range from riding my horse, going to the Wisconsin Dells, going to my cabin up North, to just watching television. It's very clear who has support at home and whose parents have the weekend off from work. It's clear who gets to do amazing things and who doesn't. Then on Monday morning we talk about what we did. The kids seem to like it. But in my opinion the nineteen kids who really like doing it do it because they can brag. Every Friday and every Monday, one African girl just says, "I pass," every time. The teacher doesn't seem to pick up on that.

In that sense, schools today don't seem that much different from when I was in school. I see very little difference in how race is talked about now and when I was in school. I think a lot of times, the issues are covered up, and the teachers make it seem like everything is peachy clean. When we talk about race in schools, it's always about Martin Luther King Jr. That is the only activist kids can name. And even when they talk about Civil Rights, the teachers still approach it like that was then and it is so much better now. But I always want to ask, "Better for who?"

Part of the problem is that in so many of the classrooms that I've been in for my field experiences, the teacher directs all of the conversation. The teacher directs all of the activities and creates the curriculum without any input or consideration from the students. When I asked my cooperating teacher why she does it that way, she told me there isn't time to incorporate everyone's ideas and she has to cover a lot of material. She also said that so much of her job is about disciplining the students.

[Sarah was prepared to stop there. She said that she had problems with the way that her teacher monitored her students' behavior. She mentioned that she did not want to go into detail because she did not want to appear

to be criticizing her cooperating teacher whom she felt was, overall, a good teacher. I reminded her that our conversations were confidential and that all names and schools would be changed. I encouraged her to share more if she felt comfortable doing so.]

In the classroom that I am in for student teaching, the teacher has a behavioral monitor that she calls the color change system. She has a bulletin board with everyone's number on it and a color next to their name. The number system is numerical, so everyone knows who is what number. Everyday students start out with green. That is the good color. But once a student has misbehaved, their color gets changed. It goes from green being the best, to yellow, red and orange—which is the worst.

Three weeks into my student teaching, my cooperating teacher pulled me aside and told me she was disappointed that I wasn't disciplining the students. When I asked her what she meant, she told me that I hadn't given any color changes. I said, "Yeah, I know. I have to work on that." But to be honest, I'm not going to work on that. She doesn't know that I strongly disagree with her discipline color chart. And I'm not going to tell her that.

I think my experiences in the education program have taught me why I would never want to use that discipline approach. I've learned that putting kids into behavioral categories is othering them. But with that said, I do see color. I do see gender. I think to pretend that I don't is doing a disservice to my students. I was raised to not see differences. It took me a long time to be able to admit that it's OK to see differences. These categories do affect how students learn and how they communicate with you and how you communicate with them.

[*Sarah and I talked about some of the discussions we had in class during the semester that we had together as teacher and student during the literacy portion of the program. I asked her to talk in general about the ways she felt the Teacher Education Program had prepared her to understand and negotiate differences within her students as a whole.*]

I think I have been prepared, through the university to teach in a socially just manner. We have all been prepared. But you do get what you put into it. If you do the readings, if you do the work, if you really think about what is discussed in class and what is in the course readings, the material is given to you. But you have to want to become socially just. Not everyone in the program does.

Right from the first semester of the education program we start talking about social justice. But a lot of the people think that is enough. But it isn't something you read about one time. You have to keep reading and experiencing life. During that first class, we had to write about how we had experienced diversity in our lives up until that point. For a lot of people that was the first time they ever thought about it.

We also had to write a biography. But we didn't even talk about that much. I didn't even include that I was white or middle class in it. We really didn't discuss who we were and how that made us see the world. I don't even remember ever talking about how our biographies made us see the world. We just wrote it for ourselves and the teacher. No one else ever even saw it.

I think we should have done more self-exploration. I also think we should have been required to do more in the community. We did work in tutoring centers and some of the neighborhood clubs. So we did get a sense of the local community. You talk to the kids and the adults in the community and you get a sense of what is important in their lives. But then you go into the schools and all of your community exposure has to be done on your own. I know I was involved in the communities I worked in, but most of the people in my cohort didn't do anything they weren't required to do. I guess the university can only do so much, and we have to take advantage of the opportunities we have.

10 Growing Up

As present identities are always shaped by past experiences and past ways of understanding the world, looking at one's emerging identity requires looking at the past events that have influenced present notions of the self. Bakhtin (1993) argues that each event in an individual's life carries with it all events leading to that moment. So to understand the participants' emerging identities as teachers, it is important to examine some of the events in their lives leading to the creation of their teacher selves.

During our first meeting, the participants spoke of life in their particular childhood communities as well as their interactions with various people within the community. Their experiences worked to establish their privileged social positioning as white individuals and the ways this influenced how they came to understand the world. Nested within the participants' stories are the ways that particular institutional and social discourses are normalized. The stories they share reveal the assumptions they make about their own positioning in the community as well as how they have come to understand the ways that the world operates.

Their stories also reveal the ways they interpreted the positioning of those whom they saw as different from themselves. In fact how one sees the other is paramount in the way one comes to understand the self. Drawing on the works of Bakhtin, Salgado (2007) argues "it is through *Others* that my-self comes to being and gains sense and meaning" (p. 54, italics in original). Indeed, the participants shared stories about their interactions with those they saw as "the other" and how they came to position "the other" within their communities. Yet, the ways the participants come to describe themselves are often in stark contrast to how they see and describe the non-white other's existence in their worlds.

Salgado (2007) maintains that "each human being is launched in a world of otherness" and that "it is through others that we enter a socio-cultural world" (p. 57). When the participants speak of the given cultural model of how one should be within their communities, they often address the ways in which the non-whites did not assimilate rather than describing what the socially accepted way of being was. Their discussions of the non-white, for the most part, represented who or what they were *not* in the social world. In other words in describing how they understood their own social positioning, they were taking an oppositional stance toward the non-white other without directly speaking of themselves.

This contrasting position, supported by social conditioning that perpetuates white dominance, allows the participants to experience the privilege of whiteness without ever having to see, name or question it. This demonstrates one of the ways that social and institutional discourses work in and through individuals.

RACE AND CLASS—THE UNNAMED CONNECTION

You're used to having a certain lifestyle.

—Desiree

Although class and race appear to be distinctive categories, in reality they are not. One's class and race often intertwine wielding advantages for some while disadvantaging others. Drawing on the works of H.B. Johnson, (2001), Shapiro (2003) and Shapiro and Johnson (2003), Johnson and Shapiro (2003) argue that "due to the structurally advantaged/privileged position of whites as a social group, and in particular because of the financial capabilities that many of them have in terms of assets, they are able to make choices and act on those choices in very real ways" (p. 186). Because white financial advantage is something that accumulates and is passed on from one generation to the next (Kendall, 2006: Lipsitz, 2006), many whites are unable to see the economic advantage they are born into. They do not connect their inherited privilege to their current life circumstances. Rather, they see their opportunities as self-made. In this sense their privileges "have the semblance of naturalness which make them appear above scrutiny" (Hurtado & Stewart, 2004, p. 318). Thus, the "naturalness" of privilege causes whites to overlook the relationship between race and class, between whiteness and privilege. Whites can't scrutinize what they can't see. Yet, when whites ignore the ways that their race influences their economic class, they are unconsciously perpetuating racial inequality.

In varying degrees, the participants partake in talk that normalizes the economic advantages they receive from their whiteness. Two of the participants talk about their parents' generational wealth and inherited privilege. Emma speaks of being raised in a house that, at one time, was affordable for a middle class family but has recently skyrocketed in cost and is available only for the wealthy. Her parents' house, she says, would presently be out of their price range as her father is a vice principal and her mother works an eight dollar an hour job. Yet, she suggests that her parents were able to live in the house and pay their bills because her grandfather owned a successful business from which her mother inherited money upon his death. Emma says, "I don't know exactly how much money she inherited when her father died, but I know he owned a very successful furniture factory. That inheritance, I think, helped them pay the bills." She admits "I never knew how much money we had, but I did know that we weren't lacking for anything."

Emma does not connect the advantages she indirectly receives from her mother being a beneficiary of a large sum of money and her opportunity to travel with her local sport teams and take multiple trips in and out of the country. Instead, she talks about enjoying the material benefits she has directly received from her parents' financial accumulation as if it were just a normal part of growing up. She briefly mentions that she played on travel sports' teams and comments that "you couldn't do that if you were poor." She says that her parents "had an educational expense account—that's what they called it—that they would use for extensive travels." Yet despite her claim of being middle class, Emma has had travel opportunities that required a great deal of expendable money. Although she qualifies how her parents afforded to pay for some of her trips by saying that her parents took the money out of their educational expense account and her education fund, she does not speak of the correlation between the expendable income her parents had and her privilege.

Like Emma, Lauren has benefited from generational class privilege. She is hesitant to admit her class distinction, however. She says, "No one wants to say they're upper class, but I guess my family is." Yet she is careful to deny that she has benefited in a materialistic sense from her parents' wealth. She says, "My parents were very careful not to spoil us. They would say, 'Yes, we have a big house, but you're not getting everything you ask for.'" Despite Lauren's attempt to downplay her privilege, she also speaks of the ways that her class status benefits her.

Lauren describes a girl she knew who was not upper class, but says, "it was never an issue. Kids don't really notice those things." She tells of going to the mall with this friend, but recalls her friend's parents never giving her any money as Lauren's parents did. She comments, "I think it was then that I realized that maybe she didn't have as much money as the rest of us." Lauren's awareness that her friend's parents never offered to give her money suggests that the handing out of money so their daughters could go to the mall might have been a normative behavior in her parents' socio-economic circle. What she does comment on is the peculiarity of parents *not* giving their children money to shop, despite the fact that she says, "kids don't really notice those things."

Lauren's father, who was a practicing attorney, chose to quit his job and stay at home with the children while her mother practiced law. Lauren tells that "my mom's brother is also an attorney who does a lot of mortgage foreclosure work and he needed someone to do it near our city. So, he hired my dad who could mostly do the work from home. So, my dad found his little niche." Lauren does not speak of the connection between her father's social position and his career choices to both be a stay at home dad and then work as an attorney out of his home. Instead, she chooses to frame her father's career opportunity as a coincidence resulting from luck that her uncle needed to hire an attorney and her father was available. What she does not talk to is the inherent privilege that he was afforded by knowing the right people in the right places.

Emma and Lauren have advantages based on opportunities that their parents had to accumulate wealth and advance within the class system. Yet, neither of them connects her economic advantage to her race. Rather each sees her parents' experiences as a unique set of circumstances. This is not uncommon. One of the reasons for this is that white privilege is not necessarily personal, but rather it is grounded in institutional privilege. As it stands, whites hold the power positions in our political, social and economic institutions; therefore, people who resemble those in power are more quickly and easily granted advantages. Kendall (2006) argues "one of the primary privileges is having greater access to power resources than people of color do; in other words, purely on the basis of [one's white] skin color doors are open to [whites] that are not open to other people" (p. 63). In looking at the economic position of Emma and Lauren, it can be seen that the advantages that are offered their families are, in part, related to their race privilege. Many whites benefit from wealth that has been accumulated over time–where the previous generations were afforded advantages through easier access to money from financial institutions than their non-white counterparts (Kendall, 2006). When this happens, whites often credit their success to the magic of merit without seeing the relationship between their opportunities and their race.

Although Desiree, Alex and Sarah did not talk overtly about the benefits they received from their class position as Emma and Lauren did, their economic classes have impacted their lives in a more subtle manner. Although Desiree's parents did not inherit economic advantages, she sees the direct connection between her parents receiving a college education and their rise in the class system. She speaks of her parents having "blue collar jobs" yet goes on to explain that when she was in elementary school her parents went back to college where her father became an engineer and her mother earned her real estate license. With their advanced educations, her parents were given more social mobility. Yet Desiree does not talk about how her parents, who worked blue collar jobs, were able to afford to go back to college while they raised three children and worked full time. Instead, she speaks of the privileges she received more as a matter of fact. She recalls, "But after my dad became an engineer, we moved into a nicer house in the same community and were able to have more of the things that our friends and neighbors had."

When her parents became divorced, Desiree recalls her mother saying "Well, it was important that you kids maintained the lifestyle you had before we got divorced." She remembers her mother trying her hardest to help the children feel like their lives were unchanged. Desiree says that even after the divorce her mother "was a big shopper and always took us with her. I always dressed in clothes from stores like J Crew or the Gap. I didn't have Chanel, but I had the kid version of expensive clothes." When she turned sixteen, she was given a car. And her mother insisted on keeping the same house that she had when she was still married. In speaking of her expensive house Desiree says, "I was kind of embarrassed. Because after a while, you just sort of feel like it's not fair or something. You kind of feel bad. But on the other hand, you're used to having a certain lifestyle." Despite the financial complications that often result when a couple divorces, Desiree talks about her life, at least materially speaking, being unaffected. While she feels that her economic privilege may not be fair, she rationalizes her advantages by feeling as if she is entitled to live the lifestyle she has grown accustomed to.

In talking about her class status, Sarah talks about her community having a range of the middle class, yet she refers to her own class position as "more middle, middle class." This is in distinction from the lower middle class "who lived on farms and in apartments" and the upper middle class who "had big houses." Sarah's parents both grew up in New York City and were able to afford to move to a small town in the Midwest to raise their children in what her father called a "safe environment." When Sarah questions her father about choosing to live in a predominantly white neighborhood when he had grown up in a racially diverse environment, he tells her, "it was a compromise he was willing to make to assure that we grew up in a safe environment. He never said that not having people of color in the community is what made it safe, but I always figured that was what he meant."

Alex says, "I always thought I was poor when I was growing up." Although he says he had a "nice house," he compared his house to those he passed on his paper route where he would "deliver papers to these amazing houses." He has memories of "hearing my parents talking in their bedrooms—our house was nice, but small, and you could hear everything—about how they couldn't pay their bills." Yet despite his perceptions of his parents' financial struggles, he speaks of attending a pre-dominantly white, private, Catholic school.

In a study identifying white families' attitudes about what makes up a "good neighborhood," Johnson and Shapiro (2003) found that to "avoid exposing their children to people that they find 'undesirable' many white parents simply move" while "many others decide to send their children to predominantly white private schools" (p. 178). Although people are limited by the choices that they can make, whites have more choices and are more able to act on them. This is witnessed in looking at the decisions that Desiree, Sarah and Alex's parents made regarding where they would live and what schools their children would attend. Desiree and Sarah's parents chose to live in a predominantly white town that was considered "safe" (good) in order to provide an environment where their children might have more advantages. Alex's parents may have had financial concerns about paying their bills, but they still chose to allocate their money to send their children to private schools. While all three see themselves as middle class, they do not speak of the possible ways that their race privileges the economic decisions that their parents were able to make. Instead, they speak of their circumstances solely as a natural result of their economic condition.

RACIAL INTEGRATION WITHIN THE COMMUNITY

My suburb was very white. Everyone was the same. Well, of course, everyone wasn't the same. Obviously there were people who looked different.

—*Lauren*

For the most part, everyone was white in my childhood neighborhood. I say maybe because I really don't remember anyone who wasn't white. I mean, well, of course you would notice if someone had different skin color than you did, but to be honest, I didn't ever think about it. Everyone was the same to me when I was a kid.

—*Desiree*

But my neighborhood, the few blocks surrounding my house, was all white. Or at least almost completely white. The kids who weren't white often had to walk through our neighborhood to get to their part of town, so it wasn't like we never saw people of color.

—*Emma*

The city was pretty much white people and then a solid amount of Hmongs. We always thought it was about a third Hmong and then two thirds white. But I think it is actually maybe a fifth, at most, Hmong.

—*Alex*

I mean my town was all white. I never thought about it. I fit in.

—*Sarah*

All of the participants at some point in the interviews referred to the community in which they grew up as either all white or mostly white. This is one of the luxuries of whiteness—never having to see the non-white other. bell hooks (1997) contends that the institutionalized notion of whiteness as the normalized race perpetuates the invisibility of blacks (although I think we can use her argument to apply to all non-whites). She argues that "since most white people do not have to 'see' black people (constantly appearing on billboards, television, movies, in magazines, etc.) and they do not need to ever be on guard, observing black people to be 'safe,' they can live as though black people are invisible and can imagine that they are also invisible to blacks" (pp. 168–169). When whites are forced to see non-whites, they see them as others who have different affinities and relations from themselves.

Although all of the participants were able to recall people of color who resided in their communities, this only happened upon my questioning their initial responses when asked about the racial make-up of their community being all or mostly white. And when most spoke of the people of color, they talked about the tension the whites experienced when they were forced to "see" the people of color in their communities.

The only participant who did not share a story of overt racial discrimination was Emma. Rather in her description of her community, she says, "The community that I live in is very liberal in its thinking and behaviors. The people accept differences, so I don't recall any community tension at all. People just kind of did their own thing and minded their own business." Although she says there were people of color, she recalls, that the people of color often "had to walk through our neighborhood to get to their part of town." So while she does not speak of any overt racial controversy in her neighborhood, she makes reference to the physical separation of races. Emma sees her neighborhood as open and accepting, yet Low (2004) argues that the physical distinction between the spaces that people of different races occupy reinforces notions of racial discrimination in a way that is unseen by most whites.

Sarah and Alex grew up in the same town in which there was a sizable Hmong population. Yet, their perception of the number of Hmong residents is quite different. Sarah recalls that her community was about 10% Hmong; whereas, Alex talks about the townspeople thinking the Hmongs represented a third of the population, (he believes Hmong represented closer to a fifth of the population). In reality, the town is approximately 86% white and 11% people of Asian descent (US Census Bureau, 2006). Yet despite a relatively small percentage of Hmong people in the community, both Sarah and Alex talk about the strong resistance toward the Hmong whom people felt would not assimilate to the white, middle-class lifestyle.

Sarah tells that the Hmongs did not move into the white neighborhoods. Instead, she says that "they lived more in the country and the outskirts of the city which makes sense for their culture. They were immigrants and had a different culture. They ate different foods, talked different languages. And they were the only people who looked different in the community." She talks about the community perception that the Hmong children were a problem. She speaks of her mother telling her that her fellow social workers would say "Oh, we have so many of these Hmong kids and they aren't able to take care of all of their children. They run all over the town and are undisciplined, and their parents are nowhere to be seen." She explains that "there were a lot of racial slurs said at places of work or school. But they were always said under the person's breath."

These criticisms were quietly spoken until an incident happened in the community that broke the silence and disrupted her normally peaceful town. She remembers, "People never really talked publicly about how they felt about the Hmong in our community until a few years ago. There was a hunting accident and a Hmong man shot and killed some white people. It was an accident, but it gave the right for people to start talking about their problems with the Hmong. And because of this one incident, people felt like it was ok to say, 'Ok, this is how I feel. This was my negative experience with a Hmong person or a group of Hmong people'."

Alex recalls similar tension in his community with the Hmong residents. "There were a lot of people in my city who didn't like that they tried to keep their culture and traditions." He tells of the townspeople's outward intolerance of the Hmong ways when he says, "If you wanted to rip on a Hmong, you would just say, 'Go eat a dog'." He explains that despite a lot of negative things said directly to the Hmong people "people would just come right out and call them "gook" or something," the comments were ignored by the Hmong.

In an attempt to relieve some of the racial tension in Alex's community, the school board mandated forced busing in order to integrate the schools. Because of boundary lines, the schools in his community were for the most part segregated, as he recalls, "schools were either all Hmong or all white." Yet, the busing project was not a success. Alex tells that "all of a sudden, the parochial school enrollment sky rocketed. And people were furious. For whatever reason, people didn't like it. They said it was inconvenient to have their kids travel across town to go to school when there was a school just a few blocks from their homes." The forced busing experience only lasted a year or two before things went back to the way they used to be and the schools were once again segregated.

In both Sarah and Alex's stories they tell that the Hmong population kept to themselves and tried to keep their cultural traditions in tact. Yet, the white people resisted this by criticizing their way of life. Sarah's discussion of the perception that the Hmong children were running wild and undisciplined reveals the unwillingness of the white social workers to accept the cultural differences in child rearing between the Hmong and the whites. The hunting accident that occurred in her community, which resulted in the death of six whites and a murder conviction for a Hmong man, Sarah feels gave right for the white townspeople to openly criticize the Hmong's way of life. Sarah recalls hearing community members talking about the Hmong man trespassing and openly ridiculing the "primitive Hmongs [who] just don't understand the notion of private property. They think they can go wherever they want and hunt on someone's land. Those people are out of control." The criticism was not directed solely at the man who killed six people, but at the Hmong community "those people" in general who were so different from themselves. It was as if the entire Hmong community was on trial and convicted for the crime of a single Hmong man. They did not see the Hmong as individuals but rather as a collective group of others who embodied their fears of difference.

The harassment of the Hmong in Alex's community, name calling as well as using the phrase "Go eat a dog," tells of the resistance to accept people who looked different from the white members of the community as well as toward those who had cultural traditions different from the accepted traditions of the white middle class. And even while the white townspeople criticized the Hmong, they resisted the attempts to help them assimilate through the integration of the schools. As Alex explains, "the parochial school enrollment sky rocketed." Many people pulled their children out of the public schools in an attempt to keep their children away from the perceived outsiders.

Both Sarah and Alex's stories reveal the anger and fear that the white community members experienced when forced to "see" the Hmong population. When whites feel that their way of life is potentially being threatened a social split often occurs. The social split allows people to both physically and psychologically distance themselves from people whom they perceive as potentially disrupting their neighborhood stability. In both cases the fear of the unknown other caused the whites to not just acknowledge differences, but to judge the Hmong way of being as threatening which resulted in distancing themselves from the entire group of people.

Lauren had a similar experience of the white members in her community "othering" non whites. When an African American family wanted to move into her upper-class neighborhood, there was a wave of resistance. She says, "there was a house for sale and an African American family was interested. I remember hearing people say that the sellers did not want to sell their home to them because they were getting pressure from their neighbors." When I asked Lauren to describe the pressure that was being placed on her neighbors, she could not recall anything overt. She just remembered a lot of angry whispering among the parents.

But despite her community being predominantly white and not wanting an African American family moving into their neighborhood, she did not recall any problems when a Latino family moved in. "We also had a Venezuelan family move into our school district. But they didn't have any problems. I think both parents were doctors or something." Lauren did not recall ever knowing the professions of the potential African Americans who wanted to buy her neighbor's house. Lauren's recollections are revealing. She accounts for the African American's rejection in the community as something that is racially motivated. Yet, the Latino family did not experience the same resistance despite being recognized as the Venezuelan family—the racial other. She says that they did not have any problems and then follows this statement with they "were doctors or something." In Lauren's version of the events in which non-whites attempted to move into her neighborhood, one's career choice, potential for economic prosperity and education could supersede one's race as far as being accepted into her community.

Like Lauren, Desiree lived in a mostly white community. She recalls, "My mom used to tell us when we were little not to have a racist attitude. It was like she was sticking up for the people of color who lived on the other side of town. But, the neighborhood that I grew up in has changed since I was a child. Now that there are more black and Hispanic people living on our street, my mom seems to have a different attitude. She refers to them as 'those people.' She'll say things like, 'Those people are throwing trash out their windows. Those people don't say hi to you when they pass you on the street. Those people don't have any respect for the neighborhood'."

Both Lauren and Desiree witnessed anger from adults in their community when people of color began moving into or attempting to move into their neighborhood. Johnson and Shapiro (2003) found this to be a common occurrence when interviewing white families. They found that most of the whites expressed fear and anger about their perception that when people of color move into a neighborhood, the white people move out. Even more upsetting to the white families was that they saw racial diversity in their neighborhoods as the beginning of the deterioration of their communities. For the most part, the adults in Lauren's community were able to keep their neighborhood "good" by preventing it from racially diversifying—at least they successfully kept one African American family out. At the time of our interview, when Lauren was twenty-two years old, her community was still all white. The Venezuelan family moved away two years after they moved into her neighborhood—they sold their house to a white family.

Desiree's mother spoke to her children about being open to people who were racially different from them and to "not have a racist attitude." But when those same people began to move into *her* neighborhood, she openly criticizes their behavior and accuses them of not having any respect for the neighborhood. On one hand she tells her children that they should welcome diversity but on the other her criticism suggests that it should not be embraced in their own community. Bush (2004) contends this contradiction is not uncommon among whites. She argues that for many whites "there appears to be a line drawn between talking and taking action to equalize opportunity where they perceive they might lose something" (p. 136) Desiree's mother accuses her non-white neighbors of being unfriendly and dirty, "those people throw trash out their windows" suggesting that they are ruining the neighborhood. Rather than referring to anyone specific, her mother has grouped her non-white neighbors into "those people" and sees her neighborhood as less desirable and less stable.

PERSONAL EXPERIENCES WITH PEOPLE OF COLOR

There were times it was awkward, though. Like if we were talking about our hair color. Everyone wanted to be a blond, but she never said anything. Or if we were comparing who was getting the most tan in the summer, she was just kind of left out. I remember thinking,

"Oh, do you talk about different skin colors? Is that something you can do?" Lauren

After I asked the participants to share memories with non-whites in their communities, I asked them to share any personal experiences they had with their non-white peers. Without exception each shared a story that had a negative connotation. It should not be assumed that they only had negative experiences. It is quite possible that their less than favorable memories with children of color came on the heels of talking about racial tensions in their communities.

Alex talks about the gang activity in his community. "There were a couple of serious gangs. I don't know what kind of violence they did. I mean you'd see the spray painted buildings and you kind of knew they were there and that they were bad, and they were dangerous." He goes on to say, "The gangs that I'm talking about were all Hmong. There weren't any other gangs in the city." Although he perceived the gangs as dangerous, Alex could not recall hearing or reading about any dangerous crimes committed by the Hmong gangs in his community. He did point to the graffiti as crime, but did not describe that as dangerous.

Alex was invited to join a gang by someone with whom he was friends. He recalls saying "No, no, Khong. That's not cool." He explains that he was afraid of the initiation "they would beat the crap out of you with bats and things." Alex laughed at this point during the interview. He could not recall ever seeing anyone who had a broken arm or a black eye from a gang initiation. He thought that perhaps the threat of potential physical harm was part of what gave gangs their power. When asked to talk about his interactions with non-whites in his community, Alex chooses to tell a story about the Hmong gangs and the potential danger they posed to the community. By focusing on the idea of the gang, Alex exonerates himself from discussing the implications of gang membership and race in his community.

When she was in elementary school, Sarah's best friend was a Hmong girl. She was enamored with her friend and speaks of "always asking questions about her family." Her friend had many siblings and as Sarah recalls, "All of their names, they had rhyming names, and I just loved it!" Although the Hmong girl had often come to Sarah's house to play, Sarah only recalls going to her house once, and that was for a sleepover. For breakfast they had eggs and rice and Sarah remembers telling the family that she was going to ask her mom to make the same thing for her some time. Sarah was never invited back. She attributes this to her friend's discomfort with having Sarah at her home. "I think she was embarrassed or something because she never asked me to sleep over again. Her parents didn't speak English, and she spoke to her parents and grandparents in a different language, but I don't know if that was the reason or not. I always assumed it was."

Sarah is not the only participant who makes assumptions about the behavior of a non-white peer. Desiree speaks of an African American girl who moved into her community when she was in junior high. She remembers that the family did not move into her neighborhood; rather, she lived in "the poorer section of town." Desiree shares that the new girl was not very well-liked. "She was a pathological liar." One lie that Desiree remembers was that the African American girl constantly told the other children that she was moving to their part of town and that "her family was going to have a pool." This appeared to annoy Desiree who says, "I remember asking her why that mattered. It was like 'We know where you live. We know you're not moving.' I don't know if she was ashamed of where she lived or if it was a culmination of other things. I never asked her."

Both Sarah and Desiree make assumptions about the person of color with whom they had an encounter. Yet, neither of the participants directly asks her peer if her assumptions are accurate. Sarah assumes that because she takes an interest in her friend's culture (finding the food amazing, loving the rhyming of the names), the reason for the absence of future invites had to be due to her friend's embarrassment that her family didn't speak English rather than something Sarah may have done. Desiree assumes that the African American girl is ashamed of where she lives. Yet, in a subtle way, Desiree's questioning of why where she lived mattered suggests that the she believed the African American girl would never belong. Desiree assumes the African American girl feels ashamed, yet her comments "We know where you live. We know you're not moving" confirm that Desiree will always see her as an outsider. Rather than looking at how they may have contributed to their alienation from their peer of color, both find blame in the other girl rather than questioning the possibility that their own behavior, and social as well as racial position, may have played a role in the actions of the other.

Whereas Emma and Lauren do not make assumptions about the children with whom they have encounters, they talk about being uncomfortable being around a non-white peer. Emma tells of being invited to sleep over at a Mexican's boy's house when she was in first grade. She explains that she did not want to go because she was afraid she would miss her mother. Emma's mother, however, insisted that Emma go. Emma did not share whether she had fun or not. She did, however, label the experience as "weird." In describing the experience she chooses to focus on the food that she ate. "I thought it was weird. They had rice and sausage for breakfast. I tried it, but I was raised as a vegetarian, so I was completely grossed out." In her telling of the experience, Emma chooses to talk about the differences in food preferences between herself and the Mexican boy as the reason for her discomfort. She focuses on being "completely grossed out" by eating meat and calls the meal "weird" despite sausage being a common breakfast food in the United States. By focusing on the meat, she has recused herself from examining other possible reasons why she might have found the experience "weird."

Lauren recalls an experience when an African American girl moved into her neighborhood. "There was a lot of excitement about that because it was someone who was different than us." She remembers the African American girl becoming popular very quickly. Yet she tells about feeling uncomfortable with different topics of conversation. "There were times it was awkward, though. Like if we were talking about our hair color. Everyone wanted to be a blond, but she never said anything. Or if we were comparing who was getting the most tan in the summer, she was just kind of left out. I remember thinking, 'Oh, do you talk about different skin colors? Is that something you can do?' But I never brought it up."

Although Lauren speaks about personally feeling uncomfortable when their racial differences were made apparent, she points to economic differences as the reason the African American girl may have been made an outsider by the white peer group. "She didn't live in one of the big houses. She lived in one of the duplexes. They were still very nice and very expensive. But still. I felt like people made some kind of correlation between how she looked and where she lived." Lauren suggests that it was "people," not herself, who drew conclusions about race and economic advantages. By speaking in general terms (people), she does not have to address her own feelings about the racialization of people.

Because whiteness as a racial distinction is for the most part unnamed, most whites are unaware of how race affects their everyday lives. Instead, they choose to look at the world as 'race*less*' for fear of being labeled as a racist. Sullivan (2006) argues that white people's habit of ignoring race appears generous, but that ignorance often works to prevent them from seeing their own oppressive tendencies. Because the participants do not name race as a central feature in their experience with non-whites, they are protected from being seen as racists. Instead, they choose to place the blame on external factors. These include but are not limited to institutions (gangs—Alex), economic differences (Lauren and Desiree), cultural differences (Emma), and non-dominant language speaking (Sarah). By looking outside of themselves for an understanding of their negative experiences with their non-white peers, the participants never have to see their own whiteness and the ways it may have been a force in the silent oppression of their peers.

PARENTAL INFLUENCE ON CAREER CHOICES

> *I think my parents' life choices and how they raised us impacted all of our career paths.*
>
> —*Sarah*

Despite sharing stories that spoke to the negative perceptions of people of color in their communities, many of the participants talked of the positive ways in which their parents modeled social advocacy. Several connected their own decisions to work with socially marginalized children with their parents' work in their own communities. Two of the women had parents who were heavily involved in the community.

Lauren describes her mother as a staunch worker for justice. She says that her mom "is one of the top voices in the major city I live near." She is on the board of many of the local organizations in the community. She is on the Board of Directors for the Women and Girls Foundation and is also on a board for a local women's shelter. Lauren specifically remembers newspaper reporters calling her mother for input when there was a controversial issue in her community. When the county board appointed people who "were old, white men over fifty" he mother was upset and was quoted by reporters saying "that is not what our county looks like. We have a lot of women who live here, too." Lauren tells of her mother critically examining the ways that the government kept the status quo. Often saying things like "we need more representation of women. Not everyone is a man. Not everyone is white. Not everyone is heterosexual. Let's spread out the power a little bit."

As an attorney for a major law firm, Lauren's mother was responsible for negotiating a deal with the city and a major sport team to build a new stadium. Lauren explains that "there were a lot of law suits because people didn't want their tax dollars going toward a new stadium." Her mother was involved in the negotiations and she eventually worked out a deal in which some of the profits would go to organizations in the city that provided services for the needy.

Sarah's parents are also active in her community. Her step mother volunteers at a community center which provides food and free daycare to the poor Hmong community.

Her mother, a teacher in the Hmong neighborhood, is active in the teacher's union. She felt the teachers and support staff were not respected because the school board didn't respect the community it served. Her mother became active on her fellow teachers' behalf and began filing grievances against the school board's treatment of the teachers. In speaking of her mother, Sarah recalls, "She was on the bargaining team and was always negotiating for higher salaries and better health insurance. The school board hated her. She's very vocal. My mom is very intelligent and would bring up things that they didn't have answers for." Sarah's father is a full time labor representative. She says, "I always felt like he was kind of a really low class lawyer even though he isn't one."

Although Lauren and Sarah came from socially privileged positions, they were able to see what social advocacy looked like by watching their parent's passion for justice. They witnessed their parents representing those who could not adequately act on their own behalf. Lauren's mother and all three of Sarah's parents became not just advocates, but leaders in the push for justice for the marginalized people in their communities. This did not go unnoticed. The impact that their parents' active community involvement had on Lauren and Sarah was a powerful impetus in their decision to become social advocates in their own lives.

Lauren expressed a desire to work with children who are marginalized in order to help them get a quality education where she feels they can have more agency in their life choices. Her decision quite possibly was influenced by her mother's work in the community. In speaking of her mother, Lauren says, "She's my role model." At least to some degree, her career ambitions can be traced to her desire to emulate the advocacy work of her role model—her mother.

Becoming a teacher is Sarah's current career path, but this was not always the case. She explains, "I didn't always know that I wanted to be a teacher. I knew I wanted to work with kids, but I always thought I'd go into medicine." But she ruled out going into medicine when she realized that she would not have the relationships she wanted with kids. Instead, she says, "I see myself working with poorer families that don't have as many—specifically, families that don't have as many resources as other families." Sarah's parents' work to assure that the marginalized people in the community were treated in a socially just manner was influential in Sarah's decision to do the same. Sarah credits her parents for directing the life choices of all of their children when she says, "I think my parents' life choices and how they raised us impacted all of our career paths."

Emma's mother, while not as active in the politics of the community as Lauren or Sarah's parents, did make a choice to work with marginalized children within the school system. In talking of her mother, Emma says, "My mother is working with ESL students as a teacher's aide making about $8.00 an hour even though she has a Master's Degree." Emma clearly sees her mother making a choice to work a low paying job, despite the fact that with a Master's Degree, she might have been able to find a job that was more economically advantageous.

It appears that Emma's mother was not just taking the job for the sake of having a job. She was committed to working with Spanish-speaking people and wanted her children to communicate with Spanish-speaking people and learn about their different cultures. She explains, "When we went to Mexico, we didn't stay at the resorts. We would fly to Mexico City and take a second class bus and stay at the hotels that the locals stay at. That was their way for us to get to know the real Mexican culture. My parents thought that if we stayed at the resorts we would grow up thinking that the world was just like America."

Her mother's choice to work with children who were marginalized because they were English Language Learners clearly has had an impact on Emma's career path. She was recently hired to teach in a school in Mexico. In discussing her teaching job, Emma explained, "I interviewed for jobs in El Salvador, Colombia, Ecuador, Puerto Rico, Nicaragua, Venezuela and Mexico. It came down to me wanting to go to a Spanish-speaking country because I would like to come back totally fluent and get a bilingual certification." Emma's decision to become certified in bilingual education and her openness to experience teaching and living in a Spanish-speaking country can be directly linked to her parents' desire to have their children speak Spanish. Her parents' insistence that they vacation in Mexican communities as a child gave her the opportunity to empathize and appreciate with the Spanish speaking cultures. Yet, this in not completely self-less as Emma believes she needs the experience working outside of the country to build up her credentials.

Neither Alex nor Desiree described their parents as being advocates for justice. In contrast, Alex saw himself as economically marginalized while Desiree spoke of resisting the words and actions of her mother. Each credits their childhood experiences as instrumental in their desire to change the way they situate themselves in the world.

Alex speaks of the shame that he felt growing up with less economic privilege than his peers. His father had an 89 Chevy "that basically had the whole front half ripped off." He recalls being embarrassed when his dad dropped him off at middle school. "I just remember getting out and walking as fast as I could so people didn't know I came out of that car. You just didn't want people to know that you were one of the ones who wasn't wealthy. Someone growing up poor doesn't want to admit it." Alex speaks of hating the feeling of being different, but feels bad that his parents have sacrificed to give him materialistic things so that he might fit in with his friends. In discussing his feeling about the iPod he received for Christmas, he says, "I knew that they had to sacrifice getting something for the house or the car or getting each other a Christmas gift so that they could give me the iPod. And that part sucks."

Alex's experience growing up economically marginalized is one of the factors that influenced him to apply for a job in Harlem. In telling about his decision to go to New York to teach, he says, "I have to get them reading and writing and thinking about the things that are important to them in their worlds. I have to help them understand the whys of discrimination and poverty and how to break those cycles." Alex's desire to help his students break the cycles of poverty and discrimination suggest that he sees his potential students as having agency in changing their future lives. Perhaps because education has afforded him the opportunity to potentially change his economic condition, he sees education as offering his students the same possibilities. However, Alex sees himself as somewhat of a missionary who he believes children need to see the "things that are important to them in their worlds." He believes that children need him as a white outsider to see what it is important to them.

When Desiree's mother make derogatory comments about people of color, she says, "I get so mad because she is being so racist." Yet she admits that her mother's attitude has affected her. She explains, "When I go home to visit, I know that I have been influenced by her changing attitude." She tells of groups of African American men who walk in the neighborhood whom she has seen looking at the cars in people's driveways. She describes feeling afraid to get out of her car if she sees a lone African American man sitting in his car and explains, "He's probably just waiting for someone, but I feel afraid all the same. And I hate myself for it."

Throughout her telling of these stories during this particular interview, Desiree appears conflicted with the feelings of fear that she has and her judgment of that fear. She contemplates, "I wonder if maybe I have always felt that way. Maybe I have always been a little afraid of black men even if those feelings are unfounded. It's like I see Mr. Smith walking down the street and I'm afraid. But Mr. Smith has never committed any crimes. So why am I suddenly afraid?"

While Desiree claims her feelings are unfounded, she tells a story from her childhood that reveals a possible source of her fear of black men. She remembers driving through the city with her mother, and if "there were darker skinned people, she would tell us to duck down. She never told us why, but when I looked around and saw people who looked different than me, I couldn't help but make assumptions. As a kid, I think I thought that if one of those people saw us, they would kidnap us and do horrible things to us."

Because Desiree's mother does not give her an explanation for why she should be afraid, Desiree makes her own assumptions and connects the inherent danger to the people who look different from herself–"darker skinned people." McCarthy et al. (2004) explain this typical stereotype of the black man as the predator and the white woman as prey as a form of institutionalized racism that is perpetuated through the mainstream media. These types of politics of fear work to keep whites fearful of the assumed inherent danger of people of color.

Yet, Desiree is uncomfortable with her perceived sense of danger. In discussing her fearful thoughts and feelings of the black men in her neighborhood, she says, "I catch myself thinking these things and I'm like, 'Oh crap. I'm one of those people. I have these racist feelings, too.' It's frustrating because I don't know how to get rid of these feelings. And then I think, 'Thank God I am at least aware that I have these feelings. At least I know what I need to change.' But as wrong as it is to feel that way, I don't know how to make myself stop feeling afraid." Desiree expresses a desire to resist her mother's outwardly racist tendencies despite acknowledging that she is affected by them. Desiree did not actively search for a job during her student teaching semester. She expressed concern about not being ready to teach diverse students because she has not been able to reconcile her feelings of being a racist with her desire to work with children of color.

WHAT THIS SAYS ABOUT IDENTITY

Because dominant social ideologies make whiteness the de facto norm, they are an integral part of the dialogic process of the becoming of self for the participants. Indeed the social discourses that privilege whiteness shape how each comes to understand the world and his or her position in it.

Chaudhary (2007) argues that "a society becomes possible only because people carry around the image of such a grouping in their heads, a group toward which they carry an affiliation" (p. 111). To belong to the dominant culture or group in which whiteness is privileged suggests that one will be granted advantages based on their affiliation while those who do not belong will be denied theses same privileges.

Yet, the matter of understanding race and its implications is complex. Oftentimes the connection between racial advantages and institutional privilege is blurred. This is especially true when we consider the relationship between whiteness and economic advantage. Social myths that suggest that all people have equal access to privilege and can earn advantages based on the merit system work to mask the connection between race and economic opportunities. Most of the participants expressed discomfort speaking about their families' privileged economic positions. Several rationalized why their families had more than others by referring to either their parents' or extended families' personal determination or their "luck." None of the participants shared that he or she ever considered how their whiteness afforded them opportunities that might not have been available to all.

This silence regarding white economic advantage perpetuates the idea that individuals, not institutions, are the sole determinant of one's economic success. This unspoken connection allows the participants to ignore the correlation between economic advantage and race and the ways this shapes how they come to understand their social positioning. Because whiteness is unnamed when they speak of their economic positioning, the participants' identities emerge in ways that insinuate that they believe there is a disconnect between their economic and racial selves.

However, the matter is even more complex than this. Much of what the participants have come to understand as social truths and laws of becoming are based on dominant discourses and images which support these fabrications. Their early life experiences within their communities and their encounters with the people who inhabit that space further reinforced the normalization of ideologies of whiteness. Chaudhary (2007) argues that "symbolic boundaries and ethnic contrasts are created that subsequently become rationalized as 'reasonable' arguments for social cohesion, personal affinity or social distancing" (pp. 112–113). For whites, it is difficult to see what has always been there. The very foundation for how whites have come to understand themselves as racialized beings is based on a privilege they have always known. That is to say, when one is born into privilege, it is difficult to see that privilege.

Yet the participants do have some notion of a white identity. Social ideologies that normalize whiteness often exhibit implicit beliefs about what it means to have a white identity through the interrogation of the non-white other. Japur, Guanaes & Rasera (2007) contend that "it is always in a relationship with other(s) that the process of making sense takes place" (p. 126). Therefore, in the evolution of the individual's identity, developing an understanding of the non-white other enables one to make sense of the self. Building on this, Boesch (2007) maintains "there is no other without an 'I'" (p. 5). If we assume that this is true, then the inverse must also be true: there is no I without the other. So in order to understand the self, we must develop some understanding of the other. Because they cannot see their own whiteness, this helps explain, at least to some degree, why the participants come to understand who they are by seeing what they are not.

Yet this undertaking is never neutral. Bakhtin (1986) argues that "understanding is impossible without evaluation. Understanding cannot be separated from evaluation: they are simultaneous and constitute a unified, integral act" (p. 142). Indeed in speaking of the non-white other, the participants take an evaluative stance when they speak of ways that they differ from their non-white counterparts. For example, while most of the participants initially described their communities as all white or mostly white, most were able to recall and talk about the differences between themselves and the non-whites who lived in their communities. In most cases, the whites and non-whites were physically separated by neighborhood boundaries suggesting a notion of a separation between us and them. In explaining this spatial separation, most of the participants spoke of how the non-whites failed to assimilate into the white cultural model. And when they talked about overt white resistance to people of color in the community, they looked to the non-whites' inability to conform to the white norms as the source of the problem. Even the "noble" pursuit of working with marginalized children suggests that the participants may see themselves as saviors rescuing non-whites from themselves. Alex embodied such an idea when he spoke about helping children see what was important to them as if these values would remain opaque unless he revealed them

When whites see people of color as faulty for not fitting into the white culture, they are demonstrating the ways that ideologies of whiteness work through them. By seeing people of color in opposition to themselves, the participants are positioning non-whites as outside or separate from themselves—as beings with whom they have no active engagement. By making this distinction, the participants insinuate that they are not responsible to or for the ways that white privilege works to create this racial disparity. Yet, this lack of answerability is in and of itself indicative of privilege—whites never have to answer to and for the privileges they receive. However, it is only through seeing the racialized other that whites can see themselves. Without acknowledging people of color, many whites develop their identities, or author themselves, in ways that ignore their accountability for how their whiteness shapes who they are becoming. Instead, they become products of unquestioned ideologies that perpetuate white dominance over people of color.

11 School Days

The second meeting with the participants addressed their K–12 experiences within the educational setting. Their stories reveal the ways they believed that they were constructed as students within their schools. Within their stories, institutional discourses speak through the participants shaping how they learned to be the "right" kind of student who was supported by teachers and rewarded with advantages that were not as easily granted to their non-white peers.

In their stories, the participants share examples of how students who did not subscribe to the social norms of the schooling system, in other words students who did not fit in, were seen as problem students who were unmotivated and lacking in cognitive ability. This group of students was mostly made up of people of color. The students who knew the accepted way to be in school, predominantly white students, were granted privileges and had access to opportunities that the others did not have. Because of the advantages they received, the participants began to see themselves and others in their racial group as naturally high achieving and elite compared to the students of color who did not fit in. They also began to internalize what the "right" ways of being were within the educational system.

Yet it is not just the dialogic relationship with institutional ideologies that influence how one comes to form an identity as a student. Actual engagement with others in the educational system also influences how one comes to understand the self. As Wortham (2001) contends, a dialogic theory takes into consideration "the positioning of the individual with respect to others in actual practice" (p. 139). The participants' daily interactions with teachers and peers shape how they come to see themselves. By engaging with others, and observing their teachers' interactions with their class members—seeing what behaviors were praised and rewarded and which were criticized and punished—the participants came to develop their identities as students.

THE "GOOD" STUDENT—PARTICIPANTS' CONSTRUCTION AS STUDENTS

I never spoke unless I raised my hand, and I never raised my hand unless I thought I had the right answer

—Emma

When asked to talk about how they thought they were constructed as students, most of the participants characterized themselves as a "good student." More specifically, they understood a "good student" to be one who received high grades, followed directions and classroom rules and spoke in an appropriate manner at the appropriate time. What they were in fact speaking to is that they understood and could successfully meet the academic expectations within the school culture. Delpit (1995) argues that there are particular codes of speaking and being that one uses to navigate institutional success. She contends that these codes "relate to linguistic forms, communicative strategies, and presentation of the self; that is, ways of talking, ways of writing, ways of dressing and ways of interacting" (p. 25). Students from the dominant culture, particularly white and middle class, are "unknowingly socialized into these codes at an early age and thus equipped, through no effort of their own, to utilize expected language forms in their classrooms" (Suarez, 2008, p. 137).

Because most whites are not cognizant of the ways they have been socialized to navigate the academic world, the notion of a "good student" has been normalized and appears to be a natural way of being. Yet Desiree and Lauren talk about knowing how to play the system to assure their success. Desiree says, "I figured out what the teachers wanted from me and then gave them exactly that." Lauren explains her school success when she says, "I knew how to meet their expectations." Both women consciously learn what the perception of a good student is and then successfully play the part.

Emma describes herself as a good student, but adds that she was "the good, white student." She explains that as a good, white student, she was expected to be high achieving and "not act out in class." She further describes the way she was constructed as a student by describing herself as someone who would always follow directions, turn everything in on time and be nice to everyone. She says, "I never spoke unless I raised my hand, and I never raised my hand unless I thought I had the right answer." Furthermore, she says that at school she "worked very hard to be the person they expected me to be." In reflection, she speaks of being unsure whether or not her "desire to be perfect at school was self-imposed or if it was a result of the expectations on me."

In speaking of the way she was constructed as a student, Lauren also describes herself as the "good kid." She describes this "good kid" as someone who sits quietly in class, gets A's on her papers and raises her hand if she wants to speak. She sees the good kid as someone who tries really hard to please the teachers and give them what they want. She explains, "you want to give the right answer, and you want the teacher to smile at you." She talks about her desire to make her teachers happy and says, "If you can't give them the right answer, it's like, 'I'm really sorry. I'll try harder'."

Like Emma and Lauren, Desiree describes herself as "the good little white student in my K–12 schooling." She says that she "never would have been someone to make waves and challenge the way things were taught."

Just as the previous two participants had mentioned, Desiree talks of not raising her hand if she didn't know what the teacher was looking for. She says that once she was in class, she "became mute."

Sarah recalls that she was "pretty much the quiet kid in the back of the room who almost never spoke in class." Because she received high grades, she assumes that her teachers thought she was smart and "knew the right answers even if I didn't raise my hand." Although Sarah says she feels her school was a safe place to question ideas, she says she didn't know how to ask questions that challenged the status quo. "I wasn't taught how to ask those questions. Don't get me wrong. I went to academically good schools. Our test scores were really high. But I will say that I felt that there was a lot of hostility toward different opinions if you ever brought them up." While she felt that she could challenge what she was being taught, she contradicts this when she says if you did bring up a controversial idea, hostility was often the result. She does not say if the hostility came from the teacher or her fellow students, but the fear of creating tension in the academic setting was enough to effectively silence her.

Sullivan (2006) suggests that in cultures outside of the dominant culture, "silence is often seen as disrespectful during a discussion of a controversial topic since if someone disagrees with a view, she or he is obligated to speak up" (pp. 28–29). She contends that the obligation to speak up stems from the idea that the "pursuit of truth is seen as a community enterprise that requires everyone's assistance" (p. 29). This is in stark contrast to the white participants who spoke of being silent for fear of "making waves." "Good students" did not challenge ideas or create tension in the classroom. In fact, they were not even taught how to ask challenging questions. On the contrary, the participants' notion of a "good student" was one who accepted, without question, the knowledge that was being passed on to her.

Emma, Lauren, Desiree and Sarah all mention not wanting to speak unless they knew the right answer. The four participants were focused on providing the answer they thought the teacher wanted rather than constructing their own knowledge. The participants understood that good students were not required to question traditional knowledge nor were they expected to produce new knowledge. Rather, their perception of a "good student" was one who was only obligated to speak when she could regurgitate knowledge and then be rewarded for doing so. In this sense being a good student means performing one's intelligence as the possession of knowledge, not the acquisition of it. Burns (2004) sees this practice of showing one's intellectual success as constituting whiteness because what is being made known by giving the "right answer" is that one is competent in the ways of being within dominant school culture.

Additionally, Sullivan argues that white, middle-class modes of behavior are viewed as appropriate in the classroom. Specifically, she contends that in the academic setting that privileges the dominant culture, turn taking is something that is authorized by the teacher. It is considered polite to raise one's hand in the school setting. For a student to "speak out of turn or before a prior speaker has finished making all of her points is to interrupt and be rude" (p. 28). She argues that in many communities where people from the non-dominant culture reside, people tend to "value individual regulation of when turns are taken" (p. 28). When considering the school culture, this is not normative behavior. Non-mainstreamed students who speak without being called on by the teacher are not following the protocol of the dominant culture, and thus are seen as disruptive and behaving inappropriately. In other words, they are not behaving as "good students" even as they are behaving in a culturally appropriate manner. Indeed, Emma, Lauren, Desiree and Sarah all describe a "good student" as one who speaks when called upon and does not "act out in class" suggesting that those that spoke otherwise were considered something other than "good." Emma and Desiree further qualify this behavior as not just good, but the behavior of the good, "white" student. This insinuates that acting out in class was not the way white students behaved; therefore, to be good, one must act like a white person would.

Yet, Alex recalls behaving in a manner that is not aligned with Emma and Desiree's notion of the good, white student. Alex sees himself as being constructed in a dual manner both as a troublemaker and high achiever. He recalls getting into the "in crowd" where he "was trying to be cool." He tells of his eighth grade English class where he could "sit in the back of the room and joke with my buddies and not pay attention." He remembers that his teacher never stopped him from goofing off. On the contrary, rather than being seen as disruptive, Alex talks about being rewarded for his behavior. His English teacher met with him during his study hall, lunch, and recesses to help him develop his literacy skills, yet did not call him out during class for his inattentive and potentially disruptive behavior.

Alex tells that he thought it was cool to be dumb and to goof off, but maintains that he "was still a good student" whose teachers knew that and believed in him. He doesn't explain why he thought his teachers made time to privately tutor him. What he does say is that he doesn't remember his eighth grade teacher affording any of his peers the time and private tutoring that she offered to him. Instead, it remains somewhat of a mystery to him as he says, "For some reason, she took a liking to me."

The findings of Fine (2004) suggest that Alex's experience might not be that unusual. She argues that whiteness is seen as merit in schools where "youths of privilege come to feel entitled to success, expect supports, and anticipate and appreciate the help that they expect, accurately, will materialize" (p. 254). In Alex's case, he knew the rules would bend for him and that he would find relative success. This was evidenced a few years later when he tells about his math teacher, Mr. Zands, "who hated my guts" and "told me that he wanted to throw me out of the window because I was a goof off." But Alex would meet with him on his free period for extra help where he says Mr. Zands "was cool and would work with me." He recalled that this happened a lot to him. He says, "I was a real trouble maker. But I was still a good student and my teachers knew that."

TRACKING—AP AND HONORS PROGRAMS

> *He honestly believed in everyone in the classroom and he believed all of us could learn*
>
> —*Sarah*

Many of the participants were placed in the AP or honors track in high school. Several spoke of the accelerated classes being made almost exclusively of white students. This trend is all too common in schools across the nation. Fine (2004) suggests that institutional white privilege continues to be produced in schools by the use of the tracking system in which people of color are excluded and opportunities are withheld from them. She argues that when students of color have access to that which is white, it is a threat to whiteness since "whiteness requires the exportation (and subversion) of color" (p. 248). In this sense, white students need students of color in order for them to fully experience their privilege. Yet, when white students look in their advanced classes and see the majority of people who look like them, they develop "a profoundly false sense of superiority premised almost entirely on denigration which requires opposition to sustain the racial hierarchy (p. 248).

Both Desiree and Alex recall that the racial make up of their AP classes was predominantly white. Desiree says that at school, she did not see non-white students very often and when she did, they "were few and far between." When asked about the incidence of non-whites in her classes, she says, "Being in the AP track, I never saw them in my classes." Alex remembers the classes at his school being mostly homogenous as well. He tells that "You might have your token Hmong in your AP class or your token white in the remedial class, but that was basically it."

While there may not have been many non-white students in Desiree's school, she claims that even if there were, they would not have been in the AP track with her. This suggests that Desiree may believe that the advanced track was not an acceptable place for the non-white students at her school. Alex's comment about having a "token" Hmong" in an honors class suggests that Alex might believe that the Hmong student did not earn his or her seat in the class. Rather, he chooses to explain the Hmong student's presence in an AP class as a representation of all students of color. This gives the illusion of fairness which insinuates that a racial hierarchy does not exist at the school.

Emma talks about being in honors classes with mostly white students. She recalls having some students of color in her honors program, but remembers that they experienced some difficulties with their non-white peers. She says that "they were constantly harassed by their peers because they were told they were acting white if they were performing academically or if they were following the rules." The students of color were not the only ones who were called out by their peers. Emma explains that "the white kids who were not performing were called black or 'whigger' by their peers."

The racial tensions that existed in Emma's high school were, in part, created by the institution itself. Fine (2004) argues that racial tensions within institutional settings are invented and sustained through the privilege and power of withholding something from one group while simultaneously granting access to another group. In the case of Emma's school, there appears to be a racially charged way of defining who can and who cannot have access to academic success. The normalized way of understanding race and achievement at Emma's school is that whites were academically successful and non-whites were lower achieving. This played out in the social interactions between the students. The students of color who were told they were acting white were shunned by their peers of color for having capitalized on advantages that were seen as predominantly for the white students. The white students in the remedial classes became outcasts from their fellow whites for not being successful in the school culture. In both cases, the students who criticized their peers were acting on the ways in which they saw the connection between race and privilege being played out in their schools.

Alex, Lauren and Sarah speak of the ways their teachers demonstrated that they believed in their students and assisted their academic success. Although Alex's experience was in eighth grade before he was tracked into an honors program, he had a teacher who fostered his academic growth. Despite being a goof off, Alex's English teacher worked with him on her free time. Rather than requiring him to do the assigned writing that everyone else had to do, he explains that "she let me write about things that I wanted to write about. She was really genuine." He speaks of knowing that she cared about him and that he knew she was authentic. He remembers that "when she told me that she thought I was a good writer, I believed her."

Lauren also speaks of a teacher that she knew cared about his students. She says that he treated them like adults by letting them use the hall pass without asking for his permission. In particular she tells about a time when she was working on a project with a group of students, and they were really "stressed out." The teacher knew it and "he called the house to make sure we were all doing ok and getting the project done." She says that he often went out of his way by doing similar things for his AP students.

Sarah tells about her Advanced Biology teacher. She says, "He honestly believed in everyone in the classroom and he believed all of us could learn. He taught me how to learn and think." She remembers going to see him because she was having difficulty understanding a specific part of the breathing system. She went to his office and he showed her how to read the text by underlining and writing questions in the margin of her book. When Sarah nervously tells him that she is going to get in trouble for defacing a textbook, he tells her not to worry because his students are "special."

Alex, Lauren and Sarah speak of having good teachers who motivated them. Burns (2004) claims that students in the AP or honors track are more likely than students in the regular, remedial or special education track to describe their teachers as responsive. While good, effective educators can and do teach the remedial students as well as the advanced students, Fine (2004) argues that less qualified teachers are more likely to teach higher numbers of students of color. She argues that "across schools we see that Black and Latino students have the very least access to qualified educators and rigorous curriculum" and that "white students enjoy disproportionate access to qualified and certified educators" (pp. 250–251). As is the case with the participants, some of the best teachers are often given the advanced classes to teach (Burns, 2004).

Additionally, all three of the participants talked of their teachers believing in them. This is not uncommon for white students. Powell Pruitt (2004) argues that when non-white students struggle in school, they are perceived as incompetent. In contrast, she contends that when white students struggle they "are supported, empowered and affirmed through the discourse of potential (as though they had no deficits) and it just feels like 'they earned it'" (p. 236). In this sense, white students often attribute their success to their hard work without recognizing that, in part, the advantages they receive through having a support network within the school system contribute to their achievement.

RACE AND THE CURRICULUM

So you have the discussion, but you don't really have the discussion.
—Desiree

Some of the participants shared stories in which they were challenged to view the world from perspectives that called into question the traditional way they had been taught to understand the world. Lauren speaks of her US History teacher who exposed his students to alternative ways of thinking during her junior year. After reading about the Civil Rights Movement from their textbooks, he would ask them to contemplate whether things could have happened a different way. Emma recalls a specific class she took during high school that dealt with racism in contemporary times. She felt like the class was important for her to understand perspectives that were different from her own. Although Lauren and Emma were able to recall moments where they were asked to consider an alternative viewpoint to their traditional curriculum, these types of stories were the exception rather than the rule.

Most of the participants expressed frustration at the ways race was presented and discussed in the school curriculum. Desiree speaks of learning about traditional history which privileges the white, male version of the past. Although she recalls learning about the evils of slavery, she does not remember having any in-depth discussions. She says, "I mean we had discussions about what was fair and what wasn't and about how to treat people. So you have the discussion, but you don't really have the discussion." She says that they never talked about white privilege. In fact she says, "I didn't even know what that was until I came to college."

Recalling his history classes, Alex says, "I didn't know it at the time, but looking back, I would say they were definitely bad." In hindsight, he was especially disappointed in the unit where he learned about the Viet Nam War. He remembers watching one movie in class to represent the entire era. He says that that was "a missed opportunity." Upon reflection he explains that because there was a significant Hmong population in the school, there was the possibility to have some meaningful discussions in class. He saw the potential for teachers to connect his community's treatment of the Hmong population with government involvement in the Viet Nam War. He felt this would have been important because there was "very real racial tension in our school." Yet, he tells that the tension was unspoken; therefore, it was never addressed.

Like Desiree and Alex, Sarah expresses concern about the way she was taught history. She remembers reading straight from the book and rarely discussing why something happened. In describing a unit on slavery, she says, "we talked about the atrocity of African-Americans being enslaved, but we never talked about why the white slave owners thought they had the right to own slaves. The teachers made it seem like it was the fault of the culture and that individual people had no responsibility." Like Alex, Sarah feels that with the large Hmong population in her community, teachers had the opportunity to address the local racial division from a historical perspective, but chose to ignore the issue. In reflection, she suspects that the reason they were never asked about or never considered their whiteness was because "being white and having white privilege . . . it's uncomfortable to talk about."

Traditional history as it has been taught in schools emphasizes the recording of events in a chronological order from a Eurocentric viewpoint. Said (2003) suggests that the teaching of traditional history educates students about what they are supposed to believe about American history and to see the events in an uncritical manner. Furthermore, Gounari (2008) argues that the notion of a "homogenous and non-threatening narrative of US history" that has "been sterilized from racial conflicts . . . and subjugated histories has been essential to the reproduction of a cultural consensus where citizens passively and uncritically accept the fateful relationship of their country to the rest of the world" (p. 99). When students are taught to simply memorize historical occurrences from a Eurocentric perspective without considering the events from the viewpoint of the non-dominant culture, they are essentially eliminating the possibility of interrogating a multidimensional understanding of history in favor of a privileged version. What they are passively learning is that whoever has the power and the resources gets to choose what to remember and what to forget when writing the nation's history. This mono-educational approach legitimizes the white version of history as the official narrative.

Although the participants found their one-sided history lessons as problematic when they reflected upon them, when they were in high school, they did not question the traditional approach. Instead, they simply accepted the version of history that was presented to them. They learned and accepted that the white people's contribution to history was more valid and more important than the contributions of people of color. It was only upon learning about white privilege at the university that the participants began to take issue with the way they were taught to understand US history. They saw the inability to connect the past with the present as a missed opportunity where they could have explored the connection between people who had historically been subjugated and people who are currently marginalized within their own communities. While racial persecution may have been discussed, as in slavery, their history lessons focused on the behavior, not that attitudes and values that allowed the behavior. Sarah explains that because the students and teachers were white, it was uncomfortable to even have that conversation. But by examining the victim and not the oppressor, they were being subtly taught the way to purify whiteness. As Desiree says, "you have the discussion, but you don't really have the discussion."

Both Lauren and Desiree are critical of their K–12 English classes. Lauren recalls reading mostly out of Basal readers in elementary school and being directed by librarians to book series with white characters. She explains that because she was white, she just assumed everyone on the book was white. She says, "I remember always reading a book and being able to see myself. I was like, 'This could be me. This little girl in the book'." Morrison (1992) claims that "regardless of the race of the author, the readers of virtually all of American literature have been positioned as white" (p. xii). This racial unconsciousness works to position whiteness as the de facto norm marginalizing all that isn't white.

Lauren also discusses the books she read in high school. She specifically recalls loving the book *To Kill a Mockingbird*. She remembers everyone in her class being outraged when an African American man is accused and found guilty of a crime that he did not commit. She recalls having some discussion about race in the book, but says, "I just remember it being taught as a book about justice more than race." There was no discussion about the relationship between race and justice.

Morrison (1992) suggests that literary criticism of American literature focuses on the "consequences on the victim—of always defining it asymmetrically from the perspective of its impact on the object of racist policy and attitudes" (p, 92). Instead what she calls for is a race conscious analysis of literature that focuses on the "impact of racism on those who perpetuate it" (p. 92). Additionally, Ladson-Billings (1995b) contends that reading and discussing texts that present positions other than the dominant cultural viewpoint "can affect the oppressor [because] most oppression does not seem like oppression to the perpetrator" (p. 54). Indeed, Lauren's explains that her class discussions regarding the wrongful conviction of an African American man focused on the injustice done *to* him because of the color of his skin not *by* whites because of the color of their skin. By focusing on the object of racism rather than the perpetuator of racism, whiteness never has to be examined as an oppressive force. This allows Lauren and her classmates to exonerate themselves from examining their own white privilege and instead innocently exclaim, "Oh, thank God this happened back then."

Desiree speaks critically of the literature she was asked to read in her English classes. She contends that she was only required to read the works of "dead white men." Even in a World Literature class, she had the opportunity to be exposed to works from a racially diverse group of people, yet she says they only read the works of Shakespeare and Dante. She comments on her required course readings of Shakespeare's work by stating, "Sadly, we read all of the tragedies except Othello. So what does that tell you about what they were and were not willing to expose us to?"

Morrison (1992) contends that what counts as knowledge in the field of literature are traditional, canonical works that are assumed to be free of the presence of people of color. She argues that to enforce the presence of the white male view while at the same time maintaining the invisibility of people of color through silence is to "allow the black body a shadowless participation in the dominant cultural body" (p.10). Howard (2006) contends that students need to actively become connected with "the other" through "authentic engagement with the reality of those whose stories are significantly different from [their] own" which can create a space to "transcend, to some degree, the limits of social positionality and can help [students] see dominance in a clearer light" (p. 39). Desiree's observation that her teachers were not willing to let their students read *Othello*, at least to some degree, demonstrates that she recognizes the way white cultural knowledge was foregrounded as the dominant and acceptable way of understanding the world.

WHAT THIS SAYS ABOUT IDENTITY

As seen, institutional ideologies and practices work to shape how individuals develop their identities within the institution. In the case of schooling, the expectations of student behavior and performance have been framed in ways that normalize white ways of being. Drawing on Bakhtin's notions of the relationship between the self and the other, Nollan (2004) claims that "the individual in his or her daily life does not exist in a vacuum, but interacts with others socially in a presumably meaningful framework" (p. xxiv). Interactions with teachers and peers often support the normalization of institutional ideologies that privilege white social codes typically resulting in more advantages for white students.

When white children begin school, they bring with them particular ways of knowing and being that promote their chances for success in the school setting. Delpit (1995) suggests that these forms of knowledge are often mirrored within the white, middle-class family unit. Therefore, when white students enter school for the very first time, they already have an idea of how to perform their student identities. More often than not, white students are rewarded for this knowledge by being granted greater access to educational opportunities.

Inherent in the educational discourse is a notion of the "right" ways that students should perform and present the self within the school system. In discussing the No Child Left Behind policy, Popkewicz (2007) argues that "the phrase *all children* functions as a determinate category that differentiates and divides the child to be reformed from 'others' not signified in the text but whose norms and values constitute the qualities 'of the average'" (p. 77). He maintains that students are shaped by social codes that reward some for having the "right" kind of knowledge while labeling others "at risk" who do not possess this same knowledge. He contends that "principles of reflection and participation inscribe a continuum of values about who 'fits' and who does not fit the notions of reason and the 'reasonable individual'" (p. 67). Most white students come to school with the "right" kinds of knowledge and are rewarded through advanced placements and highly qualified teachers while their peers of color often are labeled as "at risk" because they do not meet the prescribed norm.

The implication when white students are given advantages within the school system is that they are brighter and more deserving of privileges (being placed in honors and AP tracks) than their non-white peers. This educational advantage is created through the myth of merit which suggests that white students have fairly earned these privileges. Yet, being white means not having to acknowledge the advantages they receive within the educational hierarchy. White students never have to see the ways their whiteness has, to some degree, contributed to shaping their identities as bright and capable students. In other words white students come to feel entitled to advantages and then internalize their achievements as evidence of their "natural" intellectual ability. In their own ways, the participants make the assumption that they deserved to be placed in honors tracks without acknowledging the ways the privileges they receive resulted in their academic achievements. One of the advantages of whiteness is not having to answer for academic advantages.

However, since the accelerated tracking systems are made up of predominantly white students at their schools, the participants come to see themselves in ways that acknowledge both what they are and what they are not. When whites look in their classes and see a plethora of people who look like them, and when they discover that the remedial classes are filled with non-whites, they begin to internalize their elite status. This is often re-enforced by the special treatment they receive from their teachers. Indeed all of the participants speak of how their teachers extended themselves to support their academic success. In this sense the participants, like most white honor students, inhabit a cultural space which actively includes whites and excludes non-whites. By considering their own position as well as witnessing who is excluded from opportunities, the participants learn to understand their student selves as deserving of access to greater advantages than those who do not inhabit their cultural space.

This suggests that the participants were being molded to be particular kinds of people. Not only were their experiences within the school system shaping them, so was the curriculum. While most of the participants looked at their K–12 schooling with a critical gaze at the time of our meeting, when they were living the experience they simply accepted the ideas that were being passed on to them as truth.

The curriculum which they were exposed to, for the most part, perpetuated ideologies that favored a white version of truth without accounting for the viewpoint of the non-white other.

Indeed, the majoritarian curriculum promulgated in most schools in the United States teaches that whiteness is a powerful and good force in the world. It does not challenge students to see diverse orientations toward the same object of reflection. Bakhtin (1982) argues that "between word and object there is an elastic environment of other words about the same object, the same theme" (p. 276). Sensing there was more than they were being shown, most of the participants felt they were missing an opportunity to see another dimension of the world. They described feeling disappointed by the content of their courses which made the world appear neat and uncomplicated when their local worlds did not appear as such.

Yet there is an unspoken privilege inherent about the participants' desire to hear the perspectives of non-whites. Non-whites never have the choice to learn of perspectives different from their own. They are forced to learn the white viewpoint of the world through the teachings of the traditional curriculum. Most of the course readings and discussions in which the participants were exposed to in their classes presented the non-white but only from a white perspective. This worked to prevent the participants from seeing the ways white colonizing values are normalized. In this way, they could pretend the world was just without seeing the complexity of the way social ideologies shape individuals. Their schooling had taught them that their white heritage represented goodness and virtue, and they internalized that.

12 College Campus Life

The next time I met with the participants we talked about their experiences with racial diversity on the college campus. As previously discussed, the participants, like most white students, came to the university from racially segregated neighborhoods and communities. For many State University white students, coming to college is the first time they have sustained contact with a racially diverse group of people. The inexperience of mixing with people who are racially different from themselves often results in white college students thinking and expecting their fellow students of color to orient themselves toward the world in much the same manner they do as white people. Chesler Peet and Sevig (2003) argue that "white students' numerical and cultural dominance [has] protected them from having to know or understand others' experiences" (p. 224). Consequently, many white students never have to see or contemplate their own racialization prior to coming to college. However, once they arrive on a college campus, this changes.

The participants' experiences on the college campus challenged them (many for the first time) to seriously consider the role their race played in their understanding of themselves and the development of their identities. Many were confronted with openly blatant racist comments and behaviors toward people of color spoken from their white peers. They struggled with how to interrupt the racist words and behaviors and were unsure of how to make sense of their own responses to their peers' actions. They became suddenly unsure of who they were in relation to many of their peers—both students of color and white students.

In the same vein, many of the participants were the targets of racial intolerance from people of color on campus. This was unsettling to them perhaps because for the first time they were confronted with seeing how their whiteness and privilege were perceived by people of color. They became conscious (many of them for the first time) of the ways that their race caused them to be "othered" by people of color.

Yet in being given the opportunity to see how they were perceived by "the other," they were being given what Bakhtin called a surplus of vision. In describing Bakhtin's notion, Holquist (1990) says you see things about me . . . and the world . . . which are out of my sight. The fact that I cannot see such things does not mean that they do not exist. . . . but it is equally the case that I see things that you are unable to see. . . . you know I have a surplus, and I know you have one as well . . . by adding the surplus that has been 'given' to you to the surplus that has been given to me I can build up an image that includes the whole of me. (p. 36)

It is through the surplus of vision that the participants begin to consciously contemplate their own identities in relation to the non-white "other."

RACIAL DIVERSITY ON CAMPUS

On the campus, I would look around and see people who looked different from me, and I thought, "Yeah, this is diverse." But now I look around and think, "There's a lot of white people here."

—*Sarah*

In the past thirty years there has been substantial growth in the number of students of color who attend four-year colleges. In 1976, people of color made up 17% of the undergraduate students enrolled at four-year colleges in the United States. By 2004, the minority population had increased to 32% (National Center for Education Statistics, 2006). Yet disparities in admission patterns continue to persist with whites representing the majority of students on the college campus (Villegas & Lucas, 2002, p. 153). During the spring 2007 semester, State University's minority enrollment made up less than 15% of the total undergraduate population.

According to several of the participants, there seems to be a contradiction between the university's presentation of itself as a diverse campus and the reality of the limited number of racially diverse people they saw. In speaking of her impression of the campus when she first arrived, Sarah talks about thinking the university was racially diverse because when she looked around, she saw people who looked different from her. But upon reflection she has come to think differently. She says, "Now I look around and think, 'there's a lot of white people here.' If we were really a diverse campus, I wouldn't notice the people of color as much. But they stand out." In recalling her freshman dorm, Sarah says, "There were maybe three or four people of color. I'm sure those students felt singled out before they even opened their mouths."

Alex tells that he lived in a dorm that housed approximately 2,000 people and describes it as "one of the most diverse environments that I have ever lived in." Yet, he explains that while one of his roommates was Egyptian, the other three were white. And although he talks about getting to know three or four African American girls who lived on his floor, he hardly accounts for the many others who were not white. He speaks about the dorms being diverse, yet he only speaks of a handful of nonwhites.

Desiree was quicker to notice the lack of racial diversity. During her first days on campus, she was approached by a film maker who asked her to talk about her feelings about diversity on the campus. Her response, "I hear it's diverse, but I don't really see many people of color" reflects her perception of the campus being predominantly white. Lauren has a somewhat different take on the lack of diversity. Because she works for the university as a tour guide for prospective students and their families, one of her duties is to play up the diversity on campus. Although she says what she feels she is supposed to say, in her presentation she emphasizes the multiple layers of diversity including race, gender and sexual orientation. When she takes a look at her surroundings, she says, "I don't really see a whole lot of diversity."

Sarah thinks the university does try to welcome diversity. She sees the university targeting students who consider themselves racially diverse by providing opportunities for them to meet students who might have similar life experiences. She describes a social program called Achieve More in which students of color who are freshmen and new transfer students are invited to attend. She finds it problematic, however. On one hand, she thinks it is positive because people of color have the opportunity to meet students who might be more like themselves "really anyone who isn't white." In this sense the university is offering a community in which people might have a comfort zone with each other. So the participants assume there are a lot of diverse people on campus. But on the other hand "they go to their classes on the first day and look at their classmates who are almost all white and they think, 'What's this? This was not my impression at all'."

As most of the participants described the campus as predominantly white, many also spoke of their interactions with white peers who were critical of the people of color who were admitted into the university. Lauren recalls people in her dorm making derogatory comments about the black people they saw on campus. She tells that "people on my floor who were not athletes would always joke about how the only African Americans you would ever see on campus would be living in our dorm [she lived in the dorm that housed many of the university athletes]. They would say, 'Why else would they be on campus?'" And the African American athletes would agree and comment that the only reason they were at State University was because they were athletes.

She remembers one of her friends being upset when he heard an athlete make a comment like that. He told Lauren, "Everyone has to try hard to get in here unless they can run a nine second hundred. I don't think they should just pick someone off of the street and say, 'You have a different skin color. Why don't you come to our university? We don't really care if you can read or not'." Lauren tells him it doesn't matter because he was admitted anyway. In reflection she says, "But people are sensitive when they see other people being given privileges or what they think are unfair advantages." The "people" she is referring to are the white students.

Emma recalls similar occurrences regarding African American student athletes. She says that "whenever some of my friends see a black guy on campus they will say, 'Oh, he must play football' or 'he's here to fill the quota'." In response she tells them that she is at the university on an athletic scholarship. Yet she feels she is often silenced when she challenges her friends about their racist comments explaining, "I would say that in my circle of friends, there is an accepted way of seeing the world. It's like they will be my friends as long as I keep my political views to myself."

Like Lauren and Emma, Sarah mentions that she has heard people make comments about people who were admitted to the university that some think shouldn't have been. She explains that it seems like everyone knows a white person who they feel was more qualified to get into the university than a minority person who was admitted. This frustrates her. She says, "It's like they don't look around and see 40,000 white people that did get in. It's ridiculous."

This backlash toward students of color who are admitted to universities is tied to white privilege. The assumption many whites make is that because they have worked hard, they are entitled to be rewarded—accepted into the university. The implication is that people of color who are taking away the rewards have not earned them. Rains (1998) argues that the insinuation of meritocracy is intended to claim the rewards are and always have been available only to whites. Rains contends, "the false sense of entitlement preserves and perpetuates the status quo by ignoring the advantages gained through the system of disadvantaging of others" (p. 85). By feeling entitled, whites never have to justify the personal advantages they receive within a system that privileges them while they expect a justification when people of color are afforded what they see as advantages.

Furthermore, Chesler, Peet, and Sevig (2003) claim that "ideological commitments to American traditions of meritocracy and individual achievement are expressed in opposition to what is seen as preferential treatment or 'special rights and privileges' provided to people of color" (p. 219). These special privileges are only seen by whites when they feel they are being denied them. Lauren's friend names racial privilege to explain why the African American athletes were admitted to the university while he was deferred. He speaks of feeling victimized by the system. But he does not speak to the privilege that many white students were afforded in their K–12 schooling which gave them an advantage over students of color when being admitted to the university (see Chapter 11). The notion of white victimhood "not only acts to obscure the experiences of students of color, but further reinforces barriers to white students' abilities to acknowledge their own racial identity as members of the dominant or privileged group" (Chesler et. al, 2003, p. 226). Indeed, as Sarah argues all one has to do is look at the number of white people who attend the university to see that whites are still receiving more advantages than people of color.

SOCIAL DIVERSITY

I just like hanging out with people who have had different experiences than me

—*Alex*

Lauren speaks of the separation between races on campus which she has observed. She explains that going to football games is a big part of the social life on campus, "but if you look in the stands, you see mostly white people." And she notices that all of the African American students sit together. The night life is separated in the same way. She talks about the bars being segregated and explains that perhaps this is due to students going to places where they feel comfortable. She adds, "I mean people who are really proud of their ethnicity want to identify with people like them be it African American, Asian American or whatever. Maybe they go to specific bars, but since I don't identify that way, I don't go to those places. I wouldn't feel comfortable going there."

Emma also notes that people are racially divided on campus. She explains that The Union has live music and dancing, where people from different races go. But upon reflection she says, "If I think of it, it is mostly white people. People still tend to stay in their racial comfort zones even if they are all in the same place."

Like Lauren and Emma, Desiree speaks of the racial segregation at the bars. She describes a particular bar that plays Latin music, The Lions' Den, where many of the Latino students go at night. She says that she wants to hang out with the Latinos, but has a hard time approaching them and she feels like an outsider because people do not include her. She says, "When I'm with my friends, I would want people to feel like they could come up to us because I think that's cool to be with lots of people who have different backgrounds. But I don't feel like the Latinos at that particular place are as welcoming."

One of the myths regarding students of color is that they are self-segregating and exclusionary. Chesler et. al. (2003) argue that this "skewed perspective does not take into consideration the separatist and/or exclusionary behaviors of white students" (p. 225). By emphasizing the minority students' racial separation from whites without considering how they separate themselves from people of color, white students perpetuate the notion of whiteness as the racial norm to which all others much be compared. Lauren frames her discussion of the football stands as the African American students sitting together rather than the white students sitting together. Desiree says the Latino students at the bars did not approach her, but that she hopes at the white bars people of color would feel comfortable approaching her friends. At either place, Desiree expects the people of color to approach her.

Lauren and Desiree do not name or acknowledge whiteness as a social position. In their stories only the position of the "other" is socially marked. Both participants overlook the complex ways that dominance and oppression work in social situations. And neither discusses being conscious of the ways her whiteness (and the whiteness of others) impacts the separation of people of different races. Maher and Thompson Tetrault (1998) contend that when whites examine their experiences with others, specifically people of color, they often resist and avoid acknowledging the perception of others. Instead they overlook their own separation and instead only see people of color as exclusionary which works to normalize the social position of whites. Wildman & Davis (2005) contend that "this normalization of privilege means that the members of society are judged, and succeed or fail, measured against the characteristics that are held by those who are privileged" (p. 99).

Yet whereas some of the participants spoke of the ways people of color separate themselves from whites, several spoke of the ways they consciously attempted to socially integrate with their nonwhite peers. As they became more aware of their whiteness and its implication, many of the participants actively sought ways to interact with people of color. Emma talks about going to a bar where a lot of Latinos go in order to practice her Spanish and be around people who are different from the usual people she spends time with. Emma also took a job tutoring minority students. She says, "I love having the experience of being exposed to students who I might not normally see in my classes. I love the chance to meet people who aren't like me." She also is a conversational partner with a Korean woman whom she meets with once a week. Emma says, "She's trying to learn English, so we just talk about everyday things. She practices her English and I get to learn some Korean."

Alex tells about going to Ramadan meals with his Egyptian friends as well as going to an African American friend's party with mostly African American people. He also speaks about going to monthly Soul Sessions on campus which he finds to be a "really cool form of expression." He explains that these monthly get-togethers are a place where people of color can socialize with one another. He says, "There are just way more minorities there than anywhere on campus." Going there has provided him an opportunity to meet more people of color. He explains, "I just like hanging out with people who have had different experiences than me. But when they go to the microphone and speak their words, I feel their pain like I never have before. It's tough when you're not white"

Desiree also goes to the Soul Sessions. She speaks of enjoying watching the people dance to the hip hop music. One of her favorite things about the sessions is when people read their poetry. She says, "I am totally jealous of the people who can go up to the microphone and read their poetry. The things that come out of the minorities' mouths are just amazing. It's like they understand things that everyone should understand. They feel things I have never felt in my life. And they are so positive and full of hope. It's one of the coolest things." She does admit, however, that maybe she shouldn't be there because she thinks maybe it should be a space without white people.

Sullivan (2006) argues that people from the dominant culture, especially whites, tend to see all spaces (physical, cultural, etc) are theirs to inhabit. Yet this is not altogether the case with Emma, Alex and Desiree. While each feels entitled to inhabit any social space, they also contemplate their presence. Rather than looking to change the space by re-centering whiteness in the social situations, all speak of seeking out experiences in which they have an opportunity to learn about cultures different from their own. While Emma is often in a dominant position helping minority students who are struggling, she attempts to subordinate herself by trying to learn Korean from the native speaker and going to a bar where she is language deficient. In this sense, she becomes the novice and the stereotypically marginalized person becomes the expert.

Alex and Desiree choose to take a subordinate position (albeit a choice that only the privileged can make—marginalized people do not get to choose to be subjugated) in order to hear the voices of dominated people. The Soul Sessions provide them the opportunity to listen to the viewpoint of marginalized people who often see and understand the world differently than whites. Trepagnier (2006) sees these types of experiences as ways to heighten one's racial awareness and describes whites listening and responding to the experiences of marginalized people as empathic role-taking which involves "seeing the other's position and having an emotional response" (p. 100). Trepagnier claims that this helps whites see the effects of racism from the perspective of the oppressed.

SUBORDINATING RACISM

It's just that if you say something you feel like you're being a killjoy, but if you don't you feel guilty.

—Desiree

Many of the participants were exposed to overt forms of racism in their everyday interactions with people on campus. A few of the participants spoke of taking issue with racial jokes they heard their peers making. Emma recalls never hearing a racial joke before she came to college. She remembers learning about blatant racism when she was in elementary school, but didn't realize that it was still alive. She explains that there is an attitude among white conservative students. She says, "It's like if you don't agree with them, you need to just be quiet." She explains, "People will look at you funny or change the subject."

While working at the Union, Sarah often heard whites' attempts at humor at the expense of people of color. She remembers one time hearing someone say, "Oh, a black fraternity is having an event. Someone should make a sign that says they are serving fried chicken and watermelon." And she recalls everyone in the group laughing. Although she says it made her mad, she comments that she did not know how to approach them.

Sarah had another unsettling experience during junior year, when she was a floor fellow. She says she heard a lot of racially insensitive comments from people on the floor. She recalls, "One time I was doing rounds and I heard someone talking about *coons*." She knocked and walked in and confronted the group of guys who were watching television. She asked why they used that word, and "someone pointed to the TV, and said, 'Because of what that N—- just did'." She told him she was offended by his language use, but explains that he got defensive and told her she should not be listening to other people's conversations.

Like Emma and Sarah, Desiree has also witnessed racial comments in the form of a joke. She recalls having a friend who was nicknamed "Jewish" by his friends. She says, "Everyone laughs including him." Another time she remembers having the flu and being told to "drink some hot sauce. It will make you throw up. That's what Mexicans do because they don't have insurance." She says these types of jokes make her feel uncomfortable but explains, "it's hard to interrupt that when they are just having fun and the person it is aimed at is playing along with it. I know it's not appropriate, but I understand the reference. It's just that if you say something you feel like you're being a killjoy, but if you don't you feel guilty."

The type of racial caricatures that Emma, Sarah and Desiree speak of work to stigmatize behaviors of non-whites. Morrison (1993) refers to this linguistic feature as race talk which whites use to degrade others. Myers (2003) contends the process of creating caricatures in the name of humor is a way which "whites construct boundaries through stereotypes, generalizations, and typifications of people of color" in order to disarm "the threat of difference by dehumanizing and degrading the 'other'" (p. 137). The marking of the other with unpleasant characteristics works to establish an "us" and "them" white norm to which all others are compared. This reinscribes a notion of white dominance over people of color.

While all three of the participants take offense at the verbal act of marginalizing people of color through attempted humor discourse, none is able to effectively interrupt the behavior of their peers. When Sarah attempts to interrupt the racist comments she hears in the dorm room, she is told to stop "listening to other people's conversations" and she solicits help from a higher authority. Desiree says nothing to her friends when they make comments for fear of being recognized as "a killjoy." Sleeter (1994) argues that racist jokes and comments among whites serve to sharpen racial lines by "inviting individuals to either declare their solidarity or mark themselves as deviant" potentially resulting in the risk of "losing the other individual's approval, friendship and company" (p. 8). In most cases, rather than call out the inappropriateness of a racial joke, the participants feel unprepared to challenge the speaker's comments.

However the fact that all three speak of feeling conflicted about knowing something is wrong (personally rejecting the negative stereotype) and feeling as if they cannot address it (being silenced) demonstrates that they recognize the white joke teller as the perpetrator of oppression. Their anger and uncomfortable feeling of being silenced suggest that they have a heightened awareness regarding the workings of racial oppression and white dominance.

Unlike the other participants, Alex tells of being wrongfully accused of being a racist. He works collecting money in a booth at a parking garage on campus. When an African American male walked up the helix, Alex confronted him and asked him to take the elevator next time. Alex says, "I really debated about saying anything to him at all in the first place because he was African American and I think a lot of white people that I know don't want to be judged as racist for saying something to an African American."

When the man ignored him and reached into the booth to grab some money, Alex assumed he was stealing from him. The situation escalated and Alex discovered that the man was in fact an employee at the parking garage. Despite apologizing profusely, Alex says, "He just kept calling me a racist when I wasn't. And all the way out I kept yelling to him, 'I'm sorry, I'm sorry.' But he complained to my boss anyway, and I was going to be charged with racial profiling and all of this crap. He just would not let it go. I told my boss I felt terrible, but I wasn't profiling him."

Alex explains that he felt bad for a while until he thought about it and felt like he was being profiled as the typical white, male racist. He says, "I had thought about my whiteness before, but I hadn't experienced it in such a powerful way. Before this experience, my whiteness was a burden for others, but this time it was a burden for me."

Although he does in fact apologize, he insists on claiming his innocence. Williams (1997) argues even though one's apologies may be sincere, they manifest, "a profoundly invested disingenuousness, and innocence that amount to the transgressive refusal to know" (p. 27). What he is refusing to know by declaring himself the victim of racism is the ways that racial behavior that is both personal and structural affects his encounters with people of color. Sullivan (2006) argues that "far from being merely innocent, ignorance can operate as a shield that protects a person from realizing her complicity in an oppressive situation" (p. 127).

In speaking of race relations between blacks and whites, Alex says, "I mean, I get that there is a history there. But people use history to make their assumptions." In defense of his perceived racist tendencies, Alex says, "It's just like, yes. I was born a Caucasian. I can't control that. But I can control what I do and that is what I am working on."

Yet there is evidence that some of the participants are beginning to confront racist talk and behaviors that they are exposed to. Sarah speaks of thinking about race in her own life more consistently. While she is not comfortable addressing strangers whom she hears making racially insensitive comments, she is not afraid to confront her peers. She says that when people start talking in a racist manner, "I just try to put ideas in their heads without telling them they are wrong. I might ask them to explain something they said and then question their position. I might suggest a book for them to read that really changed the way I looked at things. I think for me, I just keep thinking about these issues and having conversations about them."

When there is a racially charged conversation in a class, Desiree tells of times she has asked people of color how they feel about what they are hearing. She says, "I'm not asking them to speak for their race. I want to know how they personally feel about what they are hearing." She acknowledges that "up until I started seeking experiences where I could be around a diverse group of people, I never thought about being an outsider." The way people of color are treated by white people embarrasses her. She says, "People who are not privileged need to figure out how to make it in a white society. White people never have to think about that." This shows she is becoming more racially aware.

Yet she still struggles with her own racist feelings. She says, "I remember one of the students of color in the class crying because she said that people treated her differently when she was growing up because of the color of her skin. I do believe that she felt those things, but part of me wonders why those stories only come out when it is convenient or when they want something." Both Sarah and Desiree are making attempts to challenge racism in their everyday lives. They are both still unsure about how to do that in a way where they will be heard, (as are the rest of the participants), but they are beginning to consciously interrogate their own understanding as a raced being in a racialized world.

WHAT THIS SAYS ABOUT IDENTITY

The participants spoke of the contradiction they saw between the university's attempt at presenting an image of a racially diverse institution and the reality of a predominantly white establishment. They witnessed the physical separation of people from different races in various aspects of university life. Without their parents and other significant adults to help them make meaning of the separatist behaviors that would align with the dominant ideologies in which they were raised, the participants were forced to make meaning for themselves regarding their college experiences.

Whereas the participants had encounters with people of color before they came to campus, the social dynamics of racial difference remained relatively unspoken. In contrast, when they interacted with their white collegiate peers, they were exposed to the verbal expression of social ideologies. The words their peers spoke were not simply from their unique ideas. Instead, as Bakhtin (1981) suggests, "each word tastes of the context and contexts in which it has lived its socially charged life" (p. 293). In their interactions with their white peers, the participants were being exposed to the articulation of social ideologies that promoted the expectation white privilege.

Yet, in hearing these ideologies spoken, many of the participants took offense suggesting their resistance to acknowledging that the spoken word represented a social reality—at least a social reality that they did not believe was their own. However, in their stories of subordinating racism, the participants speak of their conflicted feelings when they are confronted with responding to racist words and behaviors of others as well as answering for their own racist behaviors. They did not know how to interrupt or challenge blatant racism in a way where they would not be seen as outsiders from their own racial group.

This was confusing for many of them—they were not people of color, yet they did not feel as if they were aligned with the beliefs of the dominant white culture. Many were frustrated and felt trapped as they questioned who they understood themselves to be and wondered how they could move to be white allies of people of color. In this way they were beginning to more consciously author themselves. Bakhtin (1993) calls this conscious responsibility the *non-alibi in being* wherein individuals cease from making excuses for the decisions they make, but instead assume accountability for their words and actions. Nielson (2002) explains, "My non-alibi in being means to struggle with the seduction of pretending to be who I am not through imagining of how the other might see me or how I would like the other to see me" (p. 44).

Rather than expose herself to an uncomfortable situation, Lauren opted out of any situations where she would have the opportunity to share the space with people of color and potentially experience how she might be seen by others. However, many of the participants, in reaction to the racial prejudice that occurred in their own lives as well as on campus, began to intentionally interact with non-whites. The types of experiences that the participants speak of are not easily found on campus. As Emma says, "You could leave this university without really ever having to dialogue or share the same space with someone who is radically different from yourself."

Though, in many ways the vast array of social activities on campus allowed the participants the opportunity to consciously choose experiences that would provide them with ways to develop their identities in a more empathetic manner. Some of their attempts appeared superficial as they could occupy the spaces of non-whites as onlookers—observing the people of color as objects of study (going to bars, Ramadan meals, African American parties) and doing so without the surplus of vision that might allow them to see themselves from the perspective of the non-white people at these functions.

However, not all of the experiences the participants choose to have with people of color were attempts to see the "other" from their own position or viewpoint. By interacting with people of color in social circles where some of the participants were in the minority, they were able to, at times, experience the non-white other from "inside [the others'] own essence" (Bakhtin, 1993, p. 14). The Soul Sessions that Desiree and Alex attended are examples of this type of engagement. Emma's tutoring sessions, where time was allotted for the Korean woman to become the language expert, also provided Emma the chance to inhabit a space where she could experience what it was like to be a language learner. In this way, a few of the participants were taking a necessary step to developing a racial consciousness by empathizing with people of color through seeing the "other" from within the "other's" point of view.

Yet, when the participants, specifically Alex and Desiree, speak of the Soul Sessions and feeling the pain that many non-whites experience, they are, in a sense, being infected by the other's perspective and not experiencing empathy in the way Bakhtin intends it. Bakhtin (1993) says, that in active empathy

> I do not lose myself completely . . . it is not the object that unexpectedly takes possession of me as the passive one. It is *I* who empathize actively into the object, empathizing is *my* act, and only that constitutes its productiveness and newness. (p. 15, italics in the original)

By feeling what the other feels, or something that coincides with the other's feelings, the participants have not yet made the necessary turn back to the self that Bakhtin calls for. That is to say that their attempts at empathy are located outside of the self.

It is only when the participants have the experience of being "othered" by both whites and non-whites that they are moved to re-examine their understanding of themselves. It is from the surplus of vision from the other who is watching them that the participants have a chance to see themselves from a point of view which is outside of their being. Nielson (2002) argues that this surplus of vision

> allows the self to center the other and to collect the image of the other who is himself or herself struggling with the ethical dilemma of what to do. The self-other relationship provides the transgredient stability necessary for ethical choices but leaves the space open for each to determine those choices. (p. 42)

With their surplus vision which allows them to see themselves differently, several of the participants do in fact begin to interrogate their whiteness and make choices about how to act. Yet not all of the participants use their surplus of vision to develop their racial awareness and work toward social advocacy. When confronted with being called a racist, Alex feels guilty, yet refuses to accept what his new vision has afforded him—the chance to see one way that white dominance is taken up by people of color. Instead, he recuses himself from any racially motivated intentions and calls out his African American accuser as a racist against him. He adopts an understanding of race in which the white male is the new target for discrimination ignoring the opportunity to see how ideologies that perpetuate white dominance, albeit unintentional, operate through him. He says he wants to move forward, but does not want to consider the image of himself that he was able to see in his accuser's eyes.

Because she has had the chance to see how the performance of whiteness is embedded within many of her college contemporaries, Sarah has begun to examine how she enacts her own whiteness. She can no longer be silent when someone she knows makes racist comments. While she will not openly tell them they are wrong, she has begun to question how her alliance with oppressive whites marks her as a racist to others who might be watching. She has started to challenge some of her peers when they make racially uninformed comments although she admits to still feeling uncomfortable doing so.

Desiree speaks the most of the self-reflection she has done since she has had opportunities to see how she is viewed and understood by others. Her experiences in the bars and Soul Sessions where she has not been warmly accepted have afforded her the opportunity to contemplate the ways she is perceived by others and how she authors herself. Yet she still has conflicting moments where she understands the ways institutional racial oppression operates when she hears strangers on a stage speak of it, but finds herself a product of dysconscious racism (King, 1997) by mistrusting and being suspicious of the people of color in her classes who share their struggles and pain about their personal experiences with white racism and oppression.

For the most part, many of the experiences that the participants had on the college campus and at local gatherings provided them the opportunity to critically examine different attitudes and beliefs about race. Yet, not all of the participants turn the examination toward themselves. Lauren and Emma point their fingers at other whites who display their dominance over people of color; yet they do not examine how their own whiteness makes itself known in the larger social realm. While they will defend people of color against racist comments by their white peers, neither has taken the opportunity to actively engage with people of color where they might be exposed to a counter view of whites. The participants who have the opportunity to empathize with people of color, or have the experience of being "othered" themselves have had the chance to use their surplus of vision to begin to contemplate their own social position and social becoming in relation to the other.

13 How to Be a Teacher

The final meeting with the participants occurred upon the completion of their student teaching experience in the public schools. During our conversation, participants reflected on their classes at the university as well as the teaching experiences each had over a four semester period.

The previous chapters told of participants' life experiences which culminated in their choice to enter the teaching field. The encounters throughout their lives with non-whites gave them a glimpse into the reality that people of color often face as marginalized beings within the educational system and society at large. This awareness bumped up against their beliefs that all children are learners and deserve equal opportunities to experience success in the school setting. The contradiction between the ways they saw social realities being enacted and the ways that they thought the world should operate shaped their desire to develop practices that were grounded in social and racial equity.

When they began their education classes, the participants came with the question: *how should I act?* They were looking for concrete answers, a prescribed formula, to interact with their students that would prove successful in motivating all of their students and assure their schooling success. Rather than getting specific strategies for success in which they sought, they spent time in their classes discussing and reading about the subjugation of people of color and the privilege of whites. Many of the participants were frustrated at what they called a "theoretical approach." They were willing to examine the social structures that were in place to grant privileges to some while denying it to others, yet when they were asked to think about the ways they were personally granted access to advantages, they resisted both the ideologies of their readings and the instructors themselves who asked them to contemplate their own social positioning.

Once they began their practicum and student teaching work in the schools, however, they began to understand the complexity of working with children who had their own life experiences and understandings of the world. When they first began working with children, the participants thought they could inspire their students to learn by simply sharing their knowledge through engaging lessons. What they quickly learned was that their students had their own ideas about how they were viewed by their teachers. How the students saw themselves as learners in the school as well as how they were positioned as individuals in the world also impacted the ways the students imagined and experienced their academic success or failure.

Oftentimes the participants' students willingly shared their stories of subjugation by authority figures within the school. In turn, the participants came to see the power that teachers have to influence the success or lack of success that students have in their schooling. And by listening to their students, the participants came to understand that they as teachers are accountable and responsible to their students for how they use their power. This was quite different from their experiences in their courses where they read about interactions between students and teachers. As Bakhtin (1993) claims, "the actually performed act in its individual wholeness is more than rational—it is answerable" (p. 29). While the participants may have been inspired by their course readings, they were still standing outside individual stories about others' teaching moments looking in from a different time and space. The actual performed act to which Bahktin refers involves real interactions with real people.

The participants' actual engagements with their students taught them the importance of considering how their students might react in response to their actions as teachers—and the consequences if they do not acknowledge the other in their interactions. Therefore, in thinking about their teacher identity, they began to consider not only the ways their point of view may affect their students, but the ways that their students' point of view were beginning to and would continue to affect them.

The participants came to understand that a teacher identity is shaped from the process of teaching, not from a fixed set of rules about crafting their practice. As they contemplated pedagogy, they began to rethink their initial question. With their gained experiential knowledge from working with students, they began to expand their initial question (how should I act?) to asking: *how should I act responsibly knowing that there is someone whom I am addressing that can answer me back?* Drawing on Nolan's (2004) explanation of the question of ethics, what the participants actually came to be seeking was an understanding of how to act, "not because of [their] duty, or out of [their] own interests, but how [they] should act in a specific situation knowing that each act or deed is an instance of [their] whole life history acted with others who can answer back" (p. 3). Furthermore, the participants began to see the question of: *who am I being while I'm doing?* takes on just as much importance as *how should I act.*

From their interactions with their cooperating teachers, they began to see that every word spoken and every action taken was actually a performance of an ideology that teachers had about what it means to be a teacher and what it means to be a student. From actual engagement with their students, they also came to understand that their students were animated beings with whom the participants were answerable to and for the decisions that they made on a daily basis through their interactions with their students.

TEACHER EDUCATION PROGRAM

I get it. I am a child of white privilege

—Lauren

Without exception, each of the participants felt the Teacher Education Program at State University prepared them to teach a racially diverse group of students. Like many of the participants, Alex felt that they "had some really good TA's and professors" who facilitated "some really important discussions." Yet many also had concerns about the manner with which diversity was presented and discussed within the program. Desiree explains that most of the teacher education students went into education because they have always wanted to be teachers; they weren't thinking about the link between social position and teaching. She says, "It's just assumed that we have and that we are going into education to promote equity and justice. It's not like we don't want to do that. We just never thought that deeply about it before coming into the program." It is in the first class they take in the program, Introduction to Education, where they are first confronted with thinking about their own social status as well as the social status of the students they will teach.

During the first semester class, Emma remembers everyone feeling uncomfortable. She explains that it is difficult to talk about racial advantage and disadvantage when the majority of the students are middle class, whites who come from small towns. She says, "We also had two or three students who were not white, and I think everyone was on their tiptoes not wanting to say anything offensive even though some of the things in their backgrounds are not that positive toward non-whites." Many of the students in the class directed their comments and questions to the two students who did not identify as white asking them to speak on behalf of their race.

Additionally, several of the required readings for the class dealt with white privilege. Emma thinks this is good yet confesses, "At times I want to say, 'Yeah, I know it is all out there. But does that really shape every aspect of everything that happens in the world?'" She talks about feeling guilty for being white. This guilt often works to make her feel helpless as well as hopeless. In frustration, she runs her fingers through her hair and says, "It's like where do I go from here? It's like, yes, I know I'm privileged, but unless I'm given the tools and strategies, the practical things that I can use to make the situation better, I tend to put my fingers in my ears and say, 'I can't take it anymore! It's just too upsetting! Enough! I can't have this same discussion again'."

Like Emma, Lauren feels some frustration contemplating her white privilege. In reflecting about her classes at the university, she is frustrated that the discussions regarding discrimination centered on race. She says she often felt like saying, "I get it. I am a child of white privilege." She expresses her concern that the instructor never asks the students questions about themselves: "He assumed that we were all white—all of us did not identify that way. He assumed that all of us wanted to teach in the suburbs. It was like he never asked us anything about ourselves. He just made assumptions about what he knew about white people, but not the white people in front of him."

Alex has similar feelings about discussing white privilege in class although he speaks of how other people reacted rather than his own feelings. He finds the idea of the evil white man in the suburbs foregrounded in the course readings and discussions. He remembers that there were people who felt personally attacked and unjustly demonized because they were white and from the suburbs. He says, "I think a lot of the kids in the cohort thought, 'Hey wait a second. You're talking about me here. I worked my butt off to get here. I want to help kids. Don't make me the bad guy'."

Emma and Lauren express frustration regarding what they perceived as attempts to make them feel guilty for being white. Alex observes the same guilt feelings from his classmates. Bush (2004) argues that many whites, when confronted with considering the ways white privilege has advantaged them will either deny or quickly dismiss the subject. She argues that this dismissal is often caused by whites feeling overwhelmed by the possibility that their own group affiliation, at least to some degree, holds them responsible for denying opportunities to others. Both Emma's desire to plug her ears and Lauren's desire to scream out, "I get it," demonstrate their overwhelming need turn away from seeing their own whiteness and its implications.

Additionally, as Alex explains his perceptions of his classmates taking offense, "Wait a second, you're talking about me here" he demonstrates a degree of denial in their personal privilege inherited from their group affiliation. This suggests that while it may be acceptable to talk about white privilege ideologically, it is not ok to talk about it personally. Iyer, Leach and Pederson (2004) contend this is common behavior when whites develop feelings of guilt. The authors argue that "the relatively self-focused nature of guilt makes it seem more a selfish concern for one's own pain than a sympathetic concern for others" (p. 346). Rather than examining white privilege from the perspective of the non-white in order to develop a sympathetic viewpoint, whites often direct the discussion in a manner that focuses on the white perspective.

Additionally, Iyer et al. (2004) suggest that whites often challenge the reasons they feel guilty in order to alleviate any discomfort they feel. This is evidenced in the ways that many of the students in the class direct their discomfort in the form of anger at the instructor. The matter became more complicated with the participants in this study as the teacher about whom they spoke was a person of color.

Desiree explains that while she found the teacher amazing because he altered her thinking, she points out that "everyone chose to argue with him.

He was just in our face with a different perspective and for some people that was too much. So maybe his approach was too aggressive." In speaking of the same teacher whom she found aggressive, Emma says, "I don't think that's the way you win someone over. You can't attack things like family values or community ideals–things that are central to who people are—and expect them to just give up those things so easily." Lauren describes her instructor as standing on a pulpit telling them what to believe. She says this was "a little much."

Being critical of teachers of color rather than their message is one act of resistance that many white students adopt. This is a way for white students to "reclaim their perceived sense of loss of white privilege at the hands of their non-white professors" or instructors (Balderrama, 2008, p. 37). Accusations of the instructor being "too aggressive" or "in our face" or "preaching from a pulpit", as well as accusing the instructor of making unsubstantiated assumptions suggest they felt the instructor was incompetent. They justify their criticisms by attacking the instructor's approach rather than his message. By attacking the instructor who was a person of color, they were repositioning their whiteness as the dominant voice of authority in the classroom.

Another form of resistance comes when students attempt to usurp the instructor's authority as the expert in the class. Balderrama (2008) argues that resistant white students will often question "the structure of the curriculum, the relevance of the readings, and the choice of readings" in order to challenge the teacher's expertise and competence. Several of the participants spoke of spending too much time reading about white privilege and having one-sided discussions. And they talked about wanting to alter the required course readings to include other forms of discrimination. However, as Balderrama contends, "The course syllabus represents the instructor's expertise, and by challenging it, the students were attempting to "impose their supposed 'expertise'—the course outline becomes a symbolic struggle for power and authority in the classroom" (p. 37).

SOCIAL JUSTICE—THEORY AND PRACTICE

> *We talk a lot about social justice, but when it comes down to it, it is really about how we treat others*
>
> —Desiree

Lauren says, "We hear over and over again, 'You should teach for social justice. I'm never going to tell you exactly what that is, but you should do it'." This is a common experience for prospective teachers at State University. What students appear to be looking for is a quick, one dimensional, and fixed definition from which to develop their practice. In speaking of her classes where students were asked to think about social positioning, their own as well as their students, Emma says, "It's like where do I go from here? It's like . . .unless I'm given the tools and strategies, the practical things that I can use to make the situation better, I tend to put my fingers in my ears. . . . I want to know how I can fix it in the school I am working in right now."

Yet, learning to teach for social justice is a process that one develops over a lifetime. Darling-Hammond (2002) describes learning to teach for social justice as

> coming to understand oneself in relation to others; examining how society constructs privilege and inequality and how this affects one's opportunities as well as those of different people; exploring the experiences of others and appreciating how those inform worldviews, perspectives, and opportunities and evaluating how schools and classrooms operate and can be structured to value diverse human experiences and to enable learning for all students. (p. 201)

This certainly is something one cannot develop in one semester or even in the course of a single Teacher Education Certification Program. Rather it requires constant reflection of who one is as a teacher and who the students are that one will be teaching each year. It requires both reflection about social spaces (one's own and one's students') as well as being a change agent in order to make the school and classroom a place for "forging new possibilities in meaningful and dynamic and healing ways" (Keiser, 2005, p. 32)

Despite not being given a textbook, easily digestible definition, the participants came to develop an understanding of what teaching for social justice meant to them at this juncture in their careers. Through the contemplation of their course readings and class discussions and by experiencing the ways that social justice was enacted or ignored in their practicum and student teaching sites, they were able to formulate their own notion of what it means to be a socially just practitioner. Many talked about the ways they saw notions of social justice incorporated into the classrooms by their cooperating teachers as well as how they were able to practice social justice in their student teaching and personal interactions with students. Some also shared some of the concerns they have being able to challenge injustice when they witnessed it by their fellow teachers as well as from student to student.

Desiree on Social Justice

> "We talk a lot about social justice, but when it comes down to it, it is really about how we treat others. It's nothing magical. We need to think about how we understand them, how we handle situations, rethinking why things are the way they are. Those things influence how we react and what we do. I think teachers have to be listening to what their kids are saying because that gives insights into what they are thinking.

Teachers shouldn't tell their kids what to think, but we have to get them thinking about different things. It's really about showing them different perspectives. I don't think you can possibly ensure that kids will leave your room thinking about equity and justice. But teachers have to bring up these things within the curriculum and create environments where it is ok to talk about these things."

When Desiree is accused of being a racist by Becky, a female African American student, she is floored. Becky's grandmother was helping out at the school, and when Becky introduced Desiree to her grandmother, she said, "This is Miss Desiree. She doesn't like black kids." Desiree accuses Becky of lying and tells her that that isn't true. She can not recall ever doing anything to Becky that would make her feel that way. She talks about feeling as if Becky were "pulling the race card." When Desiree confronts her in front of her grandmother, Becky says, "You say things like—all you black kids, you need to pay attention. She never says it to the white kids."

Desiree had developed a friendship with a male African American teacher whom she felt was very honest with her about her perceived presence in the classroom. He warns her that "kids will say things about you. Parents will say things about you. I've had parents say to me, 'I'm so glad that you're black. My kid doesn't respond to a white teacher'." When she speaks to him about her experience with Becky, he tells her that as a white teacher, she needs to be more conscious of what she says and does in the classroom as well as what she doesn't say or do. He advises her that she needs to think about who she is and what she represents to her students as a white teacher in a school that is made up predominantly of students of color. Cautioning her, he suggests that she makes a conscious effort to be thinking about who is listening to what she is saying and how they might be hearing it.

This conversation causes Desiree to reflect on her relationships with African Americans. She defines social justice as being able to think about how people understand one another and how they handle situations. This is exactly what she has begun doing. Although she says she has no problem talking to the African American fathers at conferences, she recognizes that when they come to see her at the school, she is in her comfort zone. She fears that if she saw them on the street, she might be afraid that they would cause her harm because they are black and she is white. This contradiction bothers her; "I am really, really ashamed when these feeling creep up. I feel like such a fraud. . . . I think I never wanted to admit that, but if I'm going to be honest, that is who I am."

Yet becoming aware of these previously hidden feelings is what Desiree believes has made her committed to teaching for social justice. She explains that she sees herself as an introspective person, but is saddened that she is thinking about her subversive racist attitudes for the first time. She wants to work with young children because, as she says, "I'd like kids to be able to work through these things at a much younger age than I am."

Additionally, she has concerns about what her boundaries are as a white teacher. In speaking about her students, she asks, "Do you challenge everything that comes out of their mouths? What do I say to the biracial African American/ Korean boy who calls himself Blackie Chan? Do I make him stop? Do I have a right to impose my perceptions about the N word when I hear African American boys call each other that? How does that work when you are a white woman?" While Desiree admits that she does not have all of the answers and solutions she would like to have, she has begun contemplating how her actions might align with her teaching ideologies.

Emma on Social Justice

"Educating in a socially just way means you have to treat all children fairly. It may not be equal, but it has to be fair. You have to give each child what they need and not everyone needs the same thing at the same time. . . . I also think it means making all kids feel valued. Their cultures should be accepted and respected. You do this by making things relevant and interesting. By bringing their home cultures into the school culture. You get kids talking about racial issues, and economic issues—those kinds of things. You get them to do more reflecting on experiences in their own lives."

During her student teaching experience, Emma witnesses a racial conflict between two African American girls who are fighting. The lighter-skinned girl kept telling the darker skinned girl to "go back to Africa." Emma overhears her cooperating teacher angrily telling them to stop. Taking them aside, he explains the story of how white slave owners used to tell African slaves their skin was ugly to make them feel inferior. The girls immediately stopped. In reflection, Emma comments that "It was really good for me to see a white teacher have the guts to step into that. I think a lot of times white teachers do not know how to respond when African American kids make racially insensitive comments to one another."

Emma also tells about an African American girl who doesn't like white people telling her what to do and often accuses them of being racists. Again, she witnesses her cooperating teacher take initiative and talk with the student about her concerns. Although she remembers that this same young girl did not like her, she says, "I quickly made it a personal project of mine to get her to like me. She's a great kid, but she just doesn't like to do anything you tell her to do." So, Emma explores and successfully discovers different ways to motivate the student to do her work. For example, instead of telling the student what to do in an authoritative manner, Emma discovers that asking her to do something and then explaining to her why it would be helpful to her and the rest of the class, the student is more cooperative.

Through the modeling of her cooperating teacher, she is able to see how a white teacher might interrupt issues of racism with her students. Emma understands that her cooperating teacher values his students by witnessing him listening to them, challenging their racist comments, asking them to reflect and letting them talk about their concerns regarding race. Emily's experiences with her cooperating teacher reflect her idea of social justice This is evidenced when she examines her preconceptions about an African American student and changes her interactions with the young girl to give the student what she needed to succeed.

Alex on Social Justice:

"For me that is what teaching for social justice is. It's about bringing the world into the classroom. It's about getting kids thinking about their own place in the world and how to change that place for their own betterment. It's about teachers making the space for that to happen by listening to all perspectives. It's about teaching kids to make that space for others, too. It's about open dialogue as a first step to creating change."

Alex has what he calls a "life altering" experience while teaching in Chicago. He speaks of going into the summer job thinking he was going to change the lives of his students with his exceptional teaching abilities. Instead, he contemplates quitting in the third week. With uninspired students and no support from his cooperating teacher, he is forced to examine his own practice. One of his ideas is to have the students examine their own neighborhood and examine the correlation between the high incidence of poverty and the high crime rate. After discovering their interest in hip hop music, he asks them to research their favorite musician and study the lyrics of their favorite songs. But, Alex is still unsettled by what he calls his students' "blatant racism toward me." Early on in his experience, they start calling him "cracker" "white boy" and "whitey." One girl refuses to call him anything but "boy." He recalls, "I made the summer in Chicago about me. But I think a lot of my ego was attached to them being successful and them liking me. Those things are important still, but I am also concerned about their futures."

When Alex is bringing their world into the classroom, he describes his teaching as culturally responsive. This is part of what he describes in his understanding of social justice. He is able to see that because he connects his lessons to their lives, they become better able to see themselves as learners. In this sense, he helps them see a way to change their place in the world through education. Yet, by centering his own social positioning as a white male within the classroom, he is unable to make a space for an open dialogue about race. This prevents his development as a socially just educator.

Upon reflection, Alex says he learned a great deal from the experience. When he was in Chicago, he tried to direct much of the learning and discussion, but has learned to be more of a discussion facilitator. He also has learned to help his students be more reflective. He explains, "I understand that the kids I am going to teach are young minds. And that sometimes they will say things that might be offensive because they haven't thought deeply enough about the issues I would like to bring up. And I can't be afraid to have those conversations. . . . It's better to use your authority to interrupt behaviors than to use your authority to silence any discussion."

Lauren on Social Justice:

"I guess that's kind of what social justice is all about. It's touching on the culture of each child in the classroom. It's about having these kinds of personal moments with kids. It's about breaking down stereotypes. It's about being conscious of how we talk about differences. It's teaching kids to critically look at things, and then critically analyze those things in the world around them. This has to be done in the curriculum as well. First kids need to see themselves reflected in the curriculum. And then they need to connect the curriculum to the larger world."

Lauren tells about working with an African American boy whom she says gets pulled out of class quite a bit for special help in math and literacy. She tells that one day when she is helping him with his math, he tells her that he hates math because his math teacher is a racist. When she asks why he thinks that, he won't tell her at first. After he shares the details about an experience with the math teacher, she tells him that she will go with him to talk to the teacher if it happens again. Then he tells her, "The people in this school, they really—they really just don't like black people. I want to go to a school where there's less white kids because I don't like all of these white people." He explains that the white teachers are more concerned about correcting his English than about listening to what he is saying.

In reflection, she sees how he is called out for correction more often than the other students in the class. She says, "All day long you hear, "LeBron go over to Special Ed now. LeBron, keep working. LeBron, why are you out of your seat again? LeBron, you were late coming in for recess." Additionally, he tells that "no one gets me. No one gets how I talk, how I dress, no one likes my music." Lauren sees this as an important moment. After he tells her that he likes hip hop music, she shares that she does, too and they have a discussion about music. She says that ever since that day, "he calls me by name instead of calling me, 'Hey you.' I feel like we really connected."

As a socially just prospective educator, Lauren explains that she thinks it is important to have personal moments with students where stereotypes are broken down. Because she was able to spend one on one time with LeBron, they were able connect and have a sincere discussion where he could share how he felt about the way he was treated at the school, and she was able to be an adult figure to whom he could confide. By listening to his concerns and offering to help him confront racist behavior directed toward him, she was becoming, by her definition, more socially just through being more conscious of thinking about the ways differences are discussed and dealt with in the school environment.

Sarah on Social Justice:

"Obviously we don't live in a world that is fair or a nation that is fair. And if you look within small communities, there are definitely huge discrepancies. I think what I want to do is bring in more of the local. I mean you want to look at the big picture, but it would be good to look at the way things are on a local level, too. You know, ask kids how they see things and then build off of that. So, I guess I think teaching for social justice means teaching to educate students to look at the world around them. Even if a community seems the same, you don't have to look that far outside of the community to see all kinds of diversity. I don't know. I just see the world changing, and people really need to accept these differences and understand them.

I think we need to honor the students' perspectives and then try to bring in other perspectives. You could do that by bringing in many perspectives on a topic. You could bring outside speakers in. You could bring in movie clips or something from YouTube. Or an excerpt from a novel. It's all about having them experience ways of looking at things that they are not familiar with."

Sarah shares a story about co-teaching about the Declaration of Independence with her cooperating teacher. She explains that her cooperating teacher focused on the meaning of the text itself rather than having the students consider deeper, often unsaid, things in the text. After the cooperating teacher passes over the phrase, "All men are created equal," Sarah interrupts and asks the students to think about who isn't being talked about. The students start giving answers, "Black men. Women. Men who didn't own land." She tells me, "I was so frustrated that we were focusing on the document alone when there was so much more we could have gone into."

This is not uncommon behavior from her cooperating teacher. Sarah explains, "My cooperating teacher just kind of slides away from anything that she thinks is too controversial. Like if anything about race comes up, she skids away from it. I would bring it up. I would say, 'Let's talk about it. What do you see in the community? Where do you see this in the media?' I would ask questions and have students discuss things and bring in their own experiences."

Sarah understands teaching for social justice as bringing the world into the classroom. She shares that she would create a space where students could connect what they are learning to what they are seeing in the world around them—in the community and in the media. She will ask them to share their experiences. In this way students can experience hearing multiple perspectives. Sarah has come to frame notions of social justice around having students look at the world in ways they may not be familiar with. While she does not have the chance to see this modeled during her preservice experiences in the schools, Sarah is committed to crafting her own practice to reflect her notions of a socially just pedagogy.

WHAT THIS SAYS ABOUT IDENTITY

The experiences that the participants have in their courses at State University are a catalyst for them to think about how social ideologies shape how one comes to understand the self and be understood as a student and a teacher. As mentioned in Chapter 2, Bakhtin (1993) asserts that two factors are significant when contemplating the self. The first he calls the *emotional volitional tone*—the sincerity one feels (or doesn't feel). The second he calls the *non-alibi in Being* in which individuals regard the self without making excuses or justifications for the decisions that they have made or will make. Through their practicum and student teaching experiences, the participants are faced with making sense of their emotional responses to their encounters with their students. Additionally, through face to face experiences (and in some cases confrontations) with both their fellow students and cooperating teachers, they begin to see that they are accountable for their attitudes, perceptions and choices. This heightened consciousness of responsibility from which they choose to view and interact with the world represents the emergence of the participants' ethical selves within the framework of teacher.

Bakhtin (1993) argues that when determining how to act, "the ought becomes possible for the first time where there is an acknowledgment of the fact of a unique person's being within the person; where this fact becomes the center for answerability—where I assume answerability for my own uniqueness, for my own being" (p. 42). When determining what one ought to do in a given moment, Bakhtin claims that the ethical choice for the individual can be discerned when the individual sees the uniqueness of the self as well as the uniqueness of the other and is prepared to respond to the other who might question his or her choice. While the participants are originally looking for a formulaic pedagogy that will tell them how to teach in a socially just manner, they quickly learn that no single script can account for their own uniqueness or the uniqueness of their individual students. They are beginning to see that teaching is as much about who they are as what they teach.

In reflection, they realize that the classes in their program are designed to help them understand the cultural nuances that their students bring to the classroom. Yet even with the clarity from hindsight, they still feel unprepared to consider the ways their own understandings and worldviews might bump up against their students'. While the participants are comfortable contemplating and discussing white privilege in the abstract sense, they resist looking within their own life experiences to see how they might be constructed by others and how their whiteness shapes how they view those who they see as different from themselves.

They also resist their instructors who ask them to sincerely consider their own positioning without rationalizing their life circumstances. In fact so strong are the participants' reactions to seeing and hearing the ways that whiteness makes itself known in the lives of people of color and to taking any ownership for they advantages they have received from institutionalized white dominance, they feel a need to attack the messengers—their instructor and peers of color. Rather than sincerely listening to the stories and concerns that their instructors and peers of color share about their own subjugation and then situating themselves within the oppression, the participants choose to make excuses or recuse themselves from the behavior attributing oppression to other whites, but not themselves. When they do see themselves as part of a privileged class, they are left paralyzed with guilt looking for someone to give them a way out.

The specific course which the participants criticize is designed to help them take responsibility for how their positioning in the world shapes the choices that they make and are able to make. It is to this premise that they initially have resistance. At the time the participants were in their courses, they could not always see the intention behind the curriculum of their classes. The content of the specific course which they spoke of is designed to emphasize the idea that in order to truly see the "other" one must first truly see the self. The instructor was asking the pre-service teachers to see themselves situated in the larger world and to acknowledge and own the values that they came to know as truth.

When people can see the self within the larger world, without making excuses for the social conditions that exist, they can begin to see their acts as answerable. In other words, they begin to contemplate how they might engage with the other in their actual thoughts, words and acts. Yet part of the resistance to the ideologies presented in the participants' classes is due to the fact that they are not forced to have an active engagement with the "other." While the instructor is a person of color and there are a few students of color in their class, the participants can easily ignore (and many chose to do just that) the ways that whiteness is understood and experienced on a personal level by the people of color in their class. For most of them, the notion of white privilege is not real in their experiences. So on the occasion when one of the people of color shares his or her experiences of being marginalized by whites, the participants assume they are talking about overt forms of oppression by racist whites, not by people like them. Yet Bakhtin (1993) argues "an answerable act or deed alone surmounts anything hypothetical, for the answerable act is, after all, the actualization of a decision—inescapably, irremediably, and irrevocably" (p. 28). It is not until they are forced to actively engage with people of color—the students in the schools—that they are given the opportunity to see themselves not just as teachers but as *white* teachers through the eyes of students of color. In this sense many of the participants are afforded a surplus of vision that helps them contemplate their social position in a new way.

Yet without being given a language to make sense of the surplus of vision that they are given, the participants often feel ill-equipped to interrogate their experiences and form new meaning regarding their encounters with people of color. What the participants appear to be missing from their classes is a way to talk about and implement the ideas of social justice. Only two of the participants have mentors in their schools who take the time to talk with them about their experiences or model appropriate ways to interrupt racist words or behaviors showing them how a teacher might address concerns surrounding race.

It is only from being described as a racist teacher that Desiree is forced to consider the impact of her white skin on her students' perceptions of her. She is told by a fellow teacher (a person of color) that she must be cognizant of how she is being heard and interpreted and to be aware of how she presents herself to her students. He shares stories of how people of color in the community explained to him how they construct white teachers. By framing his conversation in this way, he is providing Desiree a surplus of vision that can help her see that she must own all of her interactions with students, parents, and community members because they are, indeed, all answerable. While she still wrestles with her own internalized racism, she is willing to confront hidden racist beliefs when they surface and admits that she will have to constantly work on challenging her assumptions about herself and others.

Emma's cooperating teacher provides her the chance to see firsthand how a white teacher might interrupt racial tensions between students of color. She is able to witness how white cultural dominance can infect the self-esteem of students of color. By observing two students of color use the shade of their skin to assume dominance over the other, she comes to see one way that whiteness is perceived by non-whites. She bears witness to her white cooperating teacher share one of the shames of whiteness. Emma is able to transfer this understanding to how she might be perceived by her students of color—as an oppressive force in the classroom. She uses this new knowledge to reach one of her African American students who claims to hate white people. While she is able to make a connection with one student, as she continues with her teaching career, Emma will have to continue to understand how her performance of whiteness is perceived by the people of color in her school community in order to incorporate these types of connections with all of her students.

Most of the participants attempt to make meaning from their experiences. While in Chicago, Alex also has an opportunity to see himself as a white teacher through the eyes of his students of color. By being referred to as "whitey," "white boy," and "cracker," Alex is forced to contemplate the ways that he might be understood by his students of color. He spends a summer working in an urban school in Chicago with pre-conceived notions about his students of color. He believes he is going into the school as a savior who will inspire his students to look past their life circumstances and work to impress him. He has a rude awakening when his students challenge him to acknowledge the assumptions he makes about them. They demand that he see himself how they see him—a privileged white male from a world largely different from their own.

Alex is forced to do some self-reflection and reconsider his notions about teaching and learning in a more sincere manner. He quickly learns that if he turns away from what his students of color are trying to help him see, he will remain in the dark and never be the teacher he imagines himself to be. While Alex holds hope for his students, his greatest struggle seems to be getting past the idea that he needs to save his students from themselves. When he ultimately realizes that he is answerable to his students, he begins to shift his paradigm of what it means to be a white teacher working with children of color.

Lauren's experience with LeBron gives her the opportunity to see how a student of color views the white authority figures within the school. She capitalizes on her private time with him to sincerely listen to his concerns and see him in his uniqueness. In this she is able to make a personal connection with him which results in LeBron seeing her as an ally. While this is an important moment in which Lauren sympathizes with a student of color, she does not see how her own whiteness is enacted with LeBron when she tells him that she will go with him to talk to the teacher. This sends him the tacit message that not only does he need a savior, but that he needs a white savior. Unlike Alex's story, in the telling of her story, Lauren does not speak of contemplating how she is part of the white adult community at the school which is often seen as the oppressor by students of color. As long as she limits herself to special moments where she can connect with one student of color at a time offering to protect them from other whites, she runs the risk of never examining her own social positioning—never seeing herself with the clarity needed to truly see her students.

Like Lauren, Sarah's experiences with her white cooperating teacher leads her to see herself as white person separate from other whites. She anguishes over the ways her cooperating teacher overlooks powerful moments where she can integrate the students' local knowledge with curricular content. When she does interrupt her cooperating teacher's discussion about the "Declaration of Independence" with the intent to talk about various forms of discrimination, she finds the students eager to participate affirming her belief that teachers need to connect the curriculum to the students' life experiences. She honors her students' personal and cultural knowledge, but she does so at a distance. As with Lauren, in all of Sarah's stories about her teaching experiences, she speaks only of her students, never addressing her own understanding of the world as it relates to her social positioning and teacher identity. Instead, she focuses her energy on the lives of her students (an honorable endeavor) but does not contemplate how her new understandings push her to think about her own identity. Neither Sarah nor Lauren has the opportunity to see herself refracted through the eyes of her students. Each one's focus remains only on the whiteness of other teachers, not her own. In this way neither has to seriously contemplate or be answerable for her social positioning or privilege.

Building on their experiences at the university and in the practicum and student teaching sites, all of the participants develop a notion of social justice to which they plan to craft their teaching practices. For all of them, providing opportunities for their students to reflect on their own positioning as well as the world around them is an important component of social justice. Many speak of honoring their students' perspectives and understandings of the world. Most share that helping their students develop respect for cultural differences is a key factor in the socially just classroom.

Indeed, the participants have incorporated many salient points of what a socially just pedagogy looks like from which to develop their emerging teacher identity. As Nielson (2002) contends, "the connection between the responsibility of the actor and the authoring of others is that each takes into consideration the animateness of the existence of the I in the other" (p. 69). And while they are still unsure if they will be the teachers they imagine themselves to be, they are at the very least in their own way beginning to forge a teacher self that is grounded in a notion of the inter-relatedness of the self and the other.

14 Merging the Past and Present

Bahktin's work on dialogism gives us a way to look at teacher candidates' emerging teacher identities within their larger life experience. As we've seen, for Bahktin, becoming is a dialogic process in which individuals come to author themselves by assimilating the words, values and attitudes of persons and ideologies with which they have come in contact throughout their lives. The dialogism to which Bakhtin speaks calls for a social interaction, an actual engagement with others, where individuals learn and determine how to act in their daily interactions with others.

White pre-service teachers come to the field of education with a lifetime of dialogic experiences that influence their ideas of what it means to be white in a diverse world. In particular, looking at the ways that ideologies of white privilege inflect teacher candidates' understanding of the world and their position in it provides insights into how they have come to author themselves. Examining the language they use to talk about their life experiences offers a glimpse into the ways that the normalization of white privilege shapes their interactions with others as well as their emerging identities as educators. Furthermore, interrogating the stories they choose to tell can suggest possible points of conflict where teacher educators can interrupt dysconscious patterns of thought and behavior in order to help pre-service teachers see all of their students and their needs in a more conscious manner.

By bringing to light perceived biases in their pre-service teachers' stories, teacher educators can be a catalyst for teacher candidates to be able to critically reflect on their own choices. Britzman (2003) argues that in considering teacher identity, we must begin with "the recognition that multiple realities, voices and discourses conjoin and clash in the process of coming to know" (p. 49). Indeed, understanding how identity takes shape for individuals, requires an examination of "what they make happen because of what has happened to them and what it is that structures their practices" (p. 70). In regards to white teacher candidates, this examination should lead to developing an understanding of the ways discourses work in and through them culminating in perspectives which shape their developing pedagogies and future curriculum design.

Obviously, none of the participants have had life experiences that completely mirror each other. Yet, there are common themes that emerge within their life circumstances. All grew up in a predominantly white neighborhood and most never had to seriously contemplate the non-white other or their own whiteness. In their K–12 schooling they were viewed as good students, placed in honors programs, and educated to learn dominant ideologies reinforcing their white privilege. Most were forced to see the implications of race for the first time, both their own race and the race of others, when they came to the university. All began to grapple with making sense of their own position in a racially diverse world by seeing what they were and what they were not. And all of the participants came to identify as advocates for social justice within the educational system. From seeing how they were viewed by their students of color and contemplating how they could develop their practice and interact with students in a way that represented the teacher they imagined themselves to be, they came to see themselves as agents for change.

Through the interrogation of the participants' stories in this study, teacher educators can gain insight into how white teacher candidates understand and respond to those who are racially different from themselves. It is a worthy and noble goal to help white teacher candidates consider their own lives as well as understand white privilege. It is also important to help them contemplate the life circumstances and experiences of the oppressed in order to develop their cultural awareness. Some teacher candidates might even see the moral reasons to become more culturally and socially aware; however, without a more compelling reason than personal growth, many pre-service teachers will develop their own practices in much the same way they were taught.

It is not enough to help white teachers recognize and understand their own bias thoughts and behaviors. With the population becoming more and more culturally diverse, it is imperative that teacher educators help pre-service teachers move beyond their own self-understanding to advocate for their minority and underserved students who will make up a considerable portion of the future work force. Teacher educators need to facilitate their pre-service teachers' exploration of their life experiences, their conscious and dysconscious thoughts and behaviors with regard to those who are racially different from themselves. This is important so that teacher educators can help pre-service teachers become advocates for the many culturally diverse and underserved students who do not have the same advantages that they have had. Armed with this awareness, teacher educators can then help pre-service teachers develop appropriate pedagogical approaches, frame curriculum content which is accessible for all students, and create a supportive social context of learning for all students, but especially marginalized populations.

REFLECTIONS ON TEACHER EDUCATION PROGRAMS

If you don't think about where you are initially coming from, how do you know how to move forward?

—Emma

At the time of our final meeting, the participants had just completed the Teacher Education Program and many were thinking ahead to the end of the summer when they would be beginning their first year of teaching. I asked them to reflect on the program as a whole and make suggestions for how they thought the program could be made more meaningful for future pre-service teachers. I found them to be candid in their answers.

What seems to go without question was that the participants felt they had been adequately prepared to teach specific subjects. They felt that their methods classes prepared them to master the content of specific disciplines which they believed would help them develop a curriculum that fostered the intellectual development of their students. They also believed that through their methods classes, they were given a foundational understanding of how to create a curriculum that was Multicultural. They had a notion, albeit somewhat limited, of developing practices that were sensitive to the cultural needs of their students. One of the ways they felt the program was lacking, however, was in giving them space to reflect on their experiences in contrast to the experiences many of their culturally diverse students would bring to the classroom. Their experience in this particular Teacher Education Program is not unique. As seen in Chapter 2, many Schools of Education throughout the country expose their students to the concept of Multiculturalism through course work and practicum experiences. But in these situations, white students often study non-whites as "others" without seeing the role whiteness plays in a culturally diverse society.

Several of the participants suggested that the pre-service teachers should be asked to do more self-reflection. Desiree thought Teacher Education Programs "need to start with understanding your own perspectives in order to begin to see value in other perspectives." In teacher education classes throughout the country, teacher candidates are often asked to reflect on their past and present ideas about culture and education. Britzman (2003) contends that

> theorizing about such connections allows individuals a double insight into the meanings of their relationships to individuals, institutions, cultural values, and political events, and into how these relationships interpellate the individual's identity, values and ideological orientations. (p. 232)

Although reflection is a good practice, the participants in this study saw the need to move beyond contemplating ideologies as separate from themselves.

Most of the participants wanted more opportunities throughout the program to reflect on their own lives. Emma said, "I would have liked to write more about my own life experiences, and I would have liked to have heard from my classmates. I think that is a really crucial part of learning to teach for social justice. Without doing reflection about your own life, what's the point about learning about other cultures? If you don't think about where you are initially coming from, how do you know how to move forward?"

Like Emma, Lauren also wished she had more of an opportunity to examine herself and her background "like I was able to do in these interviews." She felt that there was a lot of emphasis on the students she would be teaching, but not enough on herself as educator. As discussed in Chapter 2, many teacher educators have begun asking prospective teachers to write their personal biographies with the idea that individuals' personal socialization processes will reveal how their present identities have been shaped.

Indeed, the process of writing a biography can offer writers a chance to consider their life experiences and potentially gain a richer understanding of themselves as future educators. Goodson and Sikes (2001) argue that

> given that teachers play the key role in interpreting, mediating, and realizing what goes on in educational institutions, their values, motivations and understandings have considerable influence on professional practices of all kinds" and that life history "enables exploration, the tracing and tracking of influences, through the way in which it attempts to take an holistic approach to individuals in the various contexts they inhibit. (p. 57)

Because teachers play a large role in what they teach their students and what their students learn, it is important that teachers explore the ways in which their social and racial positioning inform their practices and the ways that they interact with and respond to the needs of all of their students. Alsup (2006) suggests that when pre-service teachers have the opportunity to partake in critical reflection they "might be able to avoid replaying the same old tapes and imitating the teachers of their youth, and might be able to modify the often stagnant cultural model in significant ways" (p. 45).

Moreover, teacher educators need to provide opportunities for pre-service teachers to explore the implications of their whiteness as prospective educators in an increasingly racially diverse world of learners. As McIntyre (1997) warns, the reality is that "the white classroom teacher can 'perform the multicultural tricks while never having to critique her positionality as a beneficiary of the U.S. educational system" (p. 13). Exploring the ideologies and enactment of white privilege juxtaposed with the marginalization of people of color can help pre-service teachers understand the often unspoken reasons why so many culturally diverse students struggle in schools.

The interrogation of their experiences in contrast with those of marginalized students can help white teachers understand the urgent need to develop pedagogies and practices that may look different from when they were in school. As the population of students grows to be increasingly culturally diverse, teachers need to reflect on the ways that their life experiences, specifically with schooling, may be very different from the students with whom they will teach. As Abt-Perkins and Gomez (1998) argue "to understand the possible connections between their students' heritages" and their learning, "teachers have to first recognize such connections in their own lives" (p. 12). Teacher educators need to help teacher candidates merge their past experiences with a broader understanding of the ways that their culturally diverse students experience the world.

Another suggestion the participants had was that pre-service teachers need to have class time to share their life histories with their peers and have meaningful conversations about their experiences. Sarah talked about writing biographies, but did not remember talking about "how our biographies made us see the world. We just wrote it for ourselves and the teacher." While it is true that in some cases, they were writing for the teacher who could respond to their written word, none spoke of having the opportunity to dialogue with the teacher about what they had written. They simply turned in a paper and read the teacher's response. In this sense the teacher became the authoritative voice who was the sole person to which the writer was accountable.

Practices like this are what perpetuate the use of what students call "politically correct" language. Writers write for audiences. Students are quick to figure out what teachers want to hear. They learn what they need to write to gain the approval of the teacher. They believe that if the teacher likes what they have to say, they will get a good grade (and in many cases they are right). Rather than risk writing an honest account of the biases they have grown accustomed to throughout their lives and potentially having an opportunity to deconstruct these biases, many students write what they perceive as the dogma of their Teacher Education Programs. Too often white pre-service teachers graduate from our Teacher Education Programs believing that knowing the language of educational social justice is more important than understanding the ideology and performance of a socially just practice.

What is needed in Teacher Education Programs across the country is the opportunity for authentic reflection and honest dialogue about personal life experiences among pre-service teachers and their educators. It is in the sharing of our experiences with others and listening to their feedback that we get to see potential biases that we might not see on our own. We may not recognize a personal bias that another might readily see. When blind spots are drawn to our attention, we have opportunity to see ourselves as others see us.

Yet revealing our personal stories and our potential biases makes us vulnerable to social analysis where we the potential to be personally judged by others who may have a different understanding of the world. This is where teacher educators need to help pre-service teachers develop a language to articulate differences in ways that help each other grow rather than silence one another. Berlin (1993) suggests that "only through language do we know and act upon the conditions of our experience—conditions that are socially constructed again through the agency of discourse" (pp. 71–72). White pre-service teachers need a space to reflect on their personal ideologies, discursive practices and interactions with people who are culturally different from themselves. Yet very often this space does not exist because many whites have learned to censor themselves for fear of being seen as a racist.

Teacher educators are partially to blame for this fear. Rather than censor what our students say, or create an environment where students are censoring what they say so as not offend anyone or appear to have the wrong disposition, educators need to allow a space for students to say the wrong things, the things our students might call "politically incorrect." Yet this space should allow for expression of multiple and varied beliefs. All too often in order to avoid potential conflicts, educators create what they call "safe spaces" in their classrooms. These safe spaces are explained by educators as places where students can challenge ideas, but not people. But students often do not see the distinction between the two. What usually happens is that these prescribed "safe spaces" become zones of polite silence where students refrain from any kind of outward disagreements. When we create our classrooms as places that are safe from differences, at least from talking about them, we remove any opportunity to learn how to articulate opposing views in productive ways. Too often students leave the class quietly venting their frustration to their peers. When we deny the opportunity for authentic dialogue to occur, we deny the opportunity for growth.

Teacher educators need to re-frame and re-define what safe spaces look like and how they should operate. The goal of creating an environment where honest and authentic dialogue about life experiences can occur should not be about changing another's perceptions. There is not enough time for the type of cultural therapy that this would entail. Instead, pre-service teachers need a safe place where they can share their stories without running the risk of being forced to change their understanding of the world (which took a lifetime to learn) in one or two semesters. When they believe they can share their stories with others with the understanding that they are expressing who they are and where they come from rather than believing they have to present themselves in a particular way, pre-service teachers have the chance to see themselves refracted in the eyes of their peers as they share their stories. Of course, there will always be students who will choose to present themselves in a particular way, but that should not prevent teacher educators from allowing the opportunity for the rest of the pre-service teachers to have this authentic dialogue.

Educators need to facilitate discussions that bring to light competing discourses and allow students to explore ways to negotiate the differences. Spellmeyer (1993) suggests that students should be seeking "the active pursuit of difference, because it is difference that produces an expanding horizon and involvement with a greater and more intersubjective life world" (p. 98). Students need to see these safe spaces as places where they have the opportunity to challenge one another to unpack their socially constructed notions of what it means to be successful. When there is an opportunity for authentic engagement, students are more willing to recognize, interrupt and move beyond their own biases. This was certainly true for the participants in this study. When pre-service teachers understand the critical role they play in advocating for all of their students, but especially their culturally diverse and underserved students, they are more likely to be responsive to all of their students. Teacher educators can then more successfully help pre-service teachers understand the need for creating curriculum that is accessible for all students and supports the attainment of intellectual resources all will need to contribute, participate and compete in a global society.

Looking to additional places for change in Teacher Education Programs, Desiree would like to see the School of Education become more diversified itself. She talked about the classes being too comfortable because everyone had similar backgrounds. She asked, "Where does it get you when everyone agrees with everything you say? You have the opportunity to gain a lot more if you get people in the room who are different. It's not that we're all not different, but we all come from a similar perspective. But you need other perspectives to have a meaningful conversation."

Desiree's recommendation for a more racially diverse school of education is an important one. When a white person comes from a similar orientation as her classmates, the ideologies that stand behind her words and actions may not be as likely to be called into question by those who come from a similar position. Flowers (2008) argues that

> the cultural Other that inspires reflection or critique rarely speaks back. In 'speaking up' we are often in a dialogue with ourselves, our past, our assumptions—we are not obligated to deal with the response of the Others to our words. And in 'speaking against' we are typically in a dialogue with theory, speculations, and injunctions of other academic writers. We are not obligated to be in dialogue with Others for whom we speak. We are not accountable to them for our interpretations of *their* situation or our claims for what *should* be done. (pp. 130–131)

Interacting with people different from themselves allows teacher candidates the chance to authentically expand and enhance their cultural knowledge of people from backgrounds different from their own. Furthermore through actual dialogue with those who are different from themselves, students are more apt to become conscious of their biases and take responsibility for what they say and do and what they do not say and do.

Indeed, all prospective teachers can benefit from a racially and ethnically diverse pool of students in their Teacher Education Programs. Yet, this is especially important for white teacher candidates who so often have lived their lives in white communities with little or no firsthand experiences with people of color. Whereas white students can read narrative accounts from people of color that talk about their experiences existing as minorities within the dominant culture, white teacher candidates stand to benefit more from direct experience with people rather than through experiencing decontextualized academic exercises that address racial and ethnic differences (Villegas & Lucas, 2002; Zeichner, 1992; Zeichner & Hoeft, 1996). Furthermore, direct experience with people from diverse backgrounds has been shown to increase racial understanding and sensitivity as well as social responsibility on the part of white students (Villegas & Lucas, 2002; Alger, 1997; Astin, 1993; Humphreys, 1998).

Yet there must be a significant number of students of color in classes whose experiences are genuinely valued, lest these students run the risk of being further marginalized and alienated (Villegas & Lucas, 2002). As long as schools of education are inhabited by a predominantly white population which operates in worlds shaped by similar discourses, students will not be prepared to respond to individuals who are shaped by alternative discourses. Without direct encounters with people from different racial worlds, the opportunity to develop one's identity in a way that considers the other will be difficult to cultivate. As Desiree says, "Where does it get you when everyone agrees with everything you say?"

Teacher educators have the potential to develop their teacher training programs in ways that will make a difference in the ways teacher candidates come to understand and shape their teacher selves. As Danielewicz (2001) contends, "if we want to cultivate teachers as agents who act, then our classrooms must be environments that cultivate perception and knowledge of the self" (p. 163). Skilled and thoughtful teacher educators from varying backgrounds who have contemplated their own social positioning can operate as cultural brokers helping prospective teachers unravel the ways that personal biographies and social structures influence their life experiences. Providing prospective teachers the chance to share and dialogue in meaningful ways with their peers about their own life stories can enhance their cultural knowledge. White pre-service teachers have a greater chance of becoming advocates for their culturally diverse and underserved students when they have the opportunity to critically examine their own social becoming and the social experiences of those who are different from themselves.

If teacher candidates do not have these types of experiences before they enter a classroom with a diverse group of students, they will have to do this work on their own unarmed with any personal experiences from their past to draw on to facilitate the process of becoming an advocate for their students. Without strong support from mentors and other advocates who can help pre-service and beginning teachers challenge their own assumptions about social ideologies surrounding privilege, novice teachers stand to risk teaching in a manner that perpetuates subjugation of marginalized children.

References

Alcoff, Linda Martin. (2006).*Visible identities: Race, gender, and the self.* New York: Oxford University Press.

Alger, J.R. (1997). The educational value of diversity. *Academe.* January–February: 20–23.

Alsup, J. (2006). *Teaching identity discourse: Negotiating personal and professional spaces.* Mahwah, NJ: Lawrence Erlbaum Associates.

Apple, M.W. (2000). *Official knowledge: Democratic education in a conservative age.* New York: Routledge.

Abt-Perkins, D., Gomez, M.L. (1998). A good place to begin: Examining our personal perspectives. In M. Opitz (Ed.), *Literacy instruction for culturally and linguistically diverse students.* (pp. 8–20). Newark, DE: International Reading Association.

Artiles, A.J., Barreto, R.M., Pena, L. & McClafferty, K. (1998). Pathways to teacher learning in multicultural contexts: A longitudinal case study of two novice bilingual teachers in urban schools. *Remedial and Special Education,* 19(2): 70–90.

Astin, A.W. (1993). *What matters in college: Four critical years.* San Francisco: Jossey-Bass.

Bakhtin, M. (1981). *The dialogic imagination.* Trans. C. Emerson & M. Holquist. Austin: University of Texas Press.

Bakhtin, M. (1984). *Problems of Dostoyevsky's poetics.* Trans.Caryl Emerson. Minneapolis: University of Minnesota Press.

Bakhtin, M. (1990). *Art and answerability: Early philosophical essays.* M. Holquist (Ed.). Trans. Vadim Liapunov. Austin: University of Texas Press.

Bakhtin, M. (1993). *Toward a philosophy of the act.* Trans. Vadim Liapunov. Austin: University of Texas Press.

Balderrama, M. (2008). Shooting the messenger: The consequences of practicing an ideology of social justice. In L. Bartolome (Ed.), *Ideologies in education: Unmasking the trap of teacher neutrality.* (pp. 29–45). New York: Peter Lang.

Banks, J. (1993) Multicultural education as an academic discipline. *Multicultural Education,* Winter(8)11: 39.

Banks, J. (1994). *Multiethnic education: Theory and practice,* 3rd ed. Boston: Allyn and Bacon.

Banks, J. (1996). The historical reconstruction of knowledge about race: Implications for transformative teaching. In J.A. Banks (Ed.), *Multicultural education, transformative knowledge, and action: Historical and contemporary perspectives.* (pp. 64–87). New York: Teachers College Press.

Barnes, H. (1989). Structuring knowledge for beginning teaching. In M. Reynolds (Ed.), *Knowledge base for beginning teacher.* (pp. 13–22). New York: Pergamon Press.

Becker, H.S. (1966). Introduction. In C.R. Shaw's *The Jack Roller: A delinquent boy's own story*. (pp. v–xviii). Chicago: The University of Chicago Press.

Bennett, C. (1995). Preparing teachers for cultural diversity and national standards of academic excellence. *Journal of Teacher Education*, 46(4): 259–265.

Berlin, J.A. (1996). *Rhetorics, poetics, and cultures: Refiguring college English studies*. Urbana, IL: National Council of Teachers of English.

Bernard-Donals, M. (1994) *Mikhail Bakhtin: Between phenomenology and Marxism*. New York: Cambridge University Press.

Boesch, E. (2007). The enigmatic other. In L. Mathias & J. Valsiner (Eds.), *Othernessin question: Labryrinths of the self* (pp. 3–9). Charlotte, NC: Information Age Publishing.

Borko, H. & Putnam, R. (1996). Learning to teach. In D. Berliner & R. Calfee (Eds.), *Handbook of research on educational psychology*. (pp. 673–699). New York: Macmillan.

Britzman, D.O. (2003). *Practice makes practice: A critical study of learning to teach*. Albany: State University of New York Press.

Brodkin, K. (2004). How did Jews become white folks? . In M. Fine, L. Weis, L. Powell Pruitt, & A. Burns (Eds.) *Off white: Readings in power, privilege and resistance*. (pp. 17–34). New York: Routledge.

Burns, A. (2004). The racing of capability and culpability in desegregated schools: Discourses of merit and possibility. In M. Fine, L. Weis, L. Powell Pruitt & A. Burns (Eds.), *Off white: Readings in power, privilege and resistance*. (pp. 373–394). New York: Routledge.

Bush, M. (2004). *Breaking the code of good intentions: Everyday forms of whiteness*. Lanham, MD: Rowman & Littlefield Publishers.

Chaudhary, N. (2007). Allusion and illusion: Dynamics of self and others. In L. Mathias & J. Valsiner (Eds.), *Otherness in question: Labryrinths of the self*. (pp. 107–121). Charlotte, NC: Information Age Publishing.

Chesler, M., Peet, M., & Sevig, T. (2003). Blinded by whiteness; The development of white college students' racial awareness. In A.W. Doane and E. Bonilla-Silva (Eds.), *White out: The continuing significance of racism*. (pp. 215–230). New York: Routledge.

Clandinin, J. & Connelly, F.M. (2000). *Narrative inquiry: Experience and story in qualitative research*. San Francisco: Jossey-Bass.

Clark, C. & Peterson, P. (1986). Teachers' thought processes. In M. Wittock (Ed.), *Handbook of research on teaching*, 3rd ed. (pp. 255–296). New York: Macmillan.

Cochran-Smith, M. (1993). Discussants' remarks: Symposium on race and racism in teaching and learning. Paper presented at the annual meeting of the American Educational Research Association, Atlanta.

Cochran-Smith (1994). The power of teacher research in teacher education. In S. Hollingsworth & H. Sockett (Eds.), *Teacher research and educational reform*. (pp 142–165). Chicago: University of Chicago Press.

Cochran-Smith, M. (1995). Uncertain Allies: Understanding the boundaries between race and teaching. *Harvard Educational Review* 56(1): 541–570.

Cochran-Smith, M. (2004). *Walking the road: Race, diversity, and social justice in teacher education*. New York: Teachers College Press.

Cochran-Smith, M. & Lytle, S. (1990). Research on teaching and teacher research: The issues that divide. *Educational Researcher*, 19(2): 2–11.

Danielewicz, J. (2001). *Teaching selves: Identity, pedagogy and teacher education*. Albany: State University of New York Press.

Darling-Hammond. L. (2002). Educating a profession for equitable practice. In L. Darling-Hammond, J. French & S.P. Garcia-Lopez (Eds.), *Learning to teach for social justice*. (pp. 201–216). New York: Teachers College Press.

Delpit, L. (1995). *Other people's children: Cultural conflict in the classroom*. New York: The New Press.

Doane, W. (2003). Rethinking whiteness studies. In A.W. Doane & E. Bonilla-Silva (Eds.), *White out: The continuing significance of racism*. (pp 21–34). New York: Routledge.

Dyer, R. (2005). The matter of whiteness. In P.S. Rothenberg (Ed.), *White privilege: Essential readings on the other side of racism*. (pp. 9–14). New York: Worth Publishers.

Farber, K.S. (1995). Teaching about diversity through reflectivity: Sites of uncertainty, risk, and possibility. In R.J. Martin (Ed.), *Practicing what we teach: Confronting diversity in teacher education*. (pp. 49–63). Albany: State University of New York Press.

Farmer, F. (2001). *Saying and silence: Listening to composition with Bakhtin*. Logan, Utah: Utah State University Press.

Feiman-Nemser, S. and J, Remillard. (1996). Perspectives on learning to teach. In F. Murray (Ed.), *The teacher educator's handbook: Building a knowledge base for the preparation of teachers*. (pp. 63–91). Washington D.C.: American Association of Colleges for Teacher Education.

Feiman-Nemser, S. and S, Melnick (1992). Introducing teaching. In S. Feiman-Nemser and H. Featherstone (Eds.), *Exploring teaching: Reinventing an introductory course*. (pp. 1–17). New York: Teachers College Press.

Fine, M. (2004). Witnessing whiteness/Gathering intelligence. In M. Fine, L. Weis, L. Powell Pruitt, & A. Burns (Eds.), *Off white: Readings in power, privilege and resistance*. (pp. 245–256). New York: Routledge.

Flowers, L. (2008). *Community literacy and the rhetoric of public engagement*. Carbondale: Southern Illinois University Press.

Foucault, M. (1994). Truth and power. In P. Rabinow & N. Rose (Eds.), *The essential Foucault: Selections from essential works of Foucault (1954–1984)*. (pp. 300–318). New York: The New Press.

Fullan, M. (1993). *Changing forces: Probing the depths of educational reform*. London: Falmer.

Fullan, M. (1999). *Changing forces: The sequel*. London: Falmer.

Garibaldi, A.M. (1992). Preparing teachers for culturally diverse classrooms. In M.E. Dilworth (Ed.), *Diversity in teacher education: New expectations*. (pp. 23–39). San Francisco: Jossey-Bass.

Garmon, M.A. (1998). Using dialogue journals to promote student learning in a multicultural teacher education course. *Remedial & Special Education* 19(1): 32–45.

Gee, James Paul (2005). *Discourse analysis*. New York: Routledge.

Gomez, M.L., Rodriguez, T., & Agosto. (2008). Life histories of Latino/a teacher candidates. *Teacher's College Record*, 110(8): 1639–1676.

Gomez. M.L., Walker, A.B., and& Page, M.L. (2000). Personal experience as a guide to teaching. *Teaching and Teacher Education*, 16(7): 731–747.

Gonsalves, R. (2008). Hysterical blindness and the ideology of denial: Preservice teachers' resistance to Multicultural Education. In L. Bartolome (Ed.), *Ideologies in education: Unmasking the trap of teacher neutrality*. (pp. 3–27). New York: Peter Lang.

Goodlad, J.I. (1990). Better teachers for our nation's schools. *Phi Delta Kappan*, 72: 185–194.

Goodson, I. F. (1980–81). Life histories and the study of schooling. *Interchange*. 11(4): 62–76.

Goodson, I.F. & Sikes, P. (2001). *Life history research in educational settings: Learning from lives*. Philadelphia: Open University Press.

Goodwin, A.L. (1997). Historical and contemporary perspectives on multicultural teacher education. In J. King, E. Hollins, & W. Hayman (Eds.), *Preparing teachers for cultural diversity.* (pp. 5–22) New York: Teachers College Press.

Gounari, P. (2008). Unlearning the official history: Agency and pedagogies of possibility. In L. Bartolome (Ed.), *Ideologies in education: Unmasking the trap of teacher neutrality.* (pp. 97–114). New York: Peter Lang.

Grant, C.A. (1991). Culture and teaching: What do teachers need to know? In M. Kennedy (Ed.), *Teaching academic subjects to diverse learners.* (pp. 237–256). New York: Teachers College Press.

Greenberg, E., & Weber, K. (2008). *Generation we: How millennial youth are taking over America and changing our world forever.* Emeryville, CA: Pachatusan.

Halasek, K. (1999). *A pedagogy of possibility: Bakhtinian perspectives on composition studies.* Carbondale, IL: Southern Illinois University Press.

Harding, S. (2004). A socially relevant philosophy of science? Resources from Standpoint Theory's Controversiality. *Hypatia.* 19: 25–47.

Harris, J. (1997). *A teaching subject: Composition since 1966.* Upper Saddle River, NJ: Prentice-Hall.

Holland, D., Lachicotte, W., Skinner, D., & Cain, C. (1998). *Identity and agency in cultural worlds.* Cambridge, MA: Harvard University Press.

Hollins, E.T. & Guzman, M.T. (2005). Research on preparing teachers for diverse populations. In Cochran-Smith, M & Zeichner, K. (Eds.), *Studying teacher education: The report of the AERA panel on research and teacher education.* (pp. 477–548). Mahwah, NJ: Lawrence Erlbaum Associates.

Holquist, J.M. & Clark, K, (1984). The influence of Kant in the early work of M.M. Bakhtin. In J.P. Strelka (Ed.) *Literary Theory and Criticism: Part 1: Theory.* Bern: Peter Lang Publishers.

Holquist, M. (1990). *Dialogism.* New York: Routledge.

hooks, bell. (1997). Representing whiteness in the black imagination. In R. Frankenberg (Ed.), *Displacing whiteness: Essays in social and cultural criticism.* (pp. 165–179). Durham, NC: Duke University Press.

Howard, G.R. (2006). *We can't teach what we don't know.* New York: Teacher's College Press.

Howe, N. & Strauss, W. (2000). *Millennials rising: The next great generation.* New York: Vintage.

Humphreys, D. (1998). Higher education, race, and diversity: Views from the field. Washington, DC: Association of American Colleges and Universities. (ERIC Document Reproduction Service No. 423 778).

Hurtado, A. & Stewart, A.J. (2004) Through the looking glass: Implications of studying whiteness for feminist methods. In M. Fine, L. Weis, L. Powell Pruitt, & A. Burns (Eds.), *Off white: Readings in power, privilege and resistance.* (pp. 313–330). New York: Routledge.

Iyer, A., Leach, C.W.& Pederson, A. (2004). Racial wrongs and restitutions: The role of guilt and other group based emotions. In M. Fine, L. Weis, L. Powell Pruitt & A. Burns (Eds.), *Off white: Readings in power, privilege and resistance.* (pp. 345–361). New York: Routledge.

James, D. (2000). *Dona Maria's story: Life history, memory and political identity.* Durham: Duke University Press.

Japur, M., Guanaes, C. & Rasera, E.F. (2007). Otherness in the therapeutic context: The social construction of change. In L. Mathias & J. Valsiner (Eds.), *Othernessin question: Labryrinths of the self.* (pp. 3–9). Charlotte, NC: Information AgePublishing.

Johnson, H.B. (2001), The ideology of meritocracy and the power of wealth: School selection and the reproduction of race and class inequality. Ph.D. dissertation. Department of Sociology, Northeastern University, Boston, MA.

Johnson, H.B. & Shaprio, T.M. (2003) Good neighborhoods, good schools: Race and the "good choices" of white families. In A.W. Doane and E. Bonilla-Silva (Eds.), *White out: The continuing significance of racism.* (pp. 173–188). New York: Routledge.

Katz, S.R. (2000). Promoting bilingualism in the era of Unz: Making sense of the gap between research, policy, and practice in teacher education. *Multicultural Education*: 8(1): 2–7.

Keiser, D.L. (2005). Learners not widgets: Teacher education for social justice during transformational times. In N. Michelli & D.L. Keiser (Eds.), *Teacher education for democracy and social justice.* (pp. 31–55). New York: Routledge.

Kendall, F.E. (2006). *Understanding white privilege: Creating pathways to authentic relationships across race.* New York: Routledge.

King, J. (1997). Dysconscious "racism: Ideology, identity, and miseducation. In R. Delgado & J, Stefancic (Eds.), *Critical white studies: Looking behind the mirror.* (pp. 128–132). Philadelphia: Temple University Press.

Kincheloe, Joe L. & Steinberg, Shirley R. Steinberg(1998). Addressing the crisis of whiteness:

Reconfiguring white identity in a pedagogy of whiteness. In J. L. Kincheloe, S. R. Steinberg. N. Rodriguez & R. E. Chennault (Eds.), *White Reign: Deploying whiteness in America.* (pp. 3–30). New York: St. Martin's Griffin.

Knowles, J.G. (1992). Models for understanding pre-service and beginning teachers'biographies: Illustrations from case studies. In I. F. Goodson (Ed.), *Studying teachers lives.* (pp. 99–152). New York: Teachers College Press.

Ladson-Billings, G. (1990). Culturally relevant teaching. *The College Board Review* 155: 20–25.

Ladson-Billings, G. (1995a). Toward a critical race theory of education. *Teachers College Record.* 97: 47–69.

Ladson-Billings, G. (1995b). But that's just good teaching: The case for culturally relevant pedagogy. *Theory and Practice.* 34(3): 159–165.

Ladson-Billings, G. (1999). Preparing teachers for diverse student populations: A critical race theory perspective. In A. Iran-Nejad & D. Pearson (Eds.), *Review of research in education*, vol. 24. (pp. 211–248). Washington, D.C: American Educational Research Association.

Lampert, M. (1990). When the problem is not the question and the solution is not the answer: Mathematical knowing and teaching. *American Educational Research Journal,* 27(1): 29–63.

Linde, C. (1993). *Life stories: The creation of coherence.* New York: Oxford University Press.

Lipsitz, G. (2006). *The possessive investment in whiteness: How white people profit from identity politics.* Philadelphia: Temple University Press.

Low, S. (2004). Behind the gates: Social splitting and the "other." In M. Fine, L. Weis, L. Powell Pruitt, & A. Burns (Eds.), *Off white: Readings in power, privilege and resistance.* (pp. 35–51). New York: Routledge.

Maher, F. & Thompson Tetrault, M.K. (1998). "They got the paradigm and painted it white": Whiteness and pedagogies of possibility. . In J.L. Kincheloe, S.R. Steinberg, N. Rodriguez & R.E. Chennault (Eds.), *White Reign: Deploying whiteness in America.* (pp. 137–158). New York: St. Martin's Griffin.

McAdams, D. (1993). *The stories we live by: Personal myths and the making of the self.* New York: The Guilford Press.

McCarthy, C, Rodriguez, A., Meechum, S., David, S., Wilson-Brown, C., Godina, H., Supryia, K.E. & Buendia, E. (2004). Race, suburban resentment, and the representation of the inner city. In M. Fine, L. Weis, L. Powell Pruitt & A. Burns (Eds.), *Off white: Readings in power, privilege and resistance.* (pp. 163–174). New York: Routledge.

McFalls, E.L., & Cobb-Roberts, D. (2001). Reducing resistance to diversity through cognitive dissonance instruction: Implications for teacher education. *Journal of Teacher Education*, 52(2): 164–172.

McIntyre, A. (1997). *Making meaning of whiteness: Exploring racial identity in white teachers*. Albany: State University of New York Press.

Mishler, E. (1999). *Storylines: Craftartists' narratives of identity*. Cambridge, MA: Harvard University Press.

Morrison, T. (1992). *Playing in the dark*. New York: Vintage Books.

Morrison, T. (1993). On the backs of blacks. *Time*. December 2, 1993, 57.

Moya, P. (2006). What's identity got to do with it? Mobilizing identities in the multicultural classroom. In L.M. Alcoff, M. Hames-Garcia, S. Mohanty & P. Moya (Eds.), *Identity politics reconsidered*. (pp. 96–117) New York: Palgrave Publications.

Myers, K. (2003). White fright: Reproducing white supremacy through casual discourse. In A.W. Doane and E. Bonilla-Silva (Eds.), *White out: The continuing significance of racism*. (pp 129–144). New York: Routledge.

Nielson, G.M. (2002). *The norms of answerability: Social theory between Bakhtin and Habermas*. Albany: State University of New York Press.

Nollan, V. (2004). Introduction. In V. Nollan (Ed.), *Bakhtin: Ethics and mechanics*. (pp. xiii–xxxiii). Evanston, IL: Northwestern University Press.

Obidah, J.E. (2000).Mediating boundaries of race, class, and professional authority as a critical multiculturalist. *Teacher College Record*, 102(6): 1035–1060.

Popkewitz, T. (1998). *Struggling for the soul: The politics of schooling and the construction of the teacher*. New York: Teachers College Press.

Popkewitz, T. (2007). Alchemies and governing: Or, questions about the questions we ask. *Educational Philosophy and Theory*, 39(1): 64–83.

Powell Pruitt, L. (2004). The achievement (k)not: Whiteness and black underachievement. . In M. Fine, L. Weis, L. Powell Pruitt & A. Burns (Eds.), *Off white: Readings in power, privilege and resistance*. (pp. 235–244). New York: Routledge.

Rains, F.V. (1998). Is the benign really harmless?: Deconstructing some "benign" manifestations of operationalized white privilege. In J.L. Kincheloe, S.R. Steinberg, N. Rodriguez & R.E. Chennault (Eds.), *White Reign: Deploying whiteness in America*. (pp. 77–101). New York: St. Martin's Griffin.

Rainer, T. & Rainer, J. (2011). *The millennials: Connecting to America's largest generation*. Nashville, TN: B&H Publishing Group.

Rodriguez, N.M. (2000). Projects of whiteness in critical pedagogy. In N.M. Rodriguez & L.E. Villaverdi (Eds.), *Dismantling white privilege: Pedagogy, politics and whiteness*. (pp. 1–24). New York: Peter Lang Publishing.

Rothenberg, P.S. (2005). Introduction. In P.S. Rothenberg (Ed.), *White privilege: Essential readings on the other side of racism*. (pp. 1–5). New York: Worth Publishers.

Said. E. (2003). Global Crisis. *ZNet*. March 17, 2003.

Salgado, J. (2007). The feelings of the dialogical self: Affectivity, agency and otherness. In L. Mathias, & J. Valsiner (Eds.), *Otherness in question: Labryinths of the self*. (pp. 53–71). Charlotte, NC: Information Age Publishing.

Shapiro, T. (2003). *Racial legacies: The reproduction of inequality*. New York: Oxford University Press.

Shapiro, T. & Johnson, H.B. (2003). Family assets and school access: Race and class in the structuring of educational opportunity. In M. Sherraden (Ed.), *Inclusion in asset building: Research and policy*. New York: Oxford University Press.

Shulman, L. (1987). Knowledge and teaching: Foundations of the new reform. *Harvard Educational Review*, 51: 1–22. Original work published 1983.

Sleeter, C. (1992). *Keepers of the American dream: A study of staff development and multicultural education.* London: Falmer.

Sleeter, C. (1994). White racism. *Multicultural Education.* Spring: 6.

Solomon, P.R., Portelli, J.P., Daniel, B., Campbell, A. (2005). The discourse of denial: How white teacher candidates construct race, racism and white privilege. *Race, Ethnicity and Education.* 8(2): 147–169.

Spellmeyer, G. (1993) *Common ground: Dialogue, understanding and the teaching of composition.* Englewood Cliffs, NJ: Prentice-Hall.

Su, Z. (1997). Teaching as a profession and as a career: Minority candidates' perspectives. *Teaching and Teacher Education,* 13(3): 325–340.

Suarez, S.C. (2008). Sharing the wealth: Guiding all students into the professional discourse. In L. Bartolome (Ed.), *Ideologies in education: Unmasking the trap of teacher neutrality.* (pp. 135–158). New York: Peter Lang.

Sullivan, S. (2006). *Revealing whiteness: The unconscious habits of racial privilege.* Bloomington: Indiana University Press.

Tom, A.R. (1984). *Teaching as a moral craft.* New York: Longman.

Tom, A.R. (1997). *Redesigning teacher education.* Albany: State University of New York Press.

Trepagnier, B. (2006). *Silent Racism: How well-meaning white people perpetuate the racial divide.* Boulder: Paradigm Publishers.

US Census Bureau. (2006). US Census Bureau State and County Quick Facts. http://www.quickfacts.census.gov.

US Department of Education. (2006). National Center for Educational Statistics. http://www.nces.ed.gov.

Villegas, M., Lucas, T. (2002). *Educating culturally responsive teachers: A coherent approach.* Albany: State University of New York Press.

Wideen, M., Mayer-Smith, J. & Moon, B. (1998). A critical analysis of the research on learning to teach: Making the case for an ecological perspective on inquiry. *Review of Educational Research,* 68(2): 130–178.

Wijeyesinghe, C.L., P. Griffin, and B. Love. (1997). Racism curriculum design. In M. Adams, L.A. Bell, and P. Griffin (Eds.), *Teaching for diversity and social justice: A sourcebook.* (pp. 82–09). New York: Routledge

Wildman, S.M. & Davis, A.D. (2005). Making systems of privilege visible. In P.S. Rothenberg (Ed.), *White Privilege: Essential readings on the other side of racism.* (pp. 95–101). New York: Worth Publishers.

Willams, P. (1997). *Seeing a color-blind future: The paradox of race.* New York: Farrar, Strauss & Giroux.

Wortham, S. (2001). *Narratives in action: A strategy for research and analysis.* New York: Teachers College Press.

Zeichner, K. (1996). Educating teachers for cultural diversity. In K. Zeichner, S. Melnick & M.L. Gomez (Eds.), *Currents of reform in preservice teacher education.* (pp. 133–175). New York: Teachers College Press.

Zeichner, K. (1992). *NCRTL special report: Educating teachers for cultural diversity.* East Lansing: Michigan State University, National Center for Research on Teacher Learning.

Zeichner, K. and K. Hoeft. (1996). Teacher socialization for cultural diversity. In J. Sikula, T. Buttery, & E. Guyton (Eds.), *Handbook on research on teacher education,* 2nd ed. (pp. 525–547). New York: Macmillan.

Zimpher, N.L. & E.A. Asburn (1992). Countering parochialism in teacher candidates. In M.E. Dilworh (Ed.), *Diversity in teacher education* (pp. 40–62). San Francisco: Jossey-Bass.

Index

For Product Safety Concerns and Information please contact our EU
representative GPSR@taylorandfrancis.com
Taylor & Francis Verlag GmbH, Kaufingerstraße 24, 80331 München, Germany

www.ingramcontent.com/pod-product-compliance
Lightning Source LLC
Chambersburg PA
CBHW050713280326
41926CB00088B/3017

* 9 7 8 1 1 3 8 3 7 8 0 6 3 *